ADAPTORS AND IN...

In this updated, paperback edition, *Adaptors and Innovators* presents a new approach to creativity and problem solving. It distinguishes between preferred problem solving style (the manner of mental activity) and individual capacity (e.g., IQ or management competencies), providing a new approach to such management problems as resistance to change, individual and team creativity, and conflict between individuals and groups as a result of cognitive gaps and 'coping' behaviour.

The contributors are drawn from a varied international background of teaching, research and consultancy, and they draw on Kirton's Adaption–Innovation Theory and its measure: the Kirton Adaption–Innovation Inventory (KAI). This explores the characteristic styles of thinking underlying an individual's approach to problem solving and decision making. The KAI has been validated by nearly twenty years of research worldwide and is now widely used.

With a combination of practical guidance on the appliance of KAI and clear presentation of theoretical advances, *Adaptors and Innovators* will be of interest to managers, teachers, researchers and students in the fields of psychology, sociology and management.

Michael Kirton is Director (and founder) of the Occupational Research Centre. He is the originator of the Adaption–Innovation Inventory (KAI). He was awarded a DSc by the Council for National Academic Awards, in 1991, for his work on Adaption–Innovation theory.

ADAPTORS AND INNOVATORS

Styles of creativity and problem solving

Revised edition

Edited by Michael Kirton

London and New York

First published 1989
by Routledge
11 New Fetter Lane, London EC4P 4EE

Reprinted in 1990, 1991, 1992, 1993
Revised edition first published in paperback 1994

Published in 2000
by KAI Distribution Centre
Ye Jolly Gardeners, Old Uxbridge Rd, Rickmansworth,
Hertfordshire, WD3 2XZ, UK

©1989,1994, 2000 M.J. Kirton

Typeset in Baskerville by
Florencetype Ltd, Stoodleigh, Devon

Printed and bound in 2000 in Great Britain by
Antony Rowe Ltd, Chippenham, Wiltshire

British Library Cataloguing in Publication Data
A catalogue record for this book is available from the British Libary

ISBN 0-415-11662-7

Library of Congress Cataloguing in Publication Data
Adaptors and innovators: styles of creativity and problem-solving/
written and edited by M.J. Kirton. - Updated, paperback ed.
p.cm.
Includes bibliographical references and index.
ISBN 0-415-11662-7 (pbk.)
1. Creative ability in business. 2. Problem solving.
3. Psychology, Industrial. I. Kirton, M.J.
HD53.A33 1994
650.1-dc20   94-11958
                                                      CIP

CONTENTS

FIGURES

TABLES

ACKNOWLEDGEMENTS

I owe much to all the scholars who work on my theory and measure and are quoted here, but especially to those who co-author this book. I have been much helped in the final preparation by my colleague in the Centre, Walter Glendinning and my secretary, Angela Robinson. Thanks are due also to those companies that have given the Occupational Research Centre support over the time this work was planned and written, namely: British Airways plc, The British Petroleum Company plc, Baxter Health Care Ltd (formerly Travenol), Prime Computer (UK) Ltd, National Westminster Bank plc, Shell UK Ltd, and University of Hertfordshire administration, library, computer and reprographic services are all owed our thanks. A special thanks is owed to Stan Gryskiewicz whose idea it was to have a KAI 10 year anniversary conference (held in August 1987) and who provided the theme that led to this book.

1989 M.J.K.

Chapter 6 draws on two previously published papers by the author: G.R. Foxall (1994), 'Consumer initiators: adaptors and innovators', *British Journal of Management*, 5, copyright John Wiley & Sons; and G.R. Foxall and S. Bhate (1993), 'Cognitive styles of use-innovators for home computing software applications: implications for new product strategy', *Technovation*, 13: 311–23, copyright Elsevier. The author is grateful for permission to reproduce this material and to the referees of these articles for their perceptive comments and constructive suggestions. Last but far from least, it is time to acknowledge a debt to Michael Kirton for his encouragement over nearly a decade in carrying through this research programme and for supplying ideas for the continuance of the investigations. Our collaboration confirms the commonplace observation that science is teamwork.

1994 G.R.F.

ACKNOWLEDGEMENTS

The writing of Chapter 7 has been supported by a grant of the ANO foundation. Comments and criticism from Michael Kirton, Vernon Reynolds and Robin Dunbar were of great help to improve the text, which is not to imply that they are responsible for any flaws in the basic line of argumentation defended here. The help of Benn Hoffsculte in refining and presenting this text is also gratefully acknowledged.

1989 P.P.vdM.

A THEORY EXPLORED
PREFACE TO FIRST EDITION

The mental processes that underlie concepts of creativity, problem solving and decision making are of continuing interest to researchers and teachers and are increasingly recognized by managers as directly relevant to the problems that they encounter in introducing change. There are good logical reasons for linking the three concepts. A decision is essentially based on the choice of solution to a problem – in other words, if there is no choice of solution to a problem, no decision is needed. Further, both creativity and problem solving have in common at least the generation and resolution of novelty. Most often the three concepts have been kept apart, in theory and in research design and practice. One possible reason for this may be a lack of clarity in their relationship to intelligence. All scholars class intelligence as a concept of capacity or level; most accept that intelligence is heavily implicated in observed individual differences in problem solving and subsequent decision making. There is, however, much less clarity or certainty on what relationship should be hypothesized between creativity and intelligence. Studies that are founded on comprehensive reviews of pertinent literature and involve careful measurement, have on occasion added to the general confusion by not being able to make a clear prediction.

Guilford (1950), whilst predicting a modest relationship between intelligence test scores and many types of creative performance, concludes: 'we must look well beyond the boundaries of IQ if we are to fathom the domain of creativity'. Getzels and Jackson (1962) emphasized: 'we are not saying there is no relationship between IQ and creative thinking. Obviously, the feeble minded by IQ standards are not going to be creative. But at the high average level and above, the two are sufficiently independent to warrant differentiation.' These standpoints have a tentative air that do not make for sharp hypotheses that can be the subject of a clear test.

In contrast, Adaption–Innovation theory takes an unequivocal stance. It postulates and through its measure, the Kirton Adaption–Innovation Inventory (KAI), demonstrates that the preferred cognitive style of the individual is wholly unrelated statistically to that individual's level, i.e., capacity. That key distinction between level and style has wide implications, which are explored in this book, for the management of organizations and for the direction of future research. It brings clarity to the debate when the factors affecting an individual's response in a particular situation are being considered. It makes it possible to examine the concepts of creativity, problem solving and decision making of individuals and to predict their behaviour and that of the groups which they make up, with a greater degree of confidence than has previously been possible. It is, however, made clear that level and style are only two of the variables that affect the performance of individuals.

Other individual variables – motivation, knowledge, social skills and many others and the particular activity and organizational context in which the activity takes place – will all have a powerful impact on the outcome. It is, however, apparent from the volume of research already carried out into the application of Adaption–Innovation theory, in more than a dozen countries, that there is value in being able to demonstrate the existence of a stable preferred form of behaviour in the individual and to measure it with confidence.

One example of the value of re-examining assumptions, in the light of the clear level–style distinction that Adaption–Innovation offers, is in the concept of creativity as applied to occupational groups. Artists are generally accepted as being creative people (e.g., Myers, 1962). Architects are also often so accepted, aided no doubt by MacKinnon's (1962) seminal work on them; businessmen or engineers have so far received scant attention (e.g., MacKinnon, 1987), mainly because they are so often viewed as lacking in creativity. If, however, the level–style distinction is here applied, then a more precise differentiation can be made that all people, to a degree, are creative in their own way.

The members of these or any other profession may differ in ability, and even more widely in experience and behaviour, however defined and measured. They may also range widely over the Adaption–Innovation dimension, working closely to their relevant paradigms or not, in accord as far as possible with their preferred cognitive style.

The first chapter of this book sets out the theory, explores these and other underlying assumptions, describes typical adaptors and innovators, introduces the theory's measure, the KAI, and uses it to test some of the theoretical standpoints taken. The principal issues addressed

xi

are the distinctness of cognitive capacity and cognitive style; the stability, persistence and early setting of style; the relationship to personality and the concept of coping behaviour as an intervening variable.

The second chapter is written by a psychologist in management, Ronald Goldsmith, Professor of Marketing at The Florida State University. With style firmly separated from level, the way is clearer to relate cognitive style to personality trait. Goldsmith puts forward a number of propositions: that KAI is a summary measure of behaviour, acting as a substitute for aggregate measures of behaviour over time; that Adaption–Innovation may lie in scope between personality traits and any individual behavioural act, being more specific than the former and more general than the latter; schematically, however, Adaption–Innovation may underlie personality trait clusters. He touches also on interesting measurement issues.

Chapter 3 reviews the structures, nature and performance of the KAI from the validation studies in the early 1970s, to its present widespread international use by scholars and practitioners.

Steven de Ciantis, of Shell UK Ltd, shares the authorship of the next chapter which assembles the evidence from numerous studies for the notion of cognitive climate, placing it as an element within organizational climate. We examine the possible impact on the individual and the coping behaviour and clashes that may result.

Harry Schroder built a scholarly reputation as a professor at Princeton University in the study of cognitive complexity and group functioning. He now continues to build this reputation as a scholar and practitioner in the theory and measurement of management competencies and their use in his Center for Organizational Effectiveness at the University of South Florida. He shows that as Adaption–Innovation theory predicts, management competencies being measures of capacity are unrelated to cognitive style. When taken together, the effect is that groups of adaptor managers will exhibit their competency in clearly characteristically adaptive ways. The converse for innovators is also true. This has obvious teaching value for training departments as well as academics.

The penultimate chapter is by psychologist Gordon Foxall, Professor of Consumer Research at Birmingham University. He reviews studies based on decades of expectation in marketing and marketing research that a secure link should exist between personality characteristics and early or late adoption of novel products. His research shows that 'innovative consumers' in marketing terminology cannot be simply equated to innovators as measured by the KAI. One significant complication is the differences in style of these novel products. Another significant factor is the extent to which the buyer may be assiduously collecting products within a novel range. These applications seem amenable to being unravelled by the Adaption–Innovation theory and successfully tested by use of KAI. The implications for marketing may be that old intuitions may yet be supported by more relevant theory, sounder measures and more sophisticated research design.

Popko van der Molen's work at the State University of Groningen in the Netherlands spans biology, psychology and sociology and both animal and human behaviour. In this final chapter he explores the implications of the conflict which exists in all social animals between the drive to satisfy individual physical needs and the urge to maintain social contact and interaction. The importance of the Adaption–Innovation orientation of individuals as a basic determinant of human behaviour in such conflicts, led van der Molen to theorize that the Adaption–Innovation dimension had a biological root and he marshals data from a wide range of research on human and animal behaviour to sustain the argument. He considers the impact of this approach for the apparent cyclical rise and fall of social groups and the need for man to find a compromise between the all too slow evolutionary process of change and the all too disturbing revolutionary alternative.

The central aim of the book has been to bring together the work already done in refining and applying Adaption–Innovation theory and to consider its wider implications. The conclusions in it are based on reliable data and will, I hope, lead to a wider application of the theory and measure. Where there is speculation it will, I hope, stimulate further research including cross-disciplinary research where that is appropriate.

In order to achieve fluency, the masculine personal pronoun has been used throughout the book. Where he, him and his has been used, please read also she, her and hers.

Notes have been grouped at the end of each chapter and referred to in the text.

1989

FIVE YEARS ON
PREFACE TO SECOND EDITION

As I settle down to write this, I have the feeling I am 'working to instructions'. This structure began to become manifest during a telephone call from a representative of Routledge, who mentioned, among other matters, that this book had been reissued every year since its first publication. Actually, I had noticed that. The Routledge suggestion was that it might now be republished as a paperback and so be made more accessible to many more readers. This, as every author knows, constitutes a 'guideline', influencing what I might be expected to do to prepare the original script for its republishing.

I cannot complain of undertaking a piece of problem solving or creativity in accord with some structure, because it is an axiom of this work that all creativity, indeed all thinking, occurs within structure. Since those last days of 1988, as the first script was being completed, this has become clearer and clearer, at variance with what many of those in the creativity field seem to believe. The difference between the cerebration of adaptors and innovators, or to be more precise, the continuum from adaption to innovation, is the amount of structure that each of us prefers to have, and how much of that structure needs to be consensually agreed. In general, adaptors prefer more structure, and that more be consensually agreed than do innovators. By contrast, to slip again for a moment into oversimple dichotomy, innovators prefer and can manage comfortably with less. It must be remembered always, however, that circumstances vary and there are times when all of us need more or less. There are times when, for anyone, the structure is too tight for the needed cognitive change to be achieved, as the people of whole countries find when they live under a system of government that stultifies almost all initiative. Conversely, no thought of any kind can generate, even at the lowest levels, without the help of structure, however it is called: classification, frames of reference, theories, policies, ethics and mores, paradigms and even language itself. Like it or not, even before I can comprehend the problem of addressing you through this script, much less get it done, I need structure: enough to get me going, enough to keep me on target, enough and no more than to allow me to work in what I deem to be, for me, reasonable mental comfort. This is Adaption–Innovation theory.

The first problem to solve was what changes I must undertake, either as author or editor, or both, before republication, but staying within given guidelines. I reviewed how much had been written since those last days of 1988. I noted first that the original script had been based on 77 published studies (since 1978), backed up by 30 successfully completed higher degree theses. In these following 5 years, 90 more learned works have appeared, together with 26 more theses. Simply editing the text just to mention each of these would clutter the text and make the book less accessible. Although some of these are beginning to open new ground (e.g., in the field of education, Kirton *et al.*, 1991), I have instead decided to leave most chapters untouched, except for some annotation and addition to Chapters 1, 3 and 4, and to concentrate on three more comprehensive changes. Gordon Foxall (now Professor of Consumer Research at the University of Birmingham and Director of the Research Centre for Consumer Behaviour at the Birmingham Business School) has written a new Chapter 6, since in this area research progress has turned tentative conclusions into authoritative statements. Second, I feel that the best way to give the reader an appreciation of the progress of the thinking underlying all these works is for me to pen this revision of my own first Preface. It will show the progress made as a result of a small but critical selection from the additional published work, together with information derived from practice and consultancy, both my own and that of others which I have got to know about informally. Finally, Marián Kubeš, Director of the Institute of Creativity, at Trnava University in Slovakia, provides us with his view of the impact of the theory and its measure, KAI, over the years, from the perspective of research psychologist as well as that of practitioner and trainer in industry.

DOMAIN

The field covered by Adaption–Innovation was the first matter dealt with in the 1989 Preface. Essentially there has been no revision to that position: it lies within the area of cognition that is responsible for bringing about change. As it said, that does involve much that has been thought and written for a very long time, including the concepts of creativity, problem solving and decision making. In the intervening 5 years, there has been a sharpening of this position, for although it is obvious that there are substantial overlaps between these concepts, whether or not they are facets of the same underlying concept, the links had not been developed further in any analysis. We have since found that better clarity may be achieved if one links all three by assuming them all to be concerned with the generation and resolution of novelty.

Although it might be argued that the generation of novelty may seem more related to creativity and the resolution of novelty to problem solving (which could include the term decision making), further reflection only suggests that generation and resolution are themselves dependent on each other – for instance, the perception of the problem could be viewed as the stimulus to generation, just as generation could be the means of both the resolution and the fresh perception, if not creation, of further problems. The advantage of underlining the overlaps is that the field is more complete and the thinking and findings from one subset can help another. Methodologies, too, need to be integrated; creativity has always been viewed as in a broad, human context, but the precision of its definitions and, therefore, the soundness of its measures leave much to be desired. Problem solving has had the benefit of a much better scientific approach but has too often been narrowly laboratory-based and seen to be lacking in day-to-day human relevance. Yet problem solving, from its home in the discipline of psychology, has been seen as the prerogative of all people and animals, whilst creativity is often seen as elitist – the prerogative of the clever and the innovative. This book lies firmly in the field of psychology; all mankind is creative.

POTENTIAL LEVEL AND PREFERRED STYLE

The content of the field thus delineated is explored in Chapter 1 with much attention to detail and proof, mainly in the direction of separating the variables of level (capacity) and style. More proof is now available (e.g., Hammerschmidt and Jennings, 1991 as an addition to Chapter 5; Tefft, 1990 as an addition to Chapter 1) on this core issue, but one which leaves the arguments essentially unaltered, if better buttressed. Other issues have been given more thought. Much presentation, lecture and debate has shown that less confusion arises over the face validity of the level–style separation (especially for those steeped in the creativity literature and tradition – although others, even of more modest education and experience, have little difficulty) if one first stresses that the theory and measure relate to preferred style and not to behaviour. Of course, there is a relationship between these two, but not, by any means, a perfect one. It is cognitive style that is the essential element of the ego identity – behaviour is the compromise with the environment at large.

As with (learned) attitude, which is a predisposition for consistent response to a particular class of stimulus, one can act in ways that are not in accord with one's preferred cognitive style of generating or resolving novelty – by how much and how often is governed by motive. This was known (e.g., see Chapter 4) but its relevance was underplayed in communicating that man's obvious flexibility in the face of varied difficulty does not destabilize either the theory or the integrity of an individual's personality. Behaviour is related to, but is not synonymous with, preferred style. Coping behaviour is the link between preferred style and behaviour, but it is costly. The early studies showing this cost (such as Hayward and Everett, 1983; Lindsay, 1985) have found further support (Kubeš and Spillerová, 1992; McCarthy, 1993; Rickards and Moger, 1994).

The argument then, for the conceptual separation of level and preferred style is now better secured. It is easier to respond to the quoted (1950) Guilford observation, that there is more to creativity than IQ, by saying: Yes, indeed, style too needs to be taken into account. An equally clear response can be made to Getzels and Jackson's (1962) observation: that there is no relationship between creativity and IQ except that one has to have a high IQ in order to be creative! It is that such statements do not constitute good, sharp, testable hypotheses, which are one of the bases of sound science. As level and style pose different questions, therefore they should elicit different answers. There is no reason why these different answers should be related: that is, a knowledge of one answer does not give any knowledge (prediction) of the other, so, creative style is not related to IQ, but creative level may well be.

In my first Preface, what made up the domain of problem solving and creativity, besides level and style, was only lightly touched upon. There was reference to many variables, which are often included into definitions of creativity, that the Preface placed outside the domain, even if these other variables had obvious effects on the final product. For instance, knowledge, scope, opportunity and motive all play a role in a problem-solving outcome but were excluded as an integral part of its domain. Instead they were envisaged as, for instance, the stimulus (for action, as motive is) or the material of which idea generation made use. This position, also, has not changed by any new research. It is still just as clear that, to take another example, the level of success of an outcome, especially if made by another, is not to be confused with an assessment of the level of, for example, a theory and whether it stands the test of time. Empedocles, in 440BC, was said, by Bertrand Russell (1946), to have 'suggested a statesmanlike compromise' by allowing Earth, Air, Fire and Water to be the basic elements of which the universe was composed. Before him, other great philosophers had set the structure – making Empedocles' notion more adaptive in style: 'Heraclitus believed fire to be the primordial element, out of which everything else had arisen. Thales ... thought everything was made of water; Anaximenes thought air was the primitive element.' All this thinking was, for its day, at the highest philosophical level, yielding among much other gain, the beginning of the intellectual process that separated physics from metaphysics, so laying an essential foundation to scientific progress. The fact that the theories of these philosophers, as they relate to the search for basic elements, is now all judged wrong, does not disturb the general thesis that they were of high level and highly creative. For that matter, Empedocles' notions did last longer than modern theories are wont to do – many are alive today who were taught that elements were made up of indivisible atoms consisting of protons with a varying number of electrons whizzing round them, like little planetary systems. We now have quantum physics few can yet understand.

The value of separating out orthogonally related variables is that it is a necessary step for the development of accurate knowledge and for its valid and reliable testing with adequate (separate) measures. If this is not done, and theories and their measures both conflate variables that are independent of each other (just as with physics and metaphysics), then the measures will yield unsatisfactory results. Wallach and Kogan (1965) have found that measures of creativity correlated erratically among themselves. If some were good and others poor, some measured style, others level and some were mixed, their results can be expected.

The detachment of preferred style from potential level makes it easier, theoretically and empirically, to explore the relationship with the personality domain – see Chapter 2. At least as useful is the challenge to the terminology so loosely used by so many, which is the theme of Gordon Foxall's Chapter 6. The term innovation is used in many ways, of which two are the most common:

1   The kind of change, or suggestion for change, that has an element of 'breakthrough' to it. This is the way innovation is used in this book, it lies at the end of a continuum ranging from operating within the paradigm (consensually agreed structure) to working to the edges, or towards less defined parts of the paradigm or even 'breaking out' of

some part of its boundary to end up athwart it or outside it into some other structure (the Kuhnian switch).

2 It is used to be synonymous with 'new', 'novel', 'creative', as opposed to (i.e., regarding adaption as) not new, not creative. This is an elitist definition reinforced by the belief that only intelligent innovative people, however either term is measured, are capable of creativity. This definition conflates style with level.

So one challenge this book poses is to the way we describe the domain it covers, with all its implications. Those who run conferences, publish journals, or have titles such as 'Creativity and Innovation' are shifting innovation from a style to a level; excluding improvement and the support and refinement of paradigms from the realm of creativity; suggesting that innovation is the 'best' and highest form of solving problems without regard to the situation and its needs. Readers will be faced with a choice between tight or loose definitions – the one avenue closed to the thoughtful is using both definitions at the same time. One example of the outcome of such conflation is found in Chapter 6.

PROCESS AND TECHNIQUE

There are two more concepts that are included in the problem-solving domain other than level and style. They are process and technique. These, 5 years ago, received scant attention. Process schemata have been around a long time; one still in use was devised by Wallas in 1926 (see Foreword by Campbell in Isaksen, 1987). Like all such schemata, it represents an ideal abstraction applicable to every human, derived from many real but flawed examples (from the knowledge of its author) of problem solving, creativity or whatever is the concept in review. It purports to show, the better to understand, the workings of the concept: what are its elements – no more, no less – and in what order they appear, in its progress from its presumed start to its presumed finish. This notion poses different questions and requires different answers from those of level and style. Level can be tested by a unipolar measure that deals with 'How much'; style by a bipolar measure of 'What manner'; process needs to be tested by validation – Are these the elements? Are they in this order? Do they progress from this point to that? Does it cover everyone and every relevant event? Does this dynamic schema (process) tell us more about what is happening than we knew anyway? So process needs to be evaluated in terms of its truth, precision and usefulness, in understanding the way in which the concept it purports to explain works.

In the same way that level and style cannot be conflated and built into the same measure unseparated, neither can process be conflated with either of them (de Ciantis and Kirton, 1994). From this reasoning it is possible to construct the following statements:

1 Level measures may or may not correlate highly among themselves: e.g., level measures of general creativity may well correlate with IQ; but not all measures of all talents will correlate highly among themselves.

2 Style measures may or may not correlate highly among themselves: cognitive style and Extraversion–Introversion, both ways of dealing with input, will correlate significantly, but not perfectly. Measures of affect (e.g., Neuroticism or Myers–Briggs 'Thinking–Feeling') will correlate next to zero with style.

3 Level and style measures, if pure, correlate not at all.

4 Cognitive processes (dynamic schemata) need to be validated not measured – their use depends on whether the information they impart is clear, true and useful.

5 Level and style, as measured variables, are applicable at each stage of a process.

6 The notions of level, style and process can be applied at the same time, in any problem-solving creative situation: appealing to the process to locate where we are, between start and finish; noting that, underlying our actual behaviour at every stage of the process, we are limited by our cognitive capacities (e.g., talent – the power of the 'engine') and by our cognitive style (the characteristic way we prefer to use the engine).

It follows (from points 5 and 6) that we should reject any simple notion that any stage of the process inherently implies a different particular level or style. Style, and at times even capacity, can only be deemed appropriate or not by the perceived nature of the problem and the perceived nature of the required solution, both as influenced by the perceived situation. A process is appropriate if it is accurate and useful. So, to take another example, Guilford's elements of divergence and convergence, like the other three elements in this same dimension from which they are so often unwarrantedly detached, are useful as parts of the context in which they were devised. They should not be abstracted and treated as styles in which one is inherently superior to the other, thereby confusing process, style and level.

Additionally, each stage of these cognitive processes can be executed at levels ranging from high to low and in styles ranging from, say, adaption to innovation. The naming or presumed function of any of these elements does not imply a desired level or style outside that dictated by the perceived stimulus, its setting and its desired outcome. Therefore, diverging and remaining close to the paradigm is more adaptive in style than diverging to the edges of the paradigm or wandering outside it; adaptive diverging would also be likely to cover the scanned ground more methodically than innovative diverging. Converging on a solution that lies within, and thereby protects whilst refining the paradigm, is more adaptive than converging on a solution that threatens the paradigm. Which is 'better' in, say, social terms is quite another assessment which lies outside our domain. Including the notion of 'better' or 'more valuable' into a definition of creativity is added conflation, and another source of confusion and built-in inaccuracy of measurement.

Technique is the fourth element I suggested should be inside our domain, along with level, style and process. It can be defined as the learnt ways (know-how) that allow us to use our potential mental resources to better advantage, in actual behaviour. Techniques fall into classes that also reflect the level and style difference. One technique is that if idea generation is blocked, lay off and do some gardening; try brainstorming; try redefining and tightening the key terminology. So some of these techniques are designed to lower anxiety – thereby increasing the general level of effectiveness directly. Others simulate methods of innovation; yet others simulate those of adaption – thereby indirectly increasing effectiveness by selecting an appropriate style for the specific occasion. If one knows what the key to more effectiveness is on each occasion, then the choice of technique is easier. If one is not so clear, then experiment. Try one that suits you first, try others later; try those you think will break this particular type of problem.

Mastery of technique does not alter the user's potential level, but does make for more effective use of whatever level is available. Using a technique unlike one's own style does not change the user's style, for one just temporarily uses another style – though this form of 'coping' behaviour, like any other, can be more costly of effort than one's natural preference.

Techniques tend to be taught as if each one is the complete answer to every problem in every circumstance. Clearly knocking off to do the gardening doesn't actually get the job done. It may be valuable as a technique on a particular occasion, but not as a way of life. Using brainstorming (simulated innovation) when the answer needed is adaptive or using sharper, clearer methodology within the existing paradigm (adaption) when a paradigm-cracking solution is sought, are all misuses of technique. One other error often made is to assume that the teaching of a technique leads to a better problem solver (a more creative person), when it should be seen as leading to more effectiveness in a particular situation. Most teaching of techniques does not reveal much about two important issues in their use: to recognize when they are needed (and when not); second, that for their continued successful use they need to be practised. The clear separation of techniques from level, style and process makes the strategy of their use and limitations more easily understood and acceptable. In part, now, this is because being taught them does not imply an initial inferiority as if one's basic capacity is at fault. In part also, techniques can now be applied by their practitioners with better discrimination as to aim and occasion. Even if the technique being taught is close to one's own style, it may still need training on how to exercise it, in collaboration with others. Finally, but of great importance, the idea needs to be got across that teaching one technique for all occasions is like providing a craftsman with a single tool. A kit is required, together with the training to know which to use, and when. Training and practice in the use of tools is just part of a person's continuing education and not the correction of a flaw in brain function.

IMPLICATIONS OF STABILITY OF STYLE AND FLEXIBILITY OF BEHAVIOUR

From the earliest studies, KAI scores showed both high internal and high test–retest reliabilities. Indeed, in Chapter 7 van der Molen suggests that a heredity component is implicated and the need for varying degrees of structure in a social setting may not even be confined to humans – an intriguing line of thinking! Clapp (1993) and Taylor (1994), in presenting their own data, have also reviewed past studies in the stability, over time, of KAI scores. The former used a manager sample with 41 months between first and second administration; the latter used school-children, 14 years old at the first administration and 17 at the second. All studies confirm the remarkable stability of the instrument, as theory would suggest it should (see Chapters 1 and 2). These high stabilities are reinforced by a study by Murdock *et al.* 1993 (it relates to Chapter 5) in which course participants were for months trained to be more innovative (behaviour) but showed remarkably little difference in KAI (preference) mean score at the end of the course compared with their score before the course began. Watts (1985), in an earlier similar study, had obtained the same result. The theory is not new to any of us. We all teach children to be more adaptive: before answering the question, please read it; be more methodical; present your work more neatly; nice essay, pity it is not on the topic I set; and so on. The best teachers taught most of us a lot of technique, but changed us (our preferred cognitive style) not at all. In the process they found some of us (adaptors) more receptive to working more closely within structure than others (innovators). Lesser teachers, especially when faced with the less motivated innovators, got even less far. Of course, despite the groans in the literature, not all teachers are or ever were, adaptors. The highly innovative ones delighted most of us, whether we always understood them or not; some of us (the higher adaptors) were just confused. As the saying goes: 'You just can't win 'em all'. The best teachers win more than most; the same goes for the best leaders or managers, since this structuring performance began again when we went to work. Most teaching and leadership should be based on the assumption that those who are willing are not basically unworthy.

If cognitive style is so very stable and problems or their human environments are both variable and compelling, then a problem of cognitive fit arises – correspondence between self and cognitive climate (see Chapter 4). Another issue, contained in Chapter 3, is the use of coping behaviour. Already by 1989 it was only too clear that a gap between how a person preferred to solve problems and how he was expected to do so in practice, could, if the gap were large and lasted over a long time, cause strain and stress. Difficulty also arose if there was a large, persistent cognitive preference gap between self and colleagues. More recent studies are confirming the informed hypotheses outlined earlier (e.g., Kubeš and Spillerová, 1992; McCarthy, 1993; Rickards and Moger, 1994). This work depends on being able to measure some of the key variables. By changing the KAI instructions and asking people to rate others as they perceive them, then comparing these others' estimates with own self score, the gap between the two can be attributed to either error or a part of the person's 'coping behaviour' that the perceiver accepts as natural. Error there may be, but the evidence for the measurement of coping behaviour is (a) the 'other' estimates, when the raters are well known to the rated, have high internal reliability (Clapp, 1991; McCarthy, 1993); and (b) the direction of the deviation of the other estimate from self-estimate is in the same direction as the cognitive climate norm (see again Chapter 4) – a source of social pressure (which constitutes stimulus and engenders motive) to which we respond by 'coping'.

A number of people have questioned, although so far not in print, whether it is likely that much practised coping behaviour becomes so part of a person's behavioural repertoire that it modifies their basic preference and becomes less of a source of stress. Research is absent as far as this theory is concerned, but the current assumption is that this is true of learned behaviour (such as technique) that does not conflict with preference – practice makes it easier and easier. With coping behaviour, repeated use is additional strain. The relationship between stress and cognitive gap is, since 1989, attracting more interest among practitioners (see also Hayes and Allinson, 1994). So too is the notion of using bridger's to facilitate collaboration between people and groups: potential bridgers are people who have, preferably, intermediate scores between those they intend to bridge, and whose natural skills and willingness can be enhanced by training. The social implications of cognitive style are becoming more apparent.

APPLICATIONS OF THEORY AND MEASURE

The theoretical notions advanced in 1989 are continuing to accumulate additional support and amplification, e.g., more links have been noted between cognitive style and personality. The main differences between then and now is the widening use of the theory and measure by practitioners. Once the notion of cognitive gap and the possibility of measuring it was understood – whether between individuals, between the individual and the group, or between groups – its use in training courses became more obvious. The realization that bridging, an old concept now placed in this new theoretical setting, is a social and learnt skill has also impinged on practitioners. Mainly because of the effect of the separation in practice between estimates of a person's capacity and the same person's style, a much better understanding of the dynamics within problem-solving groups – can there be any other kind of groups? – has exercised many minds in business and administration. The sharpening of the definitions of problem-solving process and problem-solving techniques that keep these concepts separate from both style and level, as I have outlined above (see also de Ciantis and Kirton, 1994), has led to more use of them in mentoring problem-solving teams. One implication for the management of groups is that the management of intra-group diversity can shift on to an efficiency-oriented basis rather than a 'Let's be kind to Bob week, he may be different but he does his best'. Diversity, at least in the very basic cognitive sense, can now be welcomed even if the management of a cognitively heterogeneous team is a more difficult task than leading a homogeneous one. What makes the extra effort worthwhile is the pay-off of having available a diversity of (potential) problem solvers for the diversity of problems that might, and usually does, confront the group.

The value of having available the diversity of problem solver is based, as stated early, on the assumption of the psychologist that all mankind is problem solving and, therefore, creative. There cannot be people who do not find novelty attractive, but that obviously does not mean that there is anyone who finds all novelty attractive. Homo sapiens is discriminating, a calculator of possible outcomes *par excellence*. He will accept those novelties that are perceived as beneficial and reject those that are perceived as not. As Foxall's chapter will give evidence, we differ on our individual calculations of outcome – innovators are, on balance more attracted to the kind of 'new' that leads to doing differently (associated with the looser cognitive structure); adaptors to the kind of 'new' that leads to doing better (associated with tighter structure). There is no inherent advantage or superiority anywhere along this range of cognitive preferences, or the people who hold them, except in situational context, when the advantage may go either way.

The balance of the diversity in any team (see Chapter 3) is today attracting more practitioner attention: What is the best balance for our affairs right now? For the foreseeable future? How do we keep track of the need to alter the balance? How do we bring about such changes needed in a cohesive, high-morale group setting? If the balance cannot readily be altered, what other options can we find, for this group, in this situation? These thoughts, shared by everyone in a group, seem to be having the side effect of greater tolerance for diversity outside the cognitive style domain. Diversity in many forms might be useful and once this thought settles in, group effectiveness is a concept that, associated with enlightened self-interest, adds substantial weight to a more abstract notion of fairness. One interesting observation in my consultancy activities is that an acceptance of diversity in style actually makes it easier to accept differences in level. If someone is not performing at a desired level, it is best that the reasons for this are not mixed up with an irritation that the person also has a (unappreciated) difference in style. The issues are better managed when considered separately, as are any other differences between people.

As long as we remember that both preferred cognitive style and potential cognitive capacity are not readily changeable, then we can concentrate our minds on all the knowledge, attributes and attitudes that *are* amenable to change by training and teaching, through both theory and practice. Rather than try to change a person's basic identity, the more attainable aim is helping them to recognize when collaborating with someone different from themselves is a good solution. If coping behaviour is a must, as it all too often is, then learning good techniques and when to use them (and when not) will help reduce tensions and increase effectiveness, without unwisely purporting or even attempting to alter the individual's ego.

A number of consultants and managers are currently using these ideas and selected measures, including KAI, in the role of mentors to top problem-solving groups. It is interesting to be able to show groups, only recently formed, (a) where problems might be expected to arise because of their cognitive and other diversities; (b) that different members of the group can sometimes be found to be operating at different stages of the creative process; (c) and that they may disagree, during the same stage, by advocating different problem-solving techniques, because they may be aiming, often unwittingly, at a different style of conclusion; and (d) that different actualized capacities and potential levels may be useful, because they often have different skills and perspectives to offer, which can be used by an integrated group. As these group phenomena are explicated, it is also possible to underline the importance and potential usefulness to each member of these same diversities, as well as others that are available to the group. This knowledge gives a powerful incentive to treat diversity as just one other resource needing insightful, careful handling *by everyone*: a resource that should be not only tolerated but also welcomed. Some of my colleagues have observed that teams so trained and mentored seem to have acquired added tolerance for disagreement within their teams, whilst finding they are having to manage less conflict. If this is found to be an attested outcome, I shall be well pleased with any contribution my work may have made.

Let me end the critique of my 1989 Preface by hoping that my work and this book may help more people get into better, more effective accord with colleagues and partners, by the use of insight rather than exhortation; that they can achieve more effectively, not with less effort but with less pain and conflict.

1994

INTRODUCTION

Marián Kubeš

In 1986, when I first became acquainted with the work of Michael Kirton, I was a research scientist in the Department for Theory of Science and Forecasting, Slovak Academy of Sciences in Bratislava. The concept of 'paradigm', as defined by T. Kuhn, was an obvious overlap between the work I was doing and the new field I was entering. As I become more familiar with the background and context of A–I theory, I realized how much the whole of Kirton's work and its acceptance in the relevant scientific communities illustrate the processes of scientific progress with its problems, dynamism, social resistance and crisis as described by Kuhn. In ways similar to other theories in the history of science, the Adaption–Innovation theory, so 'painstakingly detailed and accurate' contributes to 'normal science' in one field and yet is so 'paradigm cracking' in another one. Moreover, during the last nine years, I could repeatedly relate A–I theoretical assumptions to the everyday reality of changing systems in Eastern Europe, thus verifying its validity on a macro level. Some of these observations are described elsewhere (Kubeš and Benkovič, 1994).

Since 1976, when the Adaption–Innovation theory of cognitive style was introduced, there has been growing evidence of the concept's validity. At the same time the scope of the theory's applications has broadened. It covers studies related to the personality background of individual cognitive preferences, explains group behaviour in situations of problem solving and conflict resolution, and suggests the role of adaptive and innovative tendencies in organizational and societal development. Below are outlined several key areas in which the theory has had strong impact.

PROVOCATIVE AND PRACTICAL

If we tried to characterize the Kirton's Adaption–Innovation theory of cognitive style, several attributes would be relevant. As a theory of cognitive style, it provides possible explanations of some of the mental processes underlying problem solving, decision making and creativity. It also shows how these processes influence people's behaviour in everyday life situations. In this respect the A–I theory is very *practical*. It is not only the individual whose behaviour is better understood either in a dyad or group situation: the power of the theory has also been proven both at the level of the organization and at the level of a whole society.

There are theories in the history of science that have impact not only on the fields from which they emerged but also on other, more or less obviously related areas of man's scientific endeavour. From the history of science we know that the radically new in science is not easily accepted. It is not only the Mertonian scepticism which forces scientists to put under scrutiny each newly proposed piece of knowledge. Scientific progress does not consist of the production of successively more accurate depictions of the real world that is independent of the conceptions of scientists. The framework of assumptions that determines the observer's viewpoint and influences the construction of facts as well as their explanation is generally termed a *paradigm*. Kuhn (1970) has shown how elaboration of a paradigm occasionally leads to anomalies that cannot be fitted within its scope, and that the reasons for rejection of a new paradigm have roots deeper than scientific scepticism.

The Adaption–Innovation theory bears a highly *provocative* element in itself. The best example of this quality, we think, is its impact on the study of creativity. As the reader will find later in the book, it sharply distinguishes between level and style of creativity and views creativity as a generalized attribute of every human being. This view sharply contrasts with claims that 'innovative' creativity is the better way forward and should be supported, studied, admired, rewarded, celebrated, etc. to the denigration of creative work that redefines, elaborates, modifies and improves the paradigm. Mankind, as created, has always had to face and solve problems that have undoubtedly required contribution from both ends, and it is a real challenge for us today to accept it and forget the elitist view that only contributes to the many faces of social injustice we can see everywhere around us.

MAJOR FIELDS OF THE THEORY'S APPLICATIONS AND DEVELOPMENT

Adaption–Innovation theory precisely defines a basic principle of the degree of structure a person is comfortable with when problem solving or thinking in general. Although it makes the theory applicable in any study where structure is relevant, it is the applied side of science which has flourished most after the introduction of the A–I concept. So far neither Kirton nor any other has paid much attention to the clarification of the nature of the information processing behind the A–I concept. No comprehensive study has been carried out to link it with the large body of existing literature in cognitive psychology in general or with other concepts of cognitive style in particular. These studies would require more complex research (experimental) design with multivariate statistics, whereas the works published during the last 18 years are based predominantly on correlational analyses of KAI with other paper-and-pencil measures.

An analysis of written materials reveals several major areas of the development and applications of A–I theory which are the focus of different chapters of this book. Since its introduction, there has been a series of studies focusing on various aspects of the *validity and reliability* of the theory's measure: the Kirton Adaption–Innovation Inventory. There has also been much effort to clarify how the A–I concept relates to *personality traits*, as cognitive styles are presumed to moderate the link between personality and thinking and thus influence individual's behavioural responses in given circumstances. The broadest area is represented by the field of *management, leadership* and *organization development*. Although cognitive styles are a domain of cognitive psychology, A–I theory has been influenced by a variety of approaches to human problem solving, decision making and creativity which meet in the basic assumptions underlying the A–I concept. Not surprisingly, the theory has had an impact on the field of *creativity and problem solving*. The area of *adoption of new products and ideas* is another major application. In the following sections we deal in more detail with these areas of A–I theory applications. Besides the above-mentioned fields there are others where the theory has been successfully applied, e.g., team building, counselling and conflict resolution, cross-cultural studies, education, personnel selection, etc.

Creativity and problem solving

To begin, we must go back to Kuhn and his observation that new knowledge emerging from one field can cause a crisis in another one.

Although placed in cognitive psychology, the adoption of some of the key assumptions of A–I theory in the field of human creativity has evoked contradictory reactions from immediate acceptance to strict refusal. In spite of its presence in a variety of different approaches, the concept of creativity remains unclear. The difficulty in understanding *creativity as such* lies also in the fact that there are many layers as well as contexts in which creativity can be viewed. Csikszentmihály (1990) argues that the usual research question – What is creativity? – should be replaced by a different question – Where is creativity? Kirton substitutes the *creative vs. non-creative* point of view with *creative in different ways at different levels among all people*. His major contribution is not only the sharp distinction of level and style in theory but also a sound measure – the Kirton Adaption–Innovation Inventory (KAI) – enabling scholars to verify this supposition empirically. Isaksen and Dorval (1993) thoroughly explored the means for improving the understanding of creativity using the level-style distinction. They used the Kirton's theory of cognitive style as representative of the style dimension. They reviewed existing research on style/level distinction and conclude that:

> The distinction provides a strong conceptual foundation by making more explicit and comprehensive the linkages between creative characteristics within people, the processes they perform, their preferences for creative productivity, and the individual differences they hold in their perceptions of environments conducive to creative performance.
>
> (Isaksen and Dorval, 1993: 325)

Kirton points out that the confusion in creativity literature is not caused by mixing up the level and style aspects only. There also exists considerable confusion in using the terms 'process' and 'technique' of creativity. Kirton explores the four key concepts (style, level, process, technique), clarifies relationships amongst them and thus lays foundations for a new model of creativity that has all the advantages of a scientifically sound concept: it is clear, empirically verifiable, throwing more light on previous contradictions, and, all in all, surely provocative enough to evoke resistance amongst others who made their names in research on creativity.

Kirton's concept of creativity is centred around the process of novelty generation/resolution. He argues that to create or solve problems requires novelty generation and/or resolution which can take place within or outside the given paradigm, depending on the amount of structure the individual prefers or feels comfortable with. While the intra-paradigm breadth of search relates to level, the inter-paradigm search relates to preferred style independently of the breadth of any single paradigm. It is this clear conceptual separation not only of style and level but also of the other two components (process and technique) which makes this model hardly acceptable by those who approach the creativity phenomenon through studying the creative product. They argue that in creative output all these four components are present in a unique holistic way and therefore they are not separable. Here an analogy with human voice seems to be appropriate. While the layman appreciates the beauty of, say, an opera aria, he is not conscious of all the complexities of pattern that reach his ears. This does not mean that this pattern cannot be broken down into more simple, measurable, independent units. An expert, however, would easily recognize e.g., sound quality, pitch, loudness, length, etc. From a practical viewpoint he would also find it impossible to develop an opera singer without having a chance to study these aspects separately: to use practice techniques, focusing on them separately and evaluating the final outcome via the contribution of each of them.

There is, however, another analogy between the product of our speech mechanism and creative output. Whatever the combination and quality of the sound components, our hearing mechanism must be thought of in two ways: as a physiological mechanism that reacts to the acoustic stimuli and, second, as the psychological activity that selects from the gross acoustic information that which is relevant in terms of the linguistic system involved. Therefore a creative output at one place may not be recognized as creative at another. There is the danger that our efforts in a scientific study of creativity would be devalued if we allowed societal values (appropriateness/usefulness) to interfere with the scientific evaluation of creative output. This is, in my view, one of the major problems to be solved in the present creativity research.

Through recent decades the concept of innovation has become the synonym for technical progress and one of the main criteria for creativity. Kirton now offers a deep revision of this loosely defined concept. He abandons the traditional scheme *innovative = creative* and *adaptive = non-creative*. People are creative regardless of their absolute position on the A–I continuum ranging from highly adaptive to highly innovative, and evaluation of the appropriateness of one of these styles can be found only in its specific context, in a particular situation. There is, therefore, one more aspect that adds value to the whole A–I concept in the field of human creativity. The theory states that every person is creative. The introduction of a sound stylistic aspect into creative performance explains why some elitist theories could flourish in the past, by failing to recognize the role of style in creative production with respect to given circumstances.

Adoption of new products, marketing and consumer behaviour

Similarly, in marketing and consumer behaviour research, as Foxall points out, the weakness of equating innovation with new, and innovator with the openness to *anything* new, has led much research astray for half a century and will continue to do so until more realistic hypotheses, founded initially on Kirton theory, are formulated. Gordon Foxall, one of the contributors to the present book, has initiated research that has resulted in several important conclusions for the field of marketing. In his recent paper, Foxall (1994) outlines three areas of implications that the A–I theory has for the conceptualization of consumer innovativeness, i.e., willingness to try new products, for the depiction of the adoption decision process, and for the psychographic segmentation of new product markets. On the basis of the finding, Foxall challenges the view that the behaviour of consumer initiators can be explained by a set of personality traits that define what is misleadingly called 'inherent innovativeness'.

> The theoretical import of the results is that consumer initiators may manifest either adaptive or innovative personality characteristics rather than the profile suggested by research in marketing and cognitive/personality psychology.
>
> (Foxall, 1994: 15)

Foxall also disconfirms the widely held view that initial buyers are inevitably highly involved and engaged in extended problem solving, while late adopters show low involvement manifesting in routine decision making and purchasing. Here again, as in other fields, if A–I theory is used as the explanatory framework, the implications modify the traditionally held views and may have significant effects on marketing strategies. The prospects for further research outlined in Foxall's works show the applicability of the A–I theory in fields remote from Kirton's original work.

Organizational development

Organizational development involves the largest group of contributions applying and developing the A–I theory. The subgroups include: A–I preferences in different occupational groups; person–environment fit and coping in organizational context, stimulating change in organizations; cognitive climate; cross-cultural differences in managerial groups; and leadership and development of social systems. Kirton's work has contributed to the clarification of several concepts in this field.

Thus, the process of change in large organizations, as studied by Clapp (1991), has led to several important conclusions regarding the policies involved in human resource management.

> If steps are not taken to manage the change from a human resource view point, the more innovative individuals, with their lack of concern for job security and interpersonal relationships, will inevitably be among the first to leave or be displaced from the organisation. . . . For the more adaptive individual, where disruptive change is ongoing, effort is expended in trying to bring order and stability to the environment. When it is felt that such efforts are negated by the ongoing changes, individual dissatisfaction results again with a potential loss of staff.
>
> (Clapp, 1991: 327–8)

The work of Kirton has also contributed to the clarification and broadening of concepts of cognitive climate and coping behaviour. The latter, for decades used predominantly in psychotherapy and counselling contexts, helps us now to understand better the everyday pressures not only in work situations but also in any other setting where individuals are expected to collaborate together.

Because of its practical usefulness, the theory and its measure are extensively used, particularly in the organizational contexts. An example of this usage can be found in a case study described by Kubeš and Benkovič (1994). It illustrates how a prevailing cognitive climate, (a concept described in one of Kirton's chapters later in this book), influences the behaviour of individual employees in the first instance and thus the whole system.

A MORE PERSONAL VIEW

I have had the privilege of being involved in the KAI worldwide network since 1986. I think that some observations I can make add to the validity of the Adaption–Innovation theory on a macro level. On the political scene of the former Czechoslovakia, we have experienced several massive swings, from adaptive to innovative and vice versa, of the pendulum of change that Kirton discusses. After a long period of ossification, the innovators (dissidents) took the lead and caused the revolutionary change of the political paradigm. Perhaps the most dramatic consequence of the shifts observed is the split of former Czechoslovakia into two independent states. Within the last four years (1990–3) we can observe several 'returns' of the pendulum as the new political leaders introduce more adaptive (hopefully effective) changes. Such a trend is viewed with hope by the population, but also with a fear of the possible return of the past. Meanwhile innovators (former leaders) now constitute the political (conservative!) opposition.

From the standpoint of A–I theory, it is not surprising that those who were willing to take risks by being in disagreement with the official establishment were innovators. It was interesting to follow how the spontaneous movement started to restructure itself into a working system where the political leaders (innovators) were expected to explain their policies to the nation. This was precisely the point where new, very real problems were generated by the attempts to resolve the original ones. Since a systematic and elaborated approach now was needed, the revolutionary innovators were quite often surrounded by people whose style was similar to their own. As team members tend to accept as critics those who deviate least from the average cognitive climate of the team (Kubeš and Spillerová, 1992), the overall activity of such a team becomes 'locked within itself' and excludes corrections from outside the system. If the system is sharply innovatively oriented, as in this case, the need for adaptive input becomes increasingly critical as time passes. Being excluded, adaptors become more dissatisfied and innovators tend to keep the system 'more open', just as in the past the adaptors had kept the system too closed. The need for a Kirton 'balance' that welcomes and also manages wide diversity is sadly needed!

CONCLUSION

Kirton's strong sense of accuracy and precision challenges all concepts that do not possess the same level of precise definition as his. Coupled with the sound conceptual background of the A–I concept, the inherent incompatibility with much current work contains a considerably pro-vocative flavour. A scientific problem can easily become a social problem. All of this makes the scientific endeavour of man an exciting enterprise. If solutions to problems people solve are always new, then the correct question, as Kirton reminds us, is whether those solutions are adaptively new or innovatively new. Kirton's solution, in his own terms, is innova-tively new and therefore, the chapters that follow provide exciting reading while at the same time the book has the additional grace of being very thoroughly adaptively constructed.

1

A THEORY OF COGNITIVE STYLE

M.J. Kirton

More than for any other organism, at the core of the understanding of homo sapiens is the study of the cognitive processes at the command of the species. For a very long time there has been a fascination for probing the variables, real or assumed, that lead to successful manifestation of creativity, problem solving and decision making, whether their nature be of the physical environment, the social setting or the individual attribute. Scientific attempts to measure some of these variables, especially the social 'climate' and the individual's potential capacity to learn and to make use of the learning in problem solving, are comparatively recent. But the fascination has been so strong and the effort so great that, just as with other sciences, more knowledge in this field has been accumulated in this century than in all the previous millennia of man's existence. To date, the concentration has been on the understanding of the basic equipment – the brain and nervous system – and the measurement of its capacity as well as the environment, such as organizational climate. It is only more recently that attention has turned to the scientific measurement, as distinct from literary description, of the wide range of different stable characteristic behaviour patterns exhibited by individuals when problem solving or being creative.

One possibility for this neglect is that cognitive style is a more subtle concept than cognitive capacity, or the many extra-individual variables that facilitate or hamper, praise or damn, novel thought and action. This is because these latter variables, however hard to measure they may be, seem simpler in their strategic conception: one end of any relevant measure is judged 'good' (e.g., high IQ) and the other end less so (e.g., shortage of a necessary resource) almost wholly irrespective of specific context. It is, for instance, not often that low IQ is a positive advantage in problem solving. Cognitive style is not like this, for any style – given a specific set of circumstances, type of problem, strategic aim, social

1

climate and individual skill, know-how, persistence and every other attribute – might just succeed where other styles have not.

Adaption–Innovation theory is located in the domain of cognitive function, specifically part of the strategic stable characteristic preferred style that people (if not also animals) seek to bring about intended change. This definition implies the exclusion of some concepts and the inclusion of others that are not necessarily mirrored in other approaches. First, the term 'preferred': in this theory, there is a clear distinction between preferred style and behaviour, which in many circumstances, all essentially related to motive, may not be in accord with one's preferred style. Later we shall need to relate style to behaviour by introducing 'coping' behaviour to indicate and possibly measure when one departs from the other.

Second, the term 'style': in this theory there is a sharp distinction between style and the capacity or level of cognition of which a person is capable, whether this is inherent or learned. The latter describes the 'power of the engine'; the former the 'manner in which it is driven'. This is not a matter that can be taken on trust, especially as this distinction is not always clear in the psychology literature and is a good deal more conflated in the creativity literature. More of this chapter will be devoted to the empirical support for this basic assumption.

Third, the term 'change': in this theory there is the implicit assumption that change, intended by man or not, is a constant phenomenon. Since humans are constantly responding to change and are the world's experts in bringing about intended change, the element in the definition will buttress the theory's theme that all people are agents of (intended) change and are creative (however that may be measured); conversely it is unsound philosophically and difficult in practice to suppose that states of 'no change' can exist anywhere.

Fourth, additionally the term 'change' in this theory is taken to embrace the concepts of creativity, problem solving and decision making, for they all in some way closely relate to cognitive style and to each other. They all involve the concept of novelty, its generation or its revolution, both interacting and giving rise to each other. It can be more readily seen from this standpoint that to describe someone with an intact cortex as uncreative is an elitist view; to describe a person as incapable of problem solving is absurd. People can be measured in terms of level and in terms of style but cannot be dismissed as not having any.

Fifth, and still following through the implications of an ever-changing universe: in this theory, all living organisms must be attuned to change. To suggest that some people like change and some dislike it must be an inadequate statement. We must all surely like changes that can be perceived to suit us, and resist those we judge will not. Naturally, there will be a wariness to any change opportunity that cannot, for whatever reason, be readily assessed as to its outcome. One reason may be that the change proposed by another is outside one's style of problem-solving search – hence the hesitation. Cautious or negative judgements, however, do not automatically imply a global, quasi-pathological syndrome of 'resistance to change' though it may well be a 'resistance to your change proposal' response! Equally, it may be quite feasible to measure people's calculations of how change affects them (and so their perception of the value of any particular change). Some will be more adventurous and risk taking (or rash, depending on one's viewpoint) than others: that is not the same thing as supposing that a large percentage of people dislike all change.

Sixth, and finally, cognitively driven change implies structure. Without structure there can be no analysis of the past and no learning; no projection to the future, no prediction and no theory; no classification of events, no abstraction of principle, no order in the universe; no language and no thought. This is a challenge to much of the creativity literature, which seems to suppose that the less structure involved in idea generation (note: not also the resolution of novelty), the more the idea is creative. Adaption–Innovation theory offers a fuller variation, which, it is hoped, is more refined: the less structure a person is comfortable with in creative or problem-solving activity, the more innovative he is; the more structure a person prefers, and the more of it needs to be consensually agreed, the more adaptive the person is.

The catch is that there are limits in both directions. Beyond a particular point in any given situation, an excess of structure inhibits the generation of new thought, or if not thought, certainly action. Equally, too little structure in any given situation and the thought processes have too few frames of reference to be able to operate effectively: we are worse off than a new-born babe. The range between too much and too little may be narrower than it appears to be, because we take so much of the enabling structure for granted, since we begin to acquire it even before we are born. It is noticeable only when it impedes us and, perforce, it does so only in part. The range does, however, look large when we have to collaborate with another who has a markedly different style. Then it becomes so easy for us to overlook the disadvantages of our own preferred need in the particular situation, but we are able to see the disadvantages of others only too clearly. Of this possible ground for conflict, more later. The point can now be stated succinctly: every point on the style continuum has its advantages and disadvantages, depending on the problem-solving context. Liking some more or some less structure does not imply capacity. Next we can look at two great men and how style and not level separates them.

Carter, in searching for the undiscovered tomb of Tutankhamun, brought his high intellectual capacity, a detailed knowledge of literary resources, and a search technique not hitherto used by archaeologists into his preferred personal strategy of methodical, detailed cognitive operations. From a knowledge of sources and eschewing intuitive flights of fancy, he settled on the Valley of the Kings as his search area. Then he applied a grid to the map of the area and from a meticulous search of the records eliminated each square known to have been subject to thorough field exploration. His own fieldwork covered the remaining areas, permitting hunch only *faute de mieux* and on which of the remaining options to tackle first. He ignored the opinion from site level that none of the areas left looked archaeologically promising. His hunch or intuition did not much help him in getting to the tomb at once. He was on his last season and even more unpromising sites when the tomb was found. His preferred cognitive style was not switched off at this success. The ruthlessly ordered, painstaking opening of the tomb, the cataloguing and initial preservation of the artefacts all employed the same mental strategy of operation that found the tomb and which brought new orders of rigorous scientific method into this relatively new science.

By comparison, the search for a plausible structure for benzene with its six carbon and six hydrogen atoms defied the most persistent systematic reasoning from its discovery by Faraday in 1825 to its resolution by Kekulé in 1865. The line of his solution, as he related years later, was set up in a reverie while on a bus journey. In his half-sleep, he seemed to see chains of carbon atoms come alive and dance before his eyes, then one chain coiled like a snake taking its tail into its mouth. He awoke with a start with the answer: the benzene molecule is a ring. Although much subsequent work and theorizing was built on to this finding, it contained an awkward paradox. To fit the elegant, intuitively satisfying pattern, three double carbon links were needed: double-bonded compounds had been found to be unstable; benzene was known to be stable. It was not until 1912 that Debye was able to propose a solution to this paradox (in a ring, negative poles can link with positive poles without a break) and not until 1936 that a Nobel Prize to Debye confirmed Kekulé's intuition and all the work subsequently carried out.

One key assumption, then underlying Adaption–Innovation theory (Kirton, 1976) is that, as a cognitive style, it relates to the individual's

4

preferred cognitive strategies involved in change (ideation made manifest) and therefore also strategies of creativity, problem solving and decision making, which must themselves be overlapping concepts or even facets of the same concept. These strategies are styles and not capacities. Freed from the complication of capacity, a second key assumption is that cognitive style is related to numerous aspects (traits) of personality that appear early in life and are particularly stable, as is cognitive style. All these assumptions help define the cognitive style. Several other assumptions follow that help define cognitive style domain by distinguishing it from others that the literature often conflates with it. In this theory, cognitive style is assumed to be conceptually independent (to lie orthogonally) to:

1 cognitive capacity (cognitive style is bipolar and non-pejorative);
2 success (cognitive style is basically non-evaluative);
3 cognitive techniques (learned procedures to enhance effective performance – cognitive style seems not to be readily altered by learning or training); and
4 coping behaviour (a process that permits functioning, for limited amounts and limited periods outside preferred cognitive style when needs must).

Having distinguished these variables, it is assumed that they are all likely to have explanatory power in understanding the necessarily complex manifestations of creativity and problem solving. In other words, in particular situations all these variables, and others such as motivation, may interrelate in unique ways. These issues will be further discussed in this and succeeding chapters.

The assumption that cognitive style is distinct from cognitive capacity is gaining wider support. Both Kogan (1976) and Messick (1976) are equally clear that level of performance, with its measures ranging from high or correct to low or incorrect are sharply different from manner of mental operation, which in turn is dependent on 'the manner (in which) individuals acquire, store, retrieve and transform information' (Kogan, 1976: 105). Both Messick (1976; 1984) and Guilford (1980) assume styles to be based on individual preference in the manner of organizing and processing information, to be consistent individual differences, and to be congenial to the individual because style develops around underlying personality traits. The Adaption–Innovation theory, as a cognitive style dimension, must at least assume that it has concomitant stable characteristics. Once, however, cognitive style can be perceived as clearly detached from cognitive capacity, it can be seen not just

5

as related to but as an integral part of personality – probably an underlying explanatory dimension to which groups of traits, themselves deepseated, must be significantly related, as well as being so related to each other.

One uncomfortable contradiction may, however, be inherent in this emerging formulation of these concepts. Style is being described as a marked preference, a character difference, a stable pattern, linked to steady personality traits. Capacity has long been considered to contain in its description an upper limit to individual potential, and social conditions are often lamented as slow to reward discontinuous-type change, however afterwards seen as desirable.

With so much assumed stability then, the elbow-room for man's muchvaunted flexibility seems to be becoming unduly cramped. One way to ease the paradox is to shift from the individual standpoint to a larger perspective: however, the progress man has made over the century is not much of a contribution to an individual's current problem. Coping behaviour in its various forms is a necessary intervening concept between quite stable preferred cognitive style and actual, needed behaviour. Man is the most guileful and resourceful exponent, among the denizens of earth, of altering circumstances to suit his own comfort and taste. But the most common coping behaviour has to be based on the fact that it is 'possible for individuals not only to learn to use a variety of specialised problem-solving and learning strategies that are consonant with their general cognitive styles, but also learn to shift to less congenial strategies that are more effective for a particular task' (Messick, 1984: 62).

Some of these learned behaviours, that are not so far from preferred style and continue to pay dividends, may become part of the natural repertoire of the practitioner. Many others form part of an acceptable accommodation to society. Yet others, further from the 'congenial' heartlands of preference, require a larger, ever-conscious effort to maintain and, however useful, are abandoned as soon as possible. The postgraduate student who is good at and enjoys putting up a whole row of interesting ideas, must all too soon settle for a manageable few on which to proceed, but is, even while writing the last pages, all too easily tempted by yet another idea diversion.

'Coping behaviour' is defined as a departure from preferred style by the minimum amount for the least time needed. The term 'needed' implies that coping is motive driven. Motive switches it on; absence of motive switches it off. Switching on costs added energy and can lead to stress; switching off conserves energy. Small amounts of coping behaviour, over short periods of time, are normal and entail easily bearable costs (e.g., Koeske *et al.*,1993); the problem arises when the coping needed is far from one's style, must be kept up over a long period of time, and especially if anxiety (high penalty) is attached to the outcomes.

To summarize, then, Adaption–Innovation, as a cognitive style, is a preferred mode of tackling problems at all stages (e.g., from one's view of what is the problem; what are relevant data for its resolution; what is an appropriate solution and how it should be implemented). As a characteristic preference, it is therefore presumed to be unrelated to level or capacity, such as IQ, level of cognitive complexity or management competency (see Chapter 5). Further to this assumption, it follows that style, as well as level, is unrelated to technique (à la Osborne or de Bono) since the latter consists of ways of making better use of one's level, generally within one's preference but, if needed, outside it.

Adaption–Innovation is assumed to be a dimension of cognitive process and, as such, is not context specific. There is no implication here, for example, that artists are creative and engineers are not. The theory's instrument – the KAI – is not a measure of cognitive or intellectual level, and, therefore, should not be confused with concepts such as level of creativity, capacity for cognitive complexity or extent of some ability. The theory is essentially value-free. Very high, very low or intermediate KAI scores are neither laudatory nor pejorative; they are simply useful for understanding behaviour in a variety of situations that may or may not have elicited appropriate responses from the people involved. It is the manner, the 'how' of performance, not the level of effectiveness of performance or its success in social terms, that is the concern of Adaption–Innovation theory.

Adaption–Innovation theory is also inferred to be a basic dimension of human personality with meaningful relationships to other personality characteristics. Because Adaption–Innovation is assumed to be a basic dimension, the implication is that it should be found to exist early in life and be stable over both time and incident. This condition is likely to apply also to a number of the style's key personality correlates, such as introversion, sensation seeking and risk taking.

In this chapter, the general characteristics of the adaptor and innovator styles are presented, together with a description of the origin and development of the measuring instrument, the KAI. Normative data are provided as a whole and for its constituent parts. The status of Adaption–Innovation theory is also reviewed in relation to its underlying assumptions: that it is about cognitive style not level; that it relates to personality; that it is formed early and is stable over time and incident; that the concomitant behaviour is predictable and is manifest in social settings; that it is non-pejorative – what for a person can be seen as an advantage or disadvantage is situation specific, not some implied character deficiency. It has been noted that knowledge of the theory will provide useful insight to individuals in understanding how they work and why others may have styles naturally different from their own. They may acquire insight into the ease with which they can clash through misunderstanding and underestimating those who have a greatly different cognitive style. These insights are useful as a basis for understanding, tolerance and finally useful collaboration across a spectrum of wide rich variety of cognitive style.

This introductory chapter provides the theoretical and conceptual background for the succeeding chapters all of which are applications of Adaption–Innovation theory in different fields. All the chapters that follow also contribute to the consolidation, demonstration and amplification of the theoretical structure explicated in Chapter 1.

THE ADAPTOR AND THE INNOVATOR DESCRIBED

The amount of structure that a person feels appropriate within which to solve a problem or to embark on creativity, and the amount of this structure he prefers is consensually agreed, are the core differences, arrayed on a continuum, of people's Adaption–Innovation cognitive strategies. As a corollary a critical characteristic of the habitual adaptor when confronting a problem is to accept the generally recognized theories, policies, customary viewpoints or, in Kuhn's (1970) terms, 'paradigms' in which it appears to be embedded. By contrast, the characteristic style of the habitual innovator is eventually to detach the problem from its cocoon of accepted thought, to reconstruct the problem and its attendant paradigm whilst in the pursuit of a solution. Attendant with these approaches are equally characteristic traits that seem, intuitively, consistent to them and, in large measure, consistent to each other. Regard for paradigms and guiding (consensually agreed) boundaries will lead to thorough search within this finite space and to a taste for ordered detail and rules. The taste for an overview embracing even the guidelines within it could lead to less attention being paid, less regard being given to those guidelines and the fine detail, the rules and excepted ways that also lie within them. The first exposition of adaptors and innovators (Kirton, 1976: Table 1) contained many descriptive terms that have since been exhaustively tested by many such scholars in several countries. However, one neat survey of these differences, already touched on in the classic literature (Drucker, 1969), is that adaptors have a preference for 'doing things better' while innovators trade off immediate efficiency in their preference for 'doing things differently'. Drucker complains that organizations tend to favour the adaptive approach. This complaint is in many instances unfair as the adaptive style seems to be especially suitable for both shorter-term problem solving as well as for many elements of long-term and larger-scale change (Nyström, 1979).

The innovative approach is obviously needed in any organization that is to survive. Yet any organization that is large and has been successful over a long period of time must inevitably be adaptively oriented to guard against unacceptable risk – inherent in making drastic changes over a broad front in a short space of time. This adaptive constraint is reflected, if somewhat reluctantly, in almost all of the classic analyses of bureaucracies. It is said that organizations in general (Whyte, 1957; Bakke, 1965; Weber, 1970; Mulkay, 1972) and especially organizations that are large in size and budget (Veblen, 1928; Swatez, 1970) have a tendency to encourage bureaucracy and adaption in order to minimize risk. Weber (1970), Merton (1957) and Parsons (1951) wrote that the aims of a bureaucratic structure are precision, reliability and efficiency. The bureaucratic structure in its nature exerts constant pressure on officials to be methodical, prudent and disciplined, resulting in an unusual degree of individual conformity in that situation. These behaviours are part of the pattern that Adaption–Innovation theory attributes to the 'adaptor' personality.

The innovator, who consciously or unwittingly reconstructs the original problem as a part of resolving it, invariably has a problem of communication. That such reconstruction has occurred is not often clearly perceived at first, even by its originator. Since it can be difficult to explain, a solution dependent on innovative thought often gets a sceptical reception. This resistance tends to be reinforced by the fact that there are nearly always alternative solutions put forward by adaptors who may be seen by significant others to be just as creative, resourceful and knowledgeable as the innovator and who, in addition, have the reputation for being sound.

An historical example may help to illustrate the differences between the two types of solution. In medieval times astronomical observations increasingly found star movements not to be in accord with the prevailing paradigm (theory). Two solutions were produced. The first retained the integrity of the paradigm and invented epicycles of increasing complexity to square observation with the theory. The second broke

Table 1 Characteristics of adaptors and innovators

The adaptor	The innovator
Characterized by precision, reliability, efficiency, methodicalness, prudence, discipline, conformity.	Seen as undisciplined, thinking, tangentially approaching tasks from unsuspected angles.
Concerned with resolving residual problems thrown up by the current paradigm.	Could be said to search for problems and alternative avenues of solution, cutting across current paradigms.
Seeks solutions to problems in tried and understood ways.	Queries problems' concomitant assumptions: manipulates problems.
Reduces problems by improvement and greater efficiency, with maximum of continuity and stability.	Is catalyst to settled groups, irreverent of their consensual views; seen as abrasive, creating dissonance.
Seen as sound, conforming, safe, dependable.	Seen as unsound, impractical; often shocks his opposite.
Liable to make goals of means.	In pursuit of goals treats accepted means with little regard.
Seems impervious to boredom, seems able to maintain high accuracy in long spells of detailed work.	Capable of detailed routine (system-maintenance) work for only short bursts.
Is an authority within given structures.	Tends to take control in unstructured situations.
Challenges rules rarely, cautiously, when assured of strong support.	Often challenges rules, has little respect for past custom.
Tends to high self-doubt. Reacts to criticism by closer outward conformity. Vulnerable to social pressure and authority; compliant.	Appears to have low self-doubt when generating ideas, not needing consensus to maintain certitude in face of opposition.
Is essential to the functioning of the institution all the time, but occasionally needs to be 'dug out' of his system.	In the institution is ideal in unscheduled crises, or better still in helping to avoid them, if he can be controlled.

When collaborating with innovators:	When collaborating with adaptors:
Supplies stability, order and continuity to the partnership.	Supplies the task orientations, the break with the past and accepted theory.
Is sensitive to people, maintains group cohesion and co-operation.	Appears insensitive to people, often threatens group cohesion and co-operation.
Provides a safe base for the innovator's riskier operations.	Provides the dynamics to bring about periodic radical change, without which institutions tend to ossify.

away from the conventional geocentric theory by shifting the sun to the centre of the universe. It does not matter for the purpose of this example that one turned out to be a thought in the right direction and the other not. Both in their ways were brilliant. Both were novel thinking, but the heliocentric theory was radically new thinking. Other examples come to mind which show the benefits of high-grade adaptive problem solving. There are also innumerable examples of successful adaptive and innovative problem solving at less lofty levels. It is logical to assume, however, that because innovative proposals break down known ways, more elements of them are outside anyone's experience – they are therefore more likely to fail. If they succeed, they are more likely to be noticed, acquiring glamour for the innovative thinker.

ELEMENTS IN THE DEVELOPMENT OF THE THEORY

The development of Adaption–Innovation theory began with observations made and conclusions reached as a result of a study of management initiative (Kirton, 1961). The aim of the study was to investigate the ways by which ideas that had led to widespread, memorable changes in the companies studied were developed and implemented. In each of the examples of initiative studied, the resulting changes had required the co-operation of many managers and other personnel in more than one department. One explicitly stated assumption made in the study was that any company can be expected to have managers who are capable of both producing original ideas and implementing them. Managers constitute a highly select group, and in general, the differences in their levels of intelligence and know-how may be much less important variables influencing their decision making than their scope for action within the specific organizational circumstances of their company.

Numerous examples of successful 'corporate' initiative, such as the introduction of a new product or new accounting procedures, were examined. The analysis highlighted the stages through which such initiatives passed on the way to becoming part of the accepted routine of the company:

- perception of the problem;
- analysis of the problem;
- analysis of the solution;
- agreement to change;
- acceptance of change;
- delegation; and finally
- implementation.

The study also examined what went wrong at these various stages and how the development of a particular initiative was thus blocked.

One clear indication emerging from this study was that the personalities of individuals were having an influence, directly or indirectly, on the progress of the initiative. Despite the assertion of all managers that they were collectively both sensitive to the need for changes and willing to embark on them, the changes analysed actually had a varied history. A number of anomalies became obvious and at the time remained unexplained. The principal questions had to do with three concepts:

1 **Time lags in acceptance of change**. The delay between the first public airing of the ideas studied and the date on which an idea was clearly accepted as a possible course of action was a matter of years – usually two or three. At the same time, some ideas were accepted almost immediately with the bare minimum of in-depth analysis. (The size of proposed changes did not much affect this time scale, although all the changes studied were on a large scale in the company context.)

2 **Resistance to ideas**. All too often a new idea had been formally blocked by a series of well-argued and reasoned objections which held up until some unanticipated critical event, a 'precipitating event', occurred. For instance: a rival company unexpectedly marketing a product like the one that one's own company has just decided not to market. ('Expected' precipitating events are often the core, or at

least part of an organization's 'contingency planning', e.g., possible changes in company taxation built into alternative forward planning by company accounts.) From then on, none of these quondam cogent contrary arguments (lack of need, lack of resources, other priorities, etc.) was ever heard again. Indeed, it appeared at times as if management had been hit by almost total collective amnesia concerning past objections.

3 **Acceptance or rejection of initiators**. There was a marked tendency for the majority of ideas which encountered opposition and delays to have been put forward by managers who were themselves on the fringe, or were even unacceptable to the 'establishment' group. This lack of full acceptance occurred not only before, but after the ideas had not only become accepted, but had even been rated as highly successful. At the same time other managers putting forward the more palatable (i.e., conventional) ideas were themselves not only initially acceptable, but remained so even if their ideas were later rejected or failed.

The A–I theory now offers a rational, measured explanation of these findings.

Adaptive solutions are those that depend directly and obviously on generally agreed paradigms. This link makes them more immediately familiar and so more easily grasped intellectually. They are therefore more readily accepted by most – by adaptors as well as those many innovators not so directly involved in the resolution of the problem under scrutiny. The familiar assumptions on which the solution depends are not under attack, and help 'butter' the solution advanced, making it more palatable. Such derived ideas, being more readily acceptable, favourably affect the status of their author, often, even, when they fail – and the authors of such ideas are much more likely to be themselves adaptors, characterized as being personally more acceptable to the 'establishment' with whom they share those underlying familiar assumptions (Bakke, 1965). Indeed, almost irrespective of their rank, they are likely to be part of that establishment, which in the past has led innovators to claim somewhat crudely that adaptors owe their success to agreeing with their bosses. However, Kirton (1977) conducted a study using the superior–subordinate identification test (Chapman and Campbell, 1957) and in a sample of 93 middle managers found no connection between Adaption–Innovation and a tendency to agree with one's boss. Instead a more subtle relationship is suggested, i.e., that those in the upper hierarchy are more likely to accept the same

13

paradigms as their adaptor juniors, and that there is, therefore, a greater chance of agreement between them on broad issues and on approved courses of action. Where they disagree on detail within the accepted paradigm, innovators may be inclined to attach less significance to this and view the broad agreements reached as simple conformity.

It can thus be seen how failure of ideas is less damaging to the adaptor than to the innovator, since any erroneous assumptions upon which the ideas were based were also shared with colleagues and other influential people. The consequence is that such failure is more likely to be written off as 'bad luck' or due to 'unforseeable events', thereby directing the blame away from the individuals concerned.

In stark contrast to this, innovative ideas, not being as closely related to the group's prevailing, relevant paradigms, and even opposing such consensus views, are more strongly resisted, and their originators are liable to be treated with suspicion and even derision (Schoen, 1960). This rejection of individuals tends to persist even after their ideas are adopted and acknowledged as successful. This is because characteristics (e.g., risk taking) will not alter with one success – confidence might well do so – and communication difficulties linked to paradigm mismatch will still continue. It should be noted that both these observations and the further descriptions to come are put in a rather extreme form (as a heuristic device) and usually therefore occur in a somewhat less dramatic form.

THE MEASURE

The Kirton Adaption–Innovation Inventory (Kirton, 1976; 1987a) is the instrument on which much of the demonstration of the theory rests, because it produces a score that distinguishes operationally adaptors and innovators on a continuum. The inventory consists of 32 items, each of which is scored by the subject on a scale from 1 to 5, giving a theoretical range of total scores from 32 to 160, with a theoretical mean of 96. The observed range of the general population, based on samples totalling over 1,000 subjects, is 27 points more restricted, running from 45 to 146, with a mean value which approximates to 95. Five further general population samples (from eight countries, in five languages) yield means within one point of the British means (see Table 2). The distributions of these studies conformed almost exactly to the normal curve (e.g., see Figure 1). Internal reliability and test-retest co-efficients have been variously estimated (see Table 3).

Further evidence of the steadiness of results from the KAI in operation

14

Table 2 Means and ranges of other general population samples

	(*N*)	*Mean*	(*s.d.*)	*Range*
UK	(562)	94.99	(17.9)	45–145
Italy	(835)	94.07	(17.7)	46–146
USA	(214)	94.98	(15.9)	–
Slovakia	(385)	95.06	(15.6)	51–149
Dutch/Flemish	(422)	95.30	(17.0)	53–142
French	(265)	94.61	(19.3)	43–133

Notes:
Italy: Prato Previde (1984) – Italian version
USA: Goldsmith (1985)
Slovak, Dutch and French: see Manual Supplement

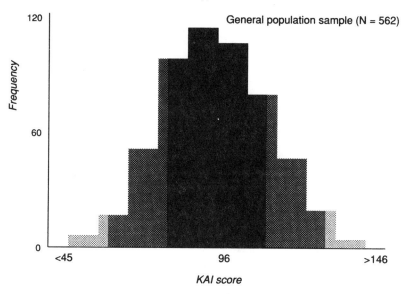

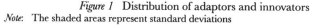

Figure 1 Distribution of adaptors and innovators
Note: The shaded areas represent standard deviations

is available from factor analytic technique (see Table 4). Studies show that in addition to the Adaptor–Innovator concept being unidimensional, it is composed of three stable, reliable factor traits (with internal reliabilities variously estimated at around 0.80). The stability of the structure is clearly seen in the percentage of items in each of the studies that load maximally on the same factor as that found in the original

Table 3 Reliabilities

Sample	Internal reliability coefficient		N	Country	Author
General	Cronbach alpha	= 0.88	562	UK	Kirton (1976)
population	Cronbach alpha	= 0.87	835	Italy	Prato Previde (1984)
	K–R20	= 0.86	214	USA	Goldsmith (1985)
Managers	K–R20	= 0.88	256	USA	Keller & Holland (1978b)
	Cronbach alpha	= 0.89	203	UK	De Ciantis (1987)
	Cronbach alpha[1]	= 0.91	142	UK	McCarthy (1993)
	Cronbach alpha	= 0.90	221	USA	Keller (1986)
Students	Cronbach alpha[2]	= 0.85	123	USA	Ettlie & O'Keefe (1982)
	Cronbach alpha[3]	= 0.84	106	USA	Goldsmith (1984)
	Cronbach alpha[3]	= 0.86	98	USA	Goldsmith (1986a)
	Cronbach alpha[3]	= 0.83	138	USA	Goldsmith & Matherly (1986a)
	Cronbach alpha[3]	= 0.87	123	USA	Goldsmith & Matherly (1986b)
	Cronbach alpha[4]	= 0.86	412	New Zealand	Kirton (1978a)
	Cronbach alpha[5]	= 0.76	374	Ireland	Hammond (1986)

Sample	Time interval	Test-retest co-efficient	N	Country	Author
Students	7 months[4]	0.82	64	New Zealand	Kirton (1978a)
Managers	5–17 months	0.84	106	USA	Gryskiewicz *et al.* (1987)
Managers	5 months	0.86	55	Italy	Prato Previde (unpub.)
Work Group	41 months	0.82	69	UK	Clapp (1993)
		Mean (1) (2)			
Students	4 months	91.2 91.1	121	South Africa	Pottas (unpub.)

Notes:
1 All women, other management samples wholly or predominately men
2 Graduates and undergraduates
3 Undergraduates
4 Students 17–18 years old
5 Students 15–19 years old

16

Table 4 Factor analyses: comparative data

The percentage of the 32 items appearing in the same factors as allocated in Kirton (1976)

	N	FA method	No. of factors	Sample characteristics	Country	% consistency against Kirton
Kirton (1976)	286	(SPSS) Principal Component/Varimax	(3)	General population	UK	
Beene and Zelhart (1986)	289	(SPSS) Principal Component/Varimax	(3)	Undergraduates	USA	97
Goldsmith (1985)	270	(SPSS) Principal Component/Varimax	(3)	General population	USA	94
De Ciantis (1987)	203	(SPSS) Principal Component/Varimax	(3)	Managers	UK	88
Mulligan and Martin (1980)	303	(SPSS) Principal Component/Varimax	(3)	6th form/high school students (c. 17 years old)	New Zealand	84
Hammond (1986)	374	(SPSS) Principal Component/Varimax	(3)	Students (15–19 years old)	Ireland	84
Prato Previde (1984)	835	(SPSS) Principal Component/Varimax	(3)	General population sample	Italy[1]	81
Pulvino (1979)	431	Alpha Factoring	(3)	Teachers (junior/middle high school)	USA	75
Keller and Holland (1978b) (30 items only)[2]	256	(SPSS) Principal Component/Varimax	(2)	Professional Employees in three applied R&D departments	USA	77

Notes:

1 KAI Italian translation

2 KAI subscale 'Sufficiency v. Proliferation of originality' only (these authors extracted only two factors and did not report using a Scree test or any other test to determine how many factors to extract)

study. The average percentage of items falling into the same factor as in the original Kirton (1976) study, across all studies, was 83 per cent.

The interpretation of the factors and what they contribute to the growing descriptions of typical adaptors and innovators is taken up in a later section. It is appropriate here to evaluate the data so far on offer, to determine what support is accruing to the assumptions on which Adaption–Innovation is grounded. One assumption was that this dimension is stable over time and incident. The data show an almost perfect normal curve distribution with a centrally placed mean and wide range – and these results are almost identical for the general population samples obtained in eight countries (four through translation) by different scholars. Data will later be presented to show that where subsets depart from the central mean and exhibit skewed distributions they do so in directions explainable by the theory and can be replicated in numerous samples from a dozen countries. This has led the translator of KAI into Italian – Prato Previde (1984) – to argue not only that the instrument measures the theory, but that the concept may well lie for the most part at a deeper level than culture (see also Chapter 7).

It should follow from these assumptions that social desirability influence must be low. That is, there is not one pole of the continuum that people would acknowledge as ideal, e.g., high IQ over low IQ. Several data converge on this conclusion. When nearly 3,000 responses to items from a manager sample were analysed (Kirton, 1987a: 59), 50 per cent had been marked 'hard' or 'very hard'; 46 per cent as 'easy' or 'very easy'; with 4 per cent at the midpoint. An experiment with another manager sample had shown that over a number of items there was sharp disagreement on which were to be considered flattering (if applied to oneself) and which pejorative. Adaptors found adaptor-orientated items favourable and some innovator items not; innovators took the opposite view. Table 5 shows five results of studies relating KAI scores to two lie scales and three social desirability measures, involving nearly 700 subjects, and yielding a weighted average close to zero.

The KAI was designed for use with adults with experience of life and at work. One effect that can be expected if a scale is administered to a sample for which it was not entirely suited, is that internal reliabilities will diminish. From Table 3 it appears that with only one sample, containing the youngest subjects, does this happen and the result is still a most respectable Cronbach Alpha of 0.76. Analysis of other data (Kirton, 1987a: 114–16) suggests that by about the mid-teens, individual Adaption–Innovation cognitive style preferences are already well defined and internally consistent, even when using an adult measure.

18

Table 5 Social desirability

Test	r Coefficient[1]	N	Author
EPI-lie scale[2]	–0.15	286	Kirton (1987a)
EPI-lie scale[2]	0.12	47	Goldsmith and Matherley (1986a)
Crowne-Marlowe social	0.03	138	Goldsmith and Matherley (1986a)
Desirability scale [3]	0.11	121	Goldsmith and Matherley (1987a)
YN-2 Yeasaying scale[4]	0.13	89	Goldsmith et al. (1986)

Notes:
1 All insignificant
2 Eysenck and Eysenck, 1964
3 Crowne and Marlowe, 1964
4 Wells, 1961

The experience derived from using the measure gives support to two other assumptions on which this theory is built. They are that this dimension is (a) stable over time, incident and even culture; and (b) exists early in life. Others, corollaries relating to the distinction between cognitive style and cognitive capacity or level, are next to be examined.

STYLE NOT LEVEL

Adaption–Innovation theory set out initially to describe the how or the manner of cognitive functioning, and specifically distinguished style from cognitive level. It should follow then that KAI scores will not correlate significantly with IQ, achievement tests, nor with level tests either of creativity or cognitive complexity.[1]

The measurement of the concept of problem solving goes back a long way, but from the start it was seen in the context of individual capacity or capability and expressed in terms of level or degree. The general collective term for the measures is the IQ test. These tests were nearly always intended to measure individual potential following Binet, though whether (and if so, by how much) this potential is, in whole or part, inherited is still a matter for scholarly (and not so scholarly) dispute. One problem for IQ test constructors was how to produce 'pure potential' uncontaminated by attainment – and all that that implied in the

19

individual subject's past; a 'social' as distinct from a 'psychometric' view which, *inter alia*, cast doubts on the notion of hereditary difference in mental capacity. This view seems to owe debts to Aristotle's teleological principle: each acorn has within it the potential to be a perfect oak – which it will not fully achieve, since earthly conditions are themselves short of the perfection required to permit reaching the heavenly ideal. Theoreticians and constructors were also concerned, in the development of instruments, to express the full range of the possible different sorts of intelligence. These were also conceived as level measures, not as different ways of problem solving. So whatever position a scholar may take on IQ – pure or contaminated, inherited or learnt – it follows that if cognitive style is concerned with the (preferred) how or manner of mental process, it should not theoretically be related to level, and so, perfect instruments of level and style will register zero correlation.

The concept of creativity began as a good deal less sharply defined than the seemingly clear-cut notion of intelligence. From the early literature it could sometimes be supposed that creativity, genius and even madness were synonymous (or at least, overlapping) terms. A significant change to a more practical scientific basis occurred at the time of Guilford's (1950) now classic address on creativity. In this address creativity was seen in terms of level, or to use his term, 'degree.' Measures built on Guilford or Thurston's clear approach should then also have zero relationship to KAI.

These matters, however, are not so simple, for within the field of creativity there has always been an interest in style: some writers such as Kogan (1976) have stressed the distinction with capacity though, as Messick (1976) adds, for the most part they are seen as 'intertwined'. The comparatively recent notion of right-left brain hemispheric preference is a rarity in that it seems to have been conceived purely in style mode. Unfortunately, since much of the literature does not, always and as a matter of course, distinguish between level and style whenever creativity is mentioned, it is rarely clear which is intended – occasionally (as in Cattell's (1981) higher-order factor), both are intended. Some of the confusion may have begun when style differences started to emerge from samples wholly selected from the most able (e.g., MacKinnon, 1978). Problems also arose when tests of creativity were found to correlate unevenly with tests of IQ averaging out at low positive. This gave rise to a curious, definitely unscientific formulation of the theoretical relationship as: there is no (a low) relationship between creativity and IQ – except that an individual needs a (certain) minimal (how much?) IQ to be deemed creative. This formulation is the basis of a critique, in part, of

KAI by Payne (1987). The rejoinder (Kirton, 1987b) reiterates that 'the Adaption–Innovation theory is quite explicit that only style is its domain and that level should theoretically lie orthogonally to it'. The expected relationship, then, between creativity and IQ depends in the first place on whether it is the level or style of creativity that is meant. If it is the level, then it should relate to other measures of cognitive capacity; if style is meant then an insignificant relationship should be expected.

This all supposes that the nature and quality of the creativity tests being used are known. Wallach and Kogan (1965), for instance, point out that when large batteries of inventories (scales or tests) all purporting to measure creativity are given to the same subjects, the resulting correlation matrix is less than clear to follow. Correlations often range from the small minus to the large plus, with most of them falling in between. Their explanation is twofold. The first and most important is that many of the tests have poor psychometric properties and should be weeded out of such batteries. The second is that some of the tests may be adequate psychometrically but may not be measuring creativity, either at all or in the way in which it is defined by the majority of the remaining tests. No one could argue with these conclusions. The Adaption–Innovation theory can add to these explanations. If there are measures of level and style of creativity (with the expected zero correlation between them), then every one of the tests in the battery would fall into at least one of five possible categories, producing a test that is:

1 psychometrically poor; and/or
2 invalid (not measuring creativity); and/or
3 measuring pure level; and/or
4 measuring pure style: and/or
5 measuring a mixture (to ratio unknown) of level and style.

It will be immediately apparent that if a person examining the resulting correlation matrix does not have this fivefold key, they will find it exceedingly difficult to make any sense of the results, and this is exactly the confused pattern about which Wallach and Kogan, and a good many other scholars, have complained.

To return again to the assumptions behind Adaption–Innovation theory, one is two-sided: (a) that it is a style dimension and (b) for that reason is distinct from level. Table 6 shows consistent support for the (b) assertion. None of seventeen correlations in the six separate studies between intelligence tests and cognitive complexity level tests and KAI were found to be significant.

Sub-assumption (a) needs separate proof; it is that Adaption–

Table 6 Correlations with level scales: intelligence and cognitive complexity

Test Intelligence	Correlation	N	Test reference
Otis higher, form A[1]	0.00	(413)	
English exam[1]	-0.03	(413)	
AH2 general[1]	0.12	(437)	From National Institute of
CT82 shapes[2]	-0.01	(437)	Industrial Psychology
GT90B verbal[2]	0.12	(437)	Battery: Nelson-NFER,
GT70B non-verbal[2]	-0.01	(437)	(1964–79)
EA2A arithmetic[2]	-0.09	(437)	
VMD diagrams[2]	0.04	(437)	
Shipley[3]	-0.01	(95)	Shipley (1940); Dennis (1973)
	-0.14	(83)	
	-0.04	(161)	
	-0.11	(99)	
Factor B (from 16PF)[4]	-0.06	(83)	Cattell *et al.* (1970)
Cattell culture free[5] (Scale 3/Form A)	-0.02	(182)	Cattell (1981) (Italian version)
Level of cognitive complexity			
Rep test[6]	-0.08	(106)	Bieri *et al.* (1966)
Role category questionnaire[6]	-0.07	(94)	Crockett (1965)
Barron-Welch revised art[3] scale	0.17	(95)	Barron (1953)

All correlations are insignificant

Notes:
1 Kirton, 1978a
2 Flegg, 1983 unpublished
3 Gryskiewicz, 1982
4 Kirton and de Ciantis, 1986
5 Rivera and Prato Previde, 1987 unpublished
6 Goldsmith, 1986b

Innovation is related to style of creativity. A study by Torrance and Horng (1980), when further analysed, is of help. Torrance administered, to a sample of undergraduates, the KAI together with a number of tests all purporting to measure creativity. The resulting correlation matrix yielded the usual jumble of results. He has kindly permitted the factor analysis of these data. The expectation from the preceding argument is that:

1 two principal factors should emerge, one of level and one of style;
2 pure, sound tests will load heavily on one of these factors;
3 good, mixed tests will load on both factors; and

4   those tests which do not relate to creativity (at least as it is defined in the material included), or those that have poor psychometric properties, will not find a secure place in either of these two factors. They will most likely be found each dominating its own factor and largely unrelated to any other test.

It can be seen from Table 7 that the two expected factors emerge. A number of tests are pure, a number of them are mixed; some tests do not find a place on either factor 1 or factor 2. Factor 1 contains both KAI and right/left hemispheric preference high in its list, and neither has any contribution to make to the second factor. Therefore this factor has been labelled style. In the second factor is the group of tests in the TTCT block, which owe much in their naming and concept to those originally devised by Guilford, who was patently concerned with level of creativity. Such tests were already known to be insignificantly related to KAI (Kirton, 1978a), suggesting that this second separate factor should be labelled level. This reinforces the earlier work (Kirton, 1987a) with over 400 New Zealand sixth-formers and six measures of level of creativity and two of IQ involving 20 separate results, of which 19 are $<\pm0.20$ and the remaining one is 0.21.

One seemingly interesting anomaly needs to be mentioned. The correlation between Cattell's higher-order factor of creativity and KAI is found to be (Kirton and de Ciantis, 1986) 0.25 which is either too high or too low to fit the theoretical stand taken here. However, Cattell derives his factor from several small style-type measures plus a double measure of Factor B – his estimate of IQ! This mixed style/level test gets a middling result.

The works quoted in this section, largely correlational and factorial, have cumulatively helped in the testing of some assumptions underlying Adaption–Innovation theory. They support operationally the theoretical position that cognitive style is not to be confused with cognitive level, and that KAI is a measure of style and not level.

There is elegance in separating level from style, since greater clarity and control can be achieved with each concept independently; the meaningful unravelling of correlation matrices is one gain. Many articles and manuals (e.g., Myers–Briggs Type Indicator; see Carne and Kirton, 1982) imply or state that artists and possibly architects are creative and engineers and possibly scientists are not. Examination of only a small range of ideas and artefacts from each field must show that such a crude division is nonsense. People can be found who paint within the current paradigm with originality, taste and competence or with dull repetition and lack of skill. Those who paint in a style that breaks the current

Table 7 Factor analysis of the Torrance matrix

Scales		Factors[1]	
		I	II
Left hemisphere style of thinking (Form C)	Torrance, Reynolds, Ball and Riegel, 1978	0.84	–
Right hemisphere style of thinking (Form C)		0.76	–
Creative personality (WKPAY)	Khatena and Torrance, 1976	0.72	–
KAI[3]	Kirton, 1976	0.66	–
Creative self-perception (SAM)	Khatena and Torrance, 1976	0.57	–
Creative motivation	Torrance, 1971	0.56	0.33
Cue test	Stein, 1975	0.42	–
Originality (Rorschach)	Hertz, 1946	0.35	–
TTCT fluency		–	0.87
TTCT originality	Torrance, 1974	0.35	0.84
TTCT flexibility		0.33	0.69
TTCT elaboration		0.35	0.67
Possible jobs	Gershon and Guilford, 1963	–	0.41
Similes	Schaefer, 1971	–	0.36
Movement (Rorschach)	Hertz, 1946	–	0.31
(Cumulative Eigenvalue %)		(50.5)	(67.7)

Notes:
1 Only loadings >0.30 entered
2 KAI weakened as blind item scored in error – this analysis of data is by kind permission of Professor E. Torrance (for original data, see Torrance and Horng, 1980) Tests not loading 0.30 on either factor: integrated hemisphere style of thinking (heaviest loading on Factor 3); Seeing Problems – Guilford, 1969 (Factor 4); TTCT Creative strengths checklist (Factor 5); Correlations listed in Kirton, 1987a

conventions may either (eventually) become famous or may be unable to persuade their neighbours to take their creations as a gift, much less hang them in their garages. Much the same goes for the other fields. By splitting creativity into style or level; cognitive complexity into preference or capacity; confining talent to specific capacity; skill and know-how to learned behaviour, it is possible to avoid some of the confusion in the current literature. One example that is especially muddling is: What is the 'expected' relationship between creativity and IQ? If a zero relation with style is advanced and can be sustained, then the clarity thus achieved will assist in examining another theoretical relationship, that between cognitive style and personality, which is broached here and further discussed in the next chapter.

PERSONALITY DIFFERENCES BETWEEN
ADAPTORS AND INNOVATORS

All theories of cognitive style include descriptions of their basic types in characteristic behavioural terms. For those claiming that these behaviours are applicable over time and over a wide range of situations (e.g., McKenna, 1984), it is reasonable to consider those behaviours as expressions of stable personality dimensions. Adaption–Innovation theory follows this pattern. The standard practice is to correlate a measure of the hypothesized personality dimension, in this case KAI scores, with various other measures of personality. The pattern of such correlations is studied with the intent of establishing the location of the theory in relation to other personality variables. Numerous KAI correlational results are now available (see Table 8). A critical test of a theory is the way results obtained not only are predicted by it, but also have an expected consistent magnitude. Of particular importance is the consistency between different studies carried out by different scholars on different populations in different countries.

This consistency of whole KAI scores is, as has been mentioned earlier, faithfully repeated for its trait component scores.[2] Equally as useful as their consistency is the ease with which they can be meaningfully labelled, in part because they can each be related to the works of different classical scholars, particularly Rogers, Weber and Merton. The first factor (SO) has been labelled Sufficiency *v* Proliferation of originality. A number of the items loading heavily on this factor have close similarity to Rogers' (1959) concept of the 'creative loner', except that he concentrates on the innovator pole of this dimension. Adaptors seem to prefer the production of (as distinct from being capable of producing) fewer original ideas, and these are seen as sound, useful and relevant to the situation as they perceive it. They find this production strategy manageable, efficient and satisfying. By contrast, innovators proliferate ideas, also by preference. Rogers suggests that his creative loner compulsively toys with ideas. When the two extreme types view each other pejoratively, as they tend to do (see also Myers, 1962: 76), the innovator claims that the adaptor originates with a finger on the stop button. The adaptor, in turn, sees the innovator as an originator who cannot find such a button. A consequence of these differences is that the adaptor tends to produce too few original ideas to ensure that at least some offer truly radical, paradigm-cracking solutions, while the innovator produces so many that it is difficult to select a 'good', appropriate, useful and immediately acceptable solution. Most of the

Table 8 Significant personality correlates

Test Classification	Correlation	Test reerences
Sensing-intuition	0.44[a]	Myers–Briggs Type Indicator
	0.54[b]	(Myers, 1962)
	0.56[b]	
	0.56[b]	
(Sensing)	–0.62[c]	
(Intuition)	0.55[c]	
	0.40[b]	
Judgement-perception	0.53[a]	
	0.53[b]	
	0.48[b]	
	0.48[b]	
	0.40[b]	
Dogmatism	–0.27[e];–0.25[e]	Dogmatism scale (Rokeach, 1960)
	–0.19[g]	Dogmatism scale (Troldahl and Powell, 1965)
Intolerance of ambiguity	–0.38[e], –0.30[e]	Intolerance of A (Budner, 1962)
	–0.47[e]; –0.45[e]	Intolerance of A (MacDonald, 1970; Rydell and Rosen, 1966)
	–0.44[d]	Intolerance of A (Budner, 1962)
Flexibility	0.40[e]; 0.46[e]	California Psychological Inventory (Gough, 1956 and 1975)
	0 .43[b]	
	0.49[b]	
	0.33[b]	
	0.34[b]	
Extraversion-I	0.45[e]; 0.46[e]	Eysenck Personality Inventory (Eysenck and Eysenck, 1964)
Introversion-E	–0.34[b]	Strong Campbell Inventory
	–0.34[b]	(Campbell, 1974)
	–0.25[b]	
	–0.30[b]	
Self-esteem	0. 27[d]	Self-esteem scale (Rosenberg, 1965)
Humble/assertive	0.42[f]	Sixteen personality factor
Conservative/ experimenting	0.60[f]	questionnaire
Controlled/ undisciplined	0.35[f]	(Cattell *et al.*, 1970)
Conscientious/ expedient	0. 44[f]	
Subduedness/ independent	0.55[f]	
Tender emotionality/ alert poise	0.26[f]	

Astute/forthright	0.22[b]	
Conservatism	−0.49[e]; −0.37[e]	New Measure of Conservatism (Wilson and Patterson, 1968)
Control-impulse	0.56[b] 0.43[b] 0.49[b] 0.49[b]	Tellegan's Research Scale (Tellegan, 1987)
Need for structure	−0.42[b] −0.56[b] −0.54[b] −0.45[b]	Wesley Total (Wesley, 1953)
Capacity for status	0.39[b] 0.36[b]	California Psychological Inventory(Gough, 1956 and 1975)
Social presence (self-confidence)	0.37[b] 0.26[b] 0.38[b]	
Risk taking	0.48[g] 0.64[c]	Jackson Personality Inventory (Jackson, 1976)
Sensation seeking	0.47[g] 0.67[c] 0.59[c]	Arousal tendency seeking instruments (Mehrabian and Russell, 1974) General sensation-seeking scale (Zuckerman, 1974)
Need for clarity	−0.36[d]	Need for clarity scale (Ivancevich and Donnelly, 1974)
Readiness to change	0.38[h]	Readiness to change scale (Hardin, 1967)
	0.30[h]	Change Index (Hage and Dewar, 1973)
	*0.31[i]; 0.59[i]	Innovativeness Scale (Hurt, Joseph and Cook 1977)
	**0.28[i];0.59[i]	Jackson Personality Inventory (Innovation − Jackson, 1976)
Structuring orientation	−0.30[j]	Management Position Analysis Test (Reddin, 1987) revised bureaucrat-executive scale.

Notes:
Reduced to: *0.00(h); 0.16/**0.19; 0.27
when controlled for sensation seeking
a Carne and Kirton, 1982
b Gryskiewicz, 1982
c Goldsmith, 1986a
d Keller and Holland, 1978b
e Kirton, 1976 (two samples)

f Kirton and de Ciantis, 1986
g Goldsmith, 1984
h Ettlie and O'Keefe, 1982
i Goldsmith, 1986a
j De Ciantis, 1987

idea output of the innovator will be discarded; some will be adopted and fail; only a few will be spectacularly successful. This originality factor relates to an individual's preference for idea production and must not be confused with level or capacity to produce original ideas as discussed and measured by, for instance, Guilford (1967). Adaptors tend to produce less, unless asked to produce more than they would prefer to do – the limit for anyone being the level of their capacity. Under some conditions, then, no differences of level can be shown (Kirton, 1978a; Casbolt, 1984).

The second factor (E) has a parallel with Weber's (1970) analysis of the aims of bureaucratic structure: Weber, in contrast to Rogers, concentrates on what in A–I theory is the adaptor pole. He describes bureaucrats as concerned with precision, reliability and efficiency. Innovation, the opposite, is in some measure a discontinuity, and can rarely be expected to be efficient at first. Efficiency usually can only be achieved by development which is an adaptive process. (Compare, for instance, the early, slow-loading, low-accuracy eighteenth-century musket with the deadly rapid fire of the fifteenth-century English archer with his long bow.)

The third factor (R), labelled rule/group conformity (formal or informal, as appropriate), has marked similarity to Merton's analysis of bureaucratic structure which 'exerts a constant pressure on officials to be methodical, prudent, disciplined . . . [and to attain] . . . an unusual degree of conformity' (Merton 1957: 198). These qualities yield high-quality adaption but not innovation. Innovators seem more able and willing to resist such pressures, valuing more highly the development of their ideas.

The results of these studies add the following positive descriptions to the differences already identified between adaptors and innovators. The habitual adaptor, in contrast to the habitual innovator, is more left-brain dominated, is, wrongly, inclined to perceive himself as much less creative, is more dogmatic, intolerant of ambiguity, and inflexible. The adaptor is more introverted, humble, conscientious, controlled, subdued and emotionally tender; more anxious (Beene, 1985) but no more neurotic than innovators. Furthermore, adaptors are lower in self esteem, have a lower capacity for status and less marked self-confidence. They prefer to take fewer risks, avoid over-sensation, and have a greater need for clarity. The habitual innovator is the opposite of the habitual adaptor in so far as these characteristics are concerned: for example he is right-brain dominated, less dogmatic, etc.

A relationship (0.62) has also been found between cognitive style and learning theory in the management training context (De Ciantis, 1987) using Honey and Mumfords' (1982) learning style questionnaire (LSQ). Adaptors tend to prefer a 'reflective' learning style whereas innovators tend to favour an 'active' style. This means that adaptors learn in a detailed, sequential, linear mode whereas innovators prefer the holistic 'here and now' approach which hands-on experience provides.

The relationship between KAI and personality is steadily being explored and some readily expected results are being published. However, to get some results, or to explain others, requires greater cerebration. For example, the intuitively expected link between KAI and Witkin's Embedded Figures Test (Witkin *et al.* 1962; Witkin and Goodenough, 1977) barely reached significance, and at that for males only (Kirton, 1978b). Some years later McKenna (1983) argued that, in contrast to his theory, Witkin's instrument measures level rather than style. As another example, it seems as if most people expect innovators to be readier to make changes than are adaptors. Both Ettlie and O'Keefe (1982) and Goldsmith (1984) found correlations to back up that assumption (see Table 8). If one takes the current literature position that 'innovators' (however described) welcome change – any change, any time – and the rest of us have greater or lesser degrees of 'resistance to change', then these correlations, although significant, seem both too low and erratic. The concept of resistance to change begs a number of important issues. As measured by Trumbo (1961), for instance, it ignores the obvious fact that homo sapiens is *inter alia* a problem-solving animal and so constantly liable to be change-inducing. In addition, cognitive style notwithstanding, this homo is quite likely to embrace with enthusiasm any changes affecting him favourably and resist any that do not, or anywhere the outcomes are too difficult to estimate (Kirton and Mulligan, 1973). Within these contexts the type of change and its relationship to style of change must also be taken into account. Given these factors, Ettlie and O'Keefe's correlations may seem too large, and this view is what Goldsmith can now support (see Chapter 2); his correlations sharply diminish when sensation seeking is partialled out.

A third example is equally intriguing, for numerous scholars have expected to find a significant positive relationship between the early adoption of ideas or products and personality traits, the like of which correlate with adaption–innovation. They failed to do so unambiguously, just as others (e.g., Loy, 1969) failed to get clear correlates from variables other than style (occupational status, professional status, peer status, education and intelligence – all non-correlates of KAI). At first KAI fared little better (Zaremba, 1978; Pulvino, 1979; Dershimer, 1980;

Jorde, 1984) until Mudd and McGrath (1988) suggested that powerful unique factors may conceal an underlying but consistent personality variable. Foxall (in Chapter 6) gives even clearer evidence of the complexity that must be unravelled before the expected results (this time in marketing) can be revealed.

Goldsmith (Chapter 2), is now able, given the separation of level from cognitive style, to draw the findings into a pattern that suggests that the Adaption–Innovation manifestation of cognitive style is a concept that underlies personality traits and interrelates numbers of them into meaningful expected patterns. As the personality correlates of Adaption–Innovation themselves seem early set and stable, these expected and confirmed relationships reinforce the same earlier-made assumptions underlying this theory. However, mankind is proud of that prodigious capacity to learn and profit from learning.

One way of dealing with problems is to have a wide repertoire of behaviour, or, in other words, to be flexible in accommodating to circumstance. This seems at variance with the supposition that the preferred style of problem solving may be inconveniently fixed. To resolve this conflict of concept, a sharp distinction must be made between preferred style and actual behaviour (Clapp and de Ciantis, 1987). Circumstances force individuals, from time to time, to operate outside their preference limits. A new assumption must therefore be set up that coping behaviour must bridge the 'gap' between what is preferred (which is well set) and what is perceived as necessary to achieve aims (which is variable): and coping behaviour bridges such gaps for as long as it is needed or can be tolerated. A person's capacity to maintain adequate coping behaviour depends on motive and the size and duration of this gap. So it can be further assumed that coping behaviour on any scale is a deliberate effort, to be indulged in when needed and as little, over as short a period of time, as possible. It follows that with no further need or motive, coping behaviour will cease. It also follows that if the coping behaviour effort is great, the individual can give up the particular aim (and its perceived rewards) that has given rise to this, now onerous, need to accommodate (e.g., find the task, the pay, the work-group, no longer attractive) and so return to behaviour more congruent to preferred cognitive style. In short, individuals will undertake the minimum coping-behaviour over the minimum duration necessary to make do in any particular situation. Excessive demand for coping-behaviour will not cause a change in cognitive style (i.e., preference) but will give rise to a desire to leave the situation. Of course, the individual does have other options that are part of problem-solving strategies:

1 **manipulative** – e.g., change aims, change the situation, get others to undertake the least desirable operations; and

2 **personal** – e.g., learning creativity or problem-solving techniques such as those of Osborn (1963).

The combination of this notion of coping behaviour together with the separation of level from style and the notion of cognitive styles with concomitant (or integral) personality characteristics can be applied to the literature descriptions of the attributes of, say, leaders or creative people. These descriptions are usually in the form of lists of attributes and make for depressing reading for all but the most egotistical or self-deluded. Omitting, as a start, items that seem irrelevant (not all lists are thoughtfully compiled) there are:

1 attributes essential to most sorts of success (e.g., perseverance);
2 attributes that come easier to the adaptor; and
3 those that come easier to the innovator.

What the lists do not imply is that most of us do well enough with fair back-up from (1) and (2) and modest coping behaviour to plug in such from (3) as are needed – or conversely (1) and (3) with help from (2). Being good at it all is not in the gift of even outstanding Man. The position, in artificial dichotomous form, can be summarized as follows:

1 Both adaptors and innovators need to operate within their own level limits (capacity, knowledge, know-how, permitted scope).
2 Adaptors and innovators have different attributes each of which, depending on circumstance, could be advantageous or disadvantageous.
3 One set of these attributes comes naturally to an individual, the opposing set has to be learned and exercised as part of individual coping behaviour. People are at their best when operating in their preferred mode.
4 When coping behaviour is no longer needed, there is a tendency to return to and exploit the preferred style.
5 Such (personal adjustment) coping behaviour is expensive in terms of stress (see Kirton and McCarthy, 1988; Clapp and de Ciantis, 1987; Hayward and Everitt, 1983; Lindsay, 1985; Thomson, 1985).
6 People use other forms of coping behaviour, e.g., change circumstances to suit preference; form part of a team whose assembled preferences cover expected eventuality; use intermediaries better able to reach the very different cognitive style of another; use mentors and facilitators.

In the following chapters many of the issues raised so far will be taken up in different contexts, in theory and in practice. Each chapter will deal with particular aspects or elements of the theory this chapter has outlined. The usefulness of the conceptual distinctness of style from other variables, essential to problem-solving success and especially to various forms of capacity, will be underlined or implied in succeeding chapters. In Chapter 2 Goldsmith again relates cognitive style to personality theory based on the many significant correlations now shown to exist with many stable personality traits. Many of the implications are explored, for example, that cognitive style is set early in life and that an individual's preference is not readily altered.

Individuals' style preferences may aggregate into cognitive climate. This is explored widely by van der Molen in Chapter 7, who envisages a range of group problem-solving states, from stagnant to revolutionary, that are self-reinforcing in cognitive style terms. The cognitive climate term was first used in relation to Adaption–Innovation in organizational settings and this is the theme of Chapter 4 with de Ciantis. One awkward side of these informed hypotheses is that the very stability of preference leads to clashes between people, between a person and his group, and between groups. However, education, training, insight and individual coping behaviour – in all the wide forms available to man – are the comfortable side of the theory, as are the means, as several chapters point out, by which group creativity and problem solving can be made more effective.

In Chapter 5 Schroder shows Adaption–Innovation being made obvious in courses that enhance management competency. One implication, in this practical setting, is to start the process of insight and tolerance to another's way of problem approach; such tolerance, built on understanding, has potential in enhancing the skills for more fruitful collaboration. Understanding of individual problem conception and solving is interestingly taken in the context of consumer buying by Foxall. He shows how the theory refined the usual hypothesis, and that the KAI findings have started to provide the support along the lines now expected (see Chapter 6).

Much of the book shows how new light can be thrown on familiar behaviour, setting up new lines of enquiry, offering fresh rational explanation, providing an angle of attack on old prejudices where once again natural, individual differences are seen as pejorative. While leaving man predictable, with stable cognitive preferences, it is possible to see more rationed approaches to learnt coping behaviour which leaves the individual and, even more, the group more flexible to tackle the wide range of change that is the characteristic of this epoch.

NOTES

1 One problem facing the scholar is to decide from titles and texts what these tests do measure – level or style or some mixture of the two.

2 Note that for the traits as for the whole inventory scores, below the mean indicates the adaptor mode; above the mean indicates the innovator mode.

2

CREATIVE STYLE AND PERSONALITY THEORY

R.E. Goldsmith

Most authorities agree that the concept of personality deals with consistencies in behavioural responses across situations, with behaviour described in part as the product of interactions between environmental stimuli (context) and relatively enduring dimensions of individual differences (personality traits). In general, personality researchers tend to choose one of two research paradigms: they either ignore individual differences (ID) to concentrate on the impact of situational variables on behaviour, or they neglect experimentation to focus on trait theory and relationships among individual differences (Geen, 1976). The latter research paradigm in personality theory contains five subcomponents:

1 **Personality dynamics** the effects of IDs on responses to a given situation;
2 **Personality development** the antecedents of IDs;
3 **Personality structure** the way in which IDs are combined into a total configuration;
4 **Personality change** the manner in which changes in ID come about;
5 **Personality measurement** the identification and measurement of IDs (Byrne, 1974).

The two subcomponents of personality theory relevant to this discussion are (1) and (5). That is, the focus is upon how individual differences may be used to explain different behavioural reactions to environmental stimuli, and how these individual differences may be measured reliably and validly. Why do some people behave one way and others, in a similar situation, behave another way? Do we have measures of the constructs thought to be responsible for the differences in overt behaviour? In the scope of A–I theory, the question may be posed, when a problem arises or a decision needs to be made: 'Why do individuals react differently in their preferences for particular types of solutions and can these preferences by accurately measured?'

The concept of personality consists of at least three types of individual difference variables: intellectual and spatial *abilities*, personality *traits*, and cognitive *styles*. The first of these variables is represented by concepts of both general and specific intelligence (Byrne, 1974: 265–6; McNemar, 1964) and by such concepts as field dependence (McKenna, 1984) or level of cognitive complexity (e.g., Vannoy, 1965). Scores on measures of these variables are used to rank order subjects by the level or amount of the construct the subjects possess (Gardner, 1983). Personality traits are generally thought of as consistent patterns of behaviour over time and across situations (Epstein and O'Brien, 1985). Subjects usually are scored so as to have more or less of the trait measured by a specific instrument. Cognitive styles are described as the manner in which individuals prefer to perform mental actions; styles may be distinguished from abilities because the former refer to level of performance and the latter to how the action is performed (McKenna, 1984). Cognitive style measures usually classify individuals into categories rather than ordering them by level. Theories of stylistic individual differences are offered by Myers (1962), referring to differences in the ways individuals prefer to use perception and judgement; by Kolb (Kolb *et al.* 1979), who describes different learning styles; by Snyder (1979) who argues that individuals may be differentiated by their preference for self-monitoring and by Kirton (1976; 1984), who argues that individuals differ systematically in their preferences for styles of creativity, decision making and problem solving. This topic deserves special attention because, according to Leavitt (1972: 71), 'the ways people think and solve problems are both real and important'.

In addition to Leavitt, several observers have commented on stylistic interpersonal differences in problem solving and creativity. In the context of a discussion of art, Eisner (1965) described two basic approaches to creativity which adumbrate the system developed by Kirton. Eisner termed his first type *boundary pushing*, or attaining the possible by extending the given. The second type of creativity he called *breaking the boundaries* rather than preserving them. Drucker recognized these two basic patterns of problem solving in a managerial context, referring to the need for 'adaptation rather than innovation, and ability to do better rather than courage to do differently' (Drucker, 1969: 50). Maccoby (1976) also described types of organizational behaviours based upon fundamental psychoanalytic analysis. Maccoby's descriptive labels 'Craftsman', 'Jungle-fighter', 'Organization man', and 'Gamesman', bear a striking resemblance to the problem-solving styles described by A–I theory. For instance, Jungle-fighters and Gamesmen are described as bold, innovative, and aggressive risk takers, and while Organization men and Craftsmen are described as detail-conscious plodders who seek to improve rather than change.

Zaleznik (1977) provides a lengthy exploration of these different styles of organizational problem solving in his distinction between 'leaders' and 'managers'. According to Zaleznik, the former act to 'develop fresh approaches to long-standing problems and to open issues for new options . . . leaders create excitement in work . . . leaders work from high-risk positions, indeed often are temperamentally disposed to seek out risk and danger . . . sometimes react to mundane work as an affliction'. Zaleznik's leaders are active instead of reactive, shaping ideas instead of responding to them. The contrast Zaleznik draws with 'managers' is quite striking:

> Managers tend to view work as an enabling process involving some combination of people and ideas interacting to establish strategies and make decisions. Managers help the process along . . . [they] need to coordinate and balance continually . . . [aiming] at shifting balances of power toward solutions acceptable as a compromise among conflicting values . . . the instinct for survival dominates their need for risk, and their ability to tolerate mundane, practical work assists their survival.
>
> (Zaleznik, 1977)

Although these careful observers have contributed much to our awareness that decision makers have stylistic differences, the most important advance in this area has come from Michael Kirton. Kirton's major contributions to the analysis of decision-making styles have been to articulate a theory of Adaption–Innovation linked to more basic descriptions of personality (originality, conformity and efficiency) and to develop an operationalization of the construct. The former provides an explanation of these interpersonal differences only described by earlier observers, while the latter enables researchers to propose and test hypothetical relationships as well as apply the theory in practical situations.

ADAPTION–INNOVATION THEORY AND PERSONALITY

Kirton argues that A–I theory is an individual difference construct representing different approaches to problem solving, decision making and creativity. Adaptors pose solutions that apply accepted, normal procedures, while innovators offer novel solutions that change the context in which the problem is embedded. Adaptors seem to see problem solution as the effective application of known principles to produce known (or highly predictable outcomes), and innovators see solving a problem as an opportunity to try something different, which might have unpredictable consequences. Adaptors create within the confines of a well-defined paradigm, innovators may seek new paradigms.

Adaption–Innovation contains three subconstructs that define the elements responsible for these differences in preferences for styles of behaviour. The first is *Sufficiency v. Proliferation of originality*. Adaptors and innovators may differ in their abilities to respond in an original fashion to some problem or challenge because some people find it easier to produce an original idea than do others. Many methods have been described to open up the gates and let original ideas flow forth (Osborn, 1963). With practice, most people can learn how to generate new ideas. Distinct from this well-known feature of human ability, however, is the fact that some people prefer to develop only a few original ideas at a time, and to evaluate carefully these ideas for applicability to the problem at hand. In Kirton's theory, adaptors are such people; hence the term 'sufficiency of originality'. In contrast, innovators prefer to produce many original ideas and be less attentive to their relevance to the problem. They proliferate original ideas, many of which may be merely novel and practically useless. In a similar fashion, adaptors prefer short-term efficiency and careful attention to the details of implementation and management of new ideas. They seek consensus and function best by operating in conformity with the rules and groups with which they must work. Innovators seek long-range effectiveness which they are willing to trade off against efficiency, and they are less tolerant of the rules. Adaptors may be satisfied with small improvements in a system, while innovators seem to need quantum changes in a system to achieve similar satisfaction. Thus, three distinct factors combine to produce characteristic patterns of behaviour.

The unique patterns of behaviour thus described by A–I theory represent the interaction of personality traits independent of abilities, in that adaptors and innovators may be more or less intelligent or talented than one another, but not uniquely different from one another in talent or ability. As stated, A–I theory is highly congruent with Gardner's theory of multiple intelligences in so far as Gardner (1983) admits that the behavioural characteristic called 'originality' is independent of any specific intellectual ability, is limited usually to activity within a single intelligence domain, and seems to arise quite early in the developmental process:

> But we do not actually know at which point in development such originality or novelty can come about, and whether it is, in fact, an option for every individual who has worked his way through an intellectual domain to its highest levels. If he has done so, it is up to the skilled practitioner himself whether he in fact produces original work or is simply satisfied with realizing a prior tradition. Perhaps, however, the seeds for originality date back far earlier and reflect basic temperament, personality, or cognitive style: on this analysis, individuals would be marked early on as potential creators of original works. These specially earmarked individuals would then become likely candidates for original productions even if they have not reached the top of their field; in contrast, others who lack these personal attributes will never be original, even if they attain superlative technical skills.
>
> (Gardner, 1983: 289)

The position of this chapter is that Adaption–Innovation theory describes a cognitive style or preference for certain patterns of behaviour and the KAI is a self-report summary measure of these patterns. Moreover, these patterns of behaviours deserve to be called 'cognitive styles'. They are 'trait-like' concepts resembling traits in that they refer to consistencies in behaviour; but they are different from personality traits *per se* because they are more specific in the behavioural domain to which they refer and are in fact traceable to broader traits and result from the combination or confluence of more than one underlying trait, representing thereby unique combinations of traits whose interactions produce particular styles of behaviour in particular situations.

The question may be posed: 'Is cognitive style separate from personality or part of it?' Personality refers to broad, general patterns of response to the environment which distinguish individuals, thus the phrase 'individual difference'. Personality traits are generally described as normally distributed, unipolar constructs along which individuals are arranged to the extent that they are 'more' or 'less' than others. Of course, this notion is that of level or continuum and can be compared with similar descriptions of other unipolar constructs such as intelligence, spatial or visual ability, etc. (Mischel, 1976: 16). Typical personality traits are dominance, aggressiveness, dogmatism, risk taking, or sensation seeking. In contrast, the KAI is a bipolar measure purporting to measure style, so that being an adaptor does not mean being less of what an innovator is, it means being different from an innovator. Thus Adaption–Innovation is a part of personality in that it represents consistent patterns of behaviour which are themselves the product of broader personality traits.

Traits are generally thought of as unidimensional constructs, but complex cognitive styles such as self-monitoring and Adaption–Innovation are multi-dimensional because they result from the coming together of various traits into unique combinations. In a factor analytic sense, the systematic variance accounted for by measures of cognitive styles is located in a general first factor of an unrotated factor solution, although rotated solutions will reveal multiple factors because the ideas captured by the scale items share systematic variance with each other that is not attributable to the general factor but which are themselves related (Snyder and Gangestad, 1986). Thus a factor analysis of the KAI shows a general factor (Kirton, 1976; Prato Previde, 1984; Goldsmith, 1985) which can be labelled Adaption–Innovation and a three-factor rotated solution corresponding to the three subconstructs. These three subscales, by and large, are themselves correlated rather than orthogonal because the innovators who prefer boundary-breaking solutions are most likely to be inefficient in much of their action and also behave in a non-conforming fashion with regard to rules and fellow workers. The adaptors, on the other hand, see their approach to problem solving as more efficient because their ideas will be less likely to meet obstacles and will be able to win support from others to see them smoothly implemented.

Closely related to this notion is the fact that value judgements are often placed on the levels of a trait, so that it is good to be more intelligent, bad to be more neurotic (McKenna, 1984). Such evaluative labels are inappropriate for KAI categories because each style is valuable in its own right (Kirton, 1987a; Matherley and Goldsmith, 1985). Sometimes adaptive solutions are best because they solve the problem in the most efficient and most easily administered way. In other circumstances innovative solutions are needed because only by doing something different will the problem be genuinely solved, although the innovative solution may cause much upheaval in the organization.

Further, the A–I construct is not, strictly speaking, a personality trait because it is not embedded in an underlying theory of human development of a more global nature such as Jung's or Freud's theories, and because it does not purport to account for patterns of behaviour across all situations. Rather, A–I theory is concerned with, and the KAI measures, a domain-specific characteristic, in this case, styles of problem

39

solving. Adaption–Innovation explains patterns of human behaviour in a tightly defined set of conditions or in specific situations, namely, problem solving in an organizational setting. The KAI measures these self-reported preferences or styles of organizational problem solving. By their answers to the KAI items, respondents tell the researcher how they prefer to behave in an organizational setting. These preferences seem to be quite stable over time, people vary reliably in their relationships to one another along the A–I continuum, and A–I theory describes relatively consistent behaviour across similar situations within the boundaries of the topic area.

One of the most persistent debates of twentieth-century personality psychology has revolved around the extent to which behaviour is situationally specific or to the extent that there are broad generalities in behaviour (Bowers, 1973; Epstein and O'Brien, 1985). Although it is apparent that individual personality-trait measures are not highly related to single behavioural events (this is principally because single behavioural acts themselves are highly situation specific), Epstein (1986) has shown repeatedly that aggregations of many cross-situational behaviour acts yield stable, reliable measures of behaviour that are themselves highly related to personality measures (Epstein and O'Brien, 1985). Thus there is positive evidence that broad, reliable generalities in behaviour (traits) do seem to account for cross-situational and cross-model consistencies in behaviour, even if only as 'summary behavioral descriptions' (Epstein and O'Brien, 1985: 532).

In the A–I theory context, the behavioural acts under consideration are specific decisions. The self-report KAI is able to measure this particular cognitive style because it asks respondents to give summary descriptions of their feelings and behaviours, over various situations and across times. We would not at all be surprised to find low, insigificant correlations between trait measures and individual differences for a given decision. This is because behaviour is unstable and situation-specific at the individual action level; people do discriminate and respond to situational contingencies. We would also expect, however, that if a large number of decisions could be observed over time and measured so that stable, reliable indicators of decision patterns could be derived, then large, significant correlations would be found between theoretically relevant personality measures and these behavioural measures. This is because, according to Epstein and O'Brien (1985), the appropriate test for relationships between trait and behaviour is between aggregates of items, not individual items.

My argument is that the KAI is a summary measure of behaviour acting as a substitute for aggregate measures of behaviour over time. That is, instead of observing many individual behaviours on many occasions and coding them into a measurement scheme to yield a stable, reliable aggregate measure of behaviour, individuals are asked to give a self-report of their behavioural patterns through simple responses to the 32 KAI items which ask, essentially, 'How do you prefer to behave' and 'What are you like?' 'This view in effect forces a self-rating or self-description to act as surrogate for a behavior-sample' (Meehl, 1945). This position, well described by Meehl, is to accept self-ratings such as those elicited by the KAI 'as a second best source of information when the direct observation of a segment of behavior is inaccessible for practical or other reasons'. As a summary measure of specific behaviours, the KAI may be contained within higher-order factors, such as those exemplified in Eysenck's work on extraversion–introversion. There are several reasons for taking this position, some involve the aetiology of personality traits and others stem from the trait-situation dilemma.

PERSONALITY TRAITS AND ADAPTION–INNOVATION

What then, is the relationship between the KAI and personality? Most personality researchers agree that patterns of behaviour are the complex product of many inherent individual traits combined with specific environmental stimuli. Thus, we have the classic trait-situation inter-action paradigm. One big problem with this formulation for personality researchers, however, is that (with a few exceptions) it has proved difficult to demonstrate reliable, valid and consistent relationships between measured traits and specific behaviours. Among the reasons for this are the following:

1 measurement failures – lack of reliable and valid trait measures;
2 interaction of large numbers of trait variables on the one hand with uncontrolled situational variables on the other hand;
3 idiosyncratic organization of behaviour with individuals and unique interpretations of situations;
4 uncontrolled effects of unmeasured variables;
5 situation specificity of behaviour (Mischel, 1973; Feshbach, 1978).

Since most personality research has shown few if any links between specifically measured traits and individual behavioural acts, we should not expect to find strong relationships between personality traits and specific problem solutions. One alternative approach to resolving this difficulty is suggested by Brunswick's (1956) 'lens model' and its revision presented by Petrinovich (1979). In this paradigm we may posit the KAI as a 'summary measure' of the 'trait-like' A–I continuum which occurs between the various broad personality traits and the highly specific observed behaviours that the traits are thought to determine. Adaption–Innovation is more specific than personality traits, but more general than any individual behavioural act. The KAI measures preferences for problem solutions which are themselves determined by interactions of many traits. These preferences we may describe as 'styles of problem solving' which may then lead to distinctive types of solutions and related organizational behaviour. The model in Table 9 shows the relationships graphically.

This argument has two parts: (a) that the KAI summarizes preferences or emotions about behaviour which are the result of personality traits, and (b) that these preferences are predictive of actual behaviour. Thus we might expect to find significant correlations between scores on the KAI and scores on various personality instruments as underlying and distal personality factors lead to the characteristic preferences for problem-solving styles measured by the KAI. Confirmation of hypothesized relationships between scores on the KAI and scores on personality measures yield positive evidence for the construct validity of the trait-measure and simultaneously its underlying theory. Moreover, KAI scores should be included in clearly defined, higher-order factors when a large body of trait measures is factored. We might further expect to find significant hypothesized relationships between KAI scores and aggregate measures of behaviour. The former can be taken to be evidence for the nomological validity of the A–I construct/theory/measure and the latter evidence for the criterion-related validity of the same.

Table 9 Model of relationships among abilities, traits, styles and behaviour

Primary individual difference	Cognitive styles	Behaviour
1 Intelligence		
2 Abilities		
3 Traits		
Specific traits:		Decision making ⎫
Sensation seeking ⎫	Adaption–Innovation	Problem solving ⎭
Risk taking ⎭		
Need for clarity, etc.	Self monitoring	

42

A growing body of research on the KAI has confirmed many of these nomological relationships. A profile of innovators and adaptors can be developed from the work of researchers who have investigated the relationships between scores on the KAI and scores on a variety of personality scales (see Table 8). Compared with adaptors, innovators are more likely to identify themselves as sensation or change seekers (Goldsmith, 1984; 1986c) and as greater risk takers (Goldsmith, 1984; 1986c), thus supporting empirically Zaleznik's description of leaders as risk takers. Innovators have been found to be less dogmatic and more flexible than adaptors to have more tolerance for ambiguity; and to have less need for structure (Kirton, 1987a). Innovators appear to be more extraverted than adaptors (Kirton, 1987a), but A–I is unrelated to neuroticism or to social desirability (Kirton, 1987a; Goldsmith and Matherly, 1986a). Innovators appear to possess greater self-esteem than adaptors (Goldsmith, 1985; Keller and Holland, 1978a). Adaptors seem to be more conservative, are more likely to control their impulses, and are less ready to change than innovators.

Adaptors and innovators do not seem to perform differently on the classic Einstellung problem (Goldsmith and Matherly, 1986b). Neither do they appear to differ with regard to IQ (Kirton, 1978; Chapter 1 this volume) or on two measures of cognitive complexity, namely cognitive articulation and cognitive differentiation (Goldsmith, 1985), evidence that Adaption–Innovation cannot be equated with some innate mental abilities. Walling *et al.* (1987), however, found innovators to perceive internal time as passing more rapidly than adaptors, suggesting that innovators are either processing information at a deeper level than adaptors or are experiencing a greater level of arousal and so tend to extraversion. The greater need to take risks and seek external stimulation evident in innovators suggests the latter interpretation, although further study of this point merits attention. Thus, several broad personality dispositions combine to form a distinctive pattern of problem solving.

How can personality lead to these patterns of decision making? A partial answer to this question may be found in Kahneman and Tversky's discussion of the psychology of preferences. In explaining the relationship between regret and frustration with decision making, they argue that imagining different outcomes of decisions leads to different decisional strategies: 'The reluctance to violate standard procedures and to act innovatively can also be an effective defense against subsequent regret because it is easy to imagine doing the conventional thing and more difficult to imagine doing the unconventional one.' They go on to argue:

43

In general the anticipation of regret is likely to favor inaction over action and routine behavior over innovative behavior. Our analysis traces these biases of decision to the rules of the cognitive operations by which alternative realties are constructed.

(Kahneman and Tversky, 1982: 173)

The tendency towards consistent innovative decisions thus may be rooted ultimately in individual differences in tolerance for regret, willingness to take risks, and the ability to imagine alternative outcomes for decisions. Adaptor–introverts avoid punishment, innovator–extroverts risk seeking reward. Hence, adaptors and innovators are expected to have different personality profiles.

This argument resembles that of van der Molen's (1988; Chapter 7 this volume) position that there are varying levels of analysis of personality and behaviour reaching from the genetic to the social. At the deepest level lie very general genetic dispositions, such as dominance and submission, which humans share with other species. At a higher level are found the personality traits or social role differences that result from interactions of the deeper genetic dispositions with life experience. It may be that much of the systematic variance in the KAI, which forms the general, unrotated first factor, is accounted for by deeper genetic causes which also determine individual differences measured by other scales. This would account for the correlations between the KAI and some personality traits. In fact, van der Molen argues that Adaption–Innovation is a highly specific social role distinction based in part on genetic dispositions and in part on environmental influences. A model of these relationships is shown in Figure 2.

A–I theory leads to a typology of human problem solvers similar to the typologies discussed earlier. Moreover, at least part of the behavioural differences observed by Eisner, Drucker, Zaleznik and Maccoby are probably due to the distinctive problem-solving styles under discussion here.

The KAI measures preferences for types of behaviour that are themselves partially the products of personality. In short, KAI items ask: 'How do you feel about these modes of behaviour?' 'Which descriptions are accurate representations of how you behave or would like to behave?' KAI scores are self-report surrogates for actual behaviour. Hence, the KAI has high reliability and validity because it is highly saturated with meaningful content, and this content is measured via many separate indicators. So while specific personality traits may be only weakly or insignificantly related to a given behaviour, they may

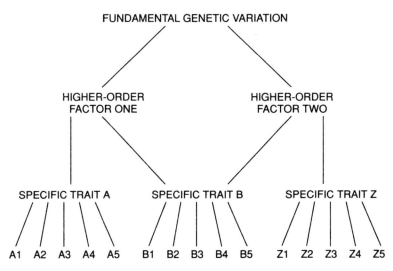

Figure 2 Relationship between KAI and underlying personality traits

be strongly related to an overall preference for a type of behaviour that may subsume many specific behaviours. These overall preferences, in turn, while lacking the theoretical elegance of typical personality theory, may be strongly related to patterns of behaviour so that we may legitimately call them 'styles' of behaviour.

Thus, the views expressed here that Adaption–Innovation is not a personality trait *per se*, that it is the result of the interactions of many traits, that it is related to patterns of behaviour, and that Adaption–Innovation may explain individual differences in patterns of behaviour, are supported by contemporary personality theory. Finally, since personality traits themselves are conceptualized as relatively stable over time, we should expect cognitive styles upon traits to be similarly stable and, moreover, to be highly resistant to change through 'training' or other short-term influences. The stability of the KAI, and presumably of adaption–innovation, is also evidenced by the fact that repeated factor analytic studies of KAI scores reveal virtually identical factor structures, reflecting more or less the three sub-components of the theory/measure (see Table 4).

MEASUREMENT ISSUES

Theory and measure are inseparable. Together they form a fundamental scientific enterprise, an iterative process of theory development, measurement study, and theoretical elaboration which can be referred to as the process of validating the theory and its measure as a trait-measure unit (Campbell and Fiske, 1959). As Cronbach and Meehl (1955) remind us: 'The investigation of a test's construct validity is not essentially different from the general scientific procedures for developing and confirming theories.'

Establishing the construct validity of the KAI within its theoretical framework should not only increase our confidence in it as a measure, but also further our understanding of the phenomena explained by A–I theory. The KAI is particularly well suited to such an endeavour because it has been so carefully constructed. Much of the power of the KAI comes from the high content validity and specificity of its situational referents. The behaviours and feelings relevant to the problem-solving styles are well identified and easily communicable to respondents (Kirton and McCarthy, 1985). Moreover, this feature leads to little item overlap with measures of other scales, another desirable psychometric property (Mischel, 1976: 143).

The psychometric requirements of a measure of behaviour are that the items overlap with a common construct, although they do not have to overlap highly with themselves, and that they are stable over time (Epstein and O'Brien, 1985). The KAI seems to meet both requirements because analyses of scores for several populations have shown that items seem to be indicative of a single general factor and the test-retest reliability scores are quite high.

Tests for the nomological validity of the scale have found that KAI scores are correlated with scores on personality scales both in magnitude and direction as descriptions of the personality traits and of Adaption–Innovation would suggest. This evidence is well summarized by Kirton (1987a). Furthermore, KAI scores are uncorrelated with measures of intelligence, spatial visualization, and fluid ability (Kirton, 1978a) or with cognitive complexity (Goldsmith, 1985), giving the scale excellent discriminant validity. As additional findings of this sort accumulate, 'a continuously expanding network of construct validity may be gradually established and progressively revised' (Mischel, 1976: 158).

Future measurement studies should concentrate on at least three areas. The first is exemplified by Kirton and McCarthy's (1985) study showing that individuals are able to describe validly their own standing on measures of styles and traits. The validity of the KAI is strengthened by evidence that it can accurately predict how individuals will describe consistencies in their own behaviour across situations. An extension of this research stream would be found in studies showing the efficacy of the KAI in distinguishing known groups (concurrent validity) shown perhaps by Hayward and Everett's (1983) study. Postdictive criterion validity is discussed by Kirton and Pender (1982).

The second area of measurement research to be pursued, directed to the left side of the model, is the further exploration of Adaption–Innovation's relationships with traditional personality constructs. Only a few of the potentially useful variables have been examined. Studies of such traits as aggression, locus of control, and need for achievement may give useful insight into the aetiology of these distinctive styles of problem solving. Current ambiguities in A–I theory may also be resolved.

As an example of this last contention, reference can be made to Kirton's (1987c) discussion of Ettlie and O'Keefe's (1982) 'intriguing or infuriating' finding of small, positive correlations between the KAI and two scales measuring change orientation. If innovators, argues Kirton, are open to change, the correlations seem too small; if situational factors play a major role in reaction to change, they seem too large.

One resolution to this dilemma may be found in Goldsmith's (1984; 1986b) argument that the fundamental and broadly defined construct, sensation seeking, plays a large role in shaping the specific styles of problem solving described by A–I theory. It is plausible that sensation seeking may also account for a 'willingness to change' disposition, as indeed some consumer researchers have argued (Raju, 1980; Hirschman, 1980). If this is the case, much of the positive correlation between the change scales and the KAI may be due to their common relationship with sensation seeking.

Data from two studies shed some light on this supposition (Goldsmith 1984, 1985, 1986a). Table 10 presents zero order and partial correlation coefficients between the KAI and measures of 'change orientation' with scores on measures of sensation seeking held constant.

In Table 10(a), for the 97 students (Goldsmith, 1984; 1986a), holding constant the effects of sensation seeking measured by the arousal-seeking tendency index (Mehrabian and Russell, 1974) reduced the correlation coefficients between the KAI and the innovativeness scale (Hurt et al., 1977) described by its authors as a measure of a 'willingness to change'. Jackson's (1976) innovation subscale combines 'willingness to change' with a description of the innovator as an original, creative inventor. This correlation was reduced as well. The attenuated values for the student sample may be due to skewed distributions and reduced variability.

47

Table 10 Correlations with sensation seeking and willingness to change
(a) Student sample

	SO	R	E	KAI	HJC	JI	ASTI
Upper diagonal: zero order correlations d.f. = 95							
SO		0.40*	0.01	0.69*	0.20*	0.44*	0.37*
R	0.29*		0.60*	0.90*	0.13	0.16	0.42*
E	−0.09	0.56*		0.63*	−0.10	−0.04	0.24*
KAI	0.63*	0.88*	0.60*		0.13	0.28*	0.47*
HJC	0.11	0.02	−0.18*	0.00		0.42*	0.28*
JI	0.37*	0.03	−0.12	0.16	0.36*		0.31*

Lower diaganol: First-order partials, d.f. = 94
n = 97
*P <0.05

(b) Adult sample

	SO	R	E	KAI	HJC	JI	ASTI	SS
Upper diagonal: zero order correlations, d.f. = 53								
SO		0.42*	−0.01	0.70*	0.71*	0.69*	0.63*	0.58*
R	0.09		0.47*	0.88*	0.51*	0.46*	0.51*	0.46*
E	−0.25*	0.42*		0.60*	−0.02	0.06	0.22	0.25*
KAI	0.44*	0.83*	0.61*		0.59*	0.59*	0.65*	0.60*
HJC	0.44*	0.21	−0.31*	0.19		0.79*	0.74*	0.56*
JI	0.46*	0.18	−0.13	0.27*	0.60*		0.65*	0.51*
ASTI							0.66*	

Lower diagnol: Second order partials, d.f. = 51
n = 55
*P <0.05

Notes:
SO   =   Sufficiency of originality
R   =   Rule group conformity
E   =   Efficiency
HJC =   Hurt, Joseph, and Cook innovation scale
JI   =   Jackson personality inventory innovation subscale
ASTI =   Arousal-seeking tendency index
SS   =   Zuckerman sensation-seeking scale

In Table 10(b), second-order partial correlation coefficients produced by holding scores on two measures of sensation seeking, the ASTI and the general sensation seeking scale (Zuckerman, 1974) for an adult sample (Goldsmith 1986c) showed the same result. It seems that much of the relation between Adaption–Innovation and 'willingness to change' may be accounted for by their common relationship with sensation seeking.

Finally, and perhaps most crucial of all, research attention needs to be directed towards the right side of the proposed model in Figure 2, verifying that KAI scores are valid indicators of stable, broad response dispositions. Although some evidence already shows A–I related to specific behaviour (Kirton, 1980), further work needs to be done in this area. This is especially important given the behaviour-based interpretation presented here of what it is the KAI is measuring. Thus, aggregate measures of many behaviours across time are needed as one form of criteria to which KAI scores may be compared. This type of research (see Chapter 5) may be the most difficult and demanding of all, but successful demonstration that KAI scores predict actual patterns of behaviour would be very powerful evidence for the validity and usefulness of this theory and measure.

CONCLUSIONS AND FUTURE RESEARCH

To summarize, A–I theory provides a partial explanation for observed behavioural differences in problem solving, decision making and creativity. Abandoning the concern with 'level of ability' paramount to so much discussion of these issues, A–I theory posits stylistic differences between adaptive and innovative decision strategies as the explanation for the behavioural variation, organizational reaction to changing circumstances, and the course of interpersonal relations among problem solvers.

This chapter argues that the distinctions highlighted by A–I theory and measured by the KAI is the manifestation, at least in part, of deeper underlying differences in personality; that broad predispositions to behaviour which shape many aspects of human life also interrelate to form the problem-solving patterns termed 'adaptive' and 'innovative'; and that these correlations may be measured validly and reliably via the KAI. People, in short, can summarize their preferred mode of behaviour and report them accurately. Thus A–I theory represents a major advance in the study of decision making and problem solving in both theoretical and applied areas.

What promises to be a new territory of A–I research? For the past twenty years or so, psychologists have debated a series of issues which may be summarized as a distinction among 'dispositional', 'situational' and 'interactive' perspectives on human behaviour (Malloy and Kenny, 1986). While some psychologists still locate the most important features of the aetiology of behaviour in intra-personal personality traits, and others focus on the contextual and environmental determinants of behaviour, most personality-oriented psychologists probably embrace an 'interactionist' philosophy, and focus their attention upon the degrees to which behaviour arises from the person and the situation in combination and, moreover, how the interactions actually take place (Hyland, 1985).

We may speculate, therefore, that future KAI research will concentrate upon adaptors and innovators in their situational contexts, asking, for instance: what situational factors promote which type of problem solving? How do adaptors and innovators respond to specific types of change? Can situational factors be manipulated to get the best from each type of problem-solver?

Thus, this second chapter closes with the ironic conclusion that, while A–I theory arose from the study of decision making within specific organizational settings and was then isolated from these situations for much of the psychometric research that confirmed its reliability and validity, it now needs to be returned to its original context and spread to new settings as well, where it may yield great insight and knowledge. Further advances in A–I research, it seems to me, will be found in the study of the interactions of these factors with specific situational variables. As such, the KAI offers the psychologist new perspectives and a useful tool for understanding and influencing a variety of behaviours.

3

ADAPTORS AND INNOVATORS AT WORK

M.J. Kirton

ADAPTORS AND INNOVATORS IN COLLABORATION

From the earliest inception of the Adaption–Innovation theory, it had been observed that high adaptors and high innovators do not readily combine. They often tend to irritate one another and hold pejorative views of one another. During the initial development of the KAI, intensive interviews, based on suggested items and their relationships, readily evolved descriptions of high scorers. Most were accurate, an observation which led to later studies (Kirton and McCarthy, 1985) showing that, once the theory had been explained, people's estimates of colleagues' scores was in close accord with self-report (with correlations circa 0.8). Some were misattributions. Two examples were: some adaptors mixed innovators' tendencies to extraversion and abrasion in dismissing consensually agreed standpoints as neuroticism; most innovators mistook the adaptor preference for operating within rules and consensus for subservient compliance.

So innovators are generally seen by adaptors as being abrasive and insensitive, despite the former's denial of having these traits. This misunderstanding often occurs because the innovator attacks the adaptor's theories and assumptions: explicitly when he feels that the adaptor needs a push to get him out of his rut, or to hurry him in the right direction; implicitly when he shows a disregard for the rules, conventions, standards of behaviour, etc. of his work group. What is even more upsetting for the adaptor is the fact that the innovator does not even seem to be aware of the havoc he is causing. Innovators may also appear abrasive to each other, since neither will show much respect for the other's theories, unless of course their two new points of view happen to coincide temporarily. Innovators perceive their work environment as more turbulent (Kirton, 1980) than do adaptors, who suspect innovators as disturbers of peace.

Adaptors may also be viewed pejoratively by innovators, who feel that the more extreme adaptors are far more likely to reject them and their ideas than collaborate with them. Innovators tend to see adaptors as stuffy and unenterprising, wedded to systems, rules and norms which, however useful, are too restricting for their (the innovators') liking. Innovators seem to overlook how much of the smooth running of the system around them depends on good adaptiveness, but seem acutely aware of the less acceptable face of efficient bureaucracy. It is not surprising, therefore, that a relationship has been found between Adaption–Innovation and management style (de Ciantis, 1987) using Reddin's (1970) 3-D theory of managerial effectiveness typology. Adaptors favour a 'bureaucrat' style (–0.47), and innovators an 'executive' style (0.27). De Ciantis supposes that the overall relationship might be greater than –0.3 but for the fact that KAI aims to measure a person's *preferred cognitive* style whilst Reddin aims to gauge *actual behavioural* style.

Disregard of convention when in pursuit of their own ideas has the effect of isolating innovators in a way similar to the alienation of Rogers' creative loner (Kirton, 1976). While innovators find it difficult to combine with others, adaptors find it easier. The latter will more rapidly establish common agreed ground, assumptions, guidelines and accepted practices on which to found their collaboration. Innovators must also do these things in order to fit at all into a company, but they are less good at doing so, and less likely to stick to the patterns they helped form. This tendency is at once the innovators' weakness and source of potential advantage. The implications of these differences for effective team building are emerging from management courses, in particular the practical exercises. McHale and Flegg (1985; 1986) found that teams composed primarily of adaptors or innovators were very different in their style of working when presented with a problem on a team building seminar. One team which included three highly innovative people found it extremely difficult to work together, with one innovative participant having to retire periodically from the group in order to cool down. This team produced a highly imaginative proposal as a solution to the problem, but grossly overspent their budget. As expected, the team which was primarily composed of adaptors produced a solution to the problem which conformed to the guidelines and was submitted on time. The content, however, was unexciting and had not made full use of all the available resources.

Data are accumulating, in industry and commerce, from academia, consultants and in-house observations, that large differences in scores between individuals (and groups) leads to increased difficulties in collaboration and even communications. This, of course, harks back to the initial work on the blockage and facilitation of management initiatives reviewed earlier (Kirton, 1961). It is the lack of understanding of others which, especially in crises, leads to friction and even lasting personal dislike. It appears from consulting and counselling that some individuals with intermediate scores and other personal appropriate characteristics, knowledge and skills act as 'bridges' between individuals and groups. Such people more frequently, it is thought, have KAI scores close to the population mean. Others further from the mean may, in particular situations, find themselves fulfilling this role. Again, experience suggests the hypothesis that, although centrally placed in relation to a particular group, the further one is from the population mean, the more difficulty is encountered with the role of the intermediary. Perhaps such people lack 'match practice' because the more extreme their score, the less likely they are to find themselves in an intermediate position. Training has an important role to play here.

A number of situations for 'bridgers' is being identified by those reporting such experiences. One of much importance to management occurs when a unit runs into trouble and has its head replaced by a new leader markedly different from the cognitive style orientation core of the group – someone who has been placed there by senior management to affect a change radical to that group: '. . . put in to ginger them up' or '. . .put in to bring some order out of the existing chaos' (depending on the style orientation of the group). As the circumstances of such posting are often associated with antecedent failure, the group's morale is a substantial factor. In its resentment, the group rarely sees such an 'alien' as a saviour. Group members attribute their failure in other terms, e.g., senior management, current policy, lack of appreciation of their success. The new leader and policy are viewed as threats and undeserved punishment. To cope with this situation (other than high turnover), the group throws up a mediator who seems often to become an informal leader and link with the authority. The KAI score of such individuals has, on a number of occasions, been recorded as intermediate between the leader and the (mean) core of the group. His personal success, if achieved, may be a critical factor for the continued existence of the group as a successful working unit. Although the evidence here is anecdotal, the suggestion of a role for the middle-level KAI scorer is an exciting prospect for systematic investigation. Evidence is also beginning to accumulate from practice in the field, that heterogeneous groups, even with a history of clash (Lindsay, 1985), can with training be brought to a state of successful co-operation based on tolerance, itself founded on insight into differences in cognitive style.

Innovators are more likely to move job (Thomson, 1985) or change function (e.g., from production to marketing – Foxall, 1986a) than adaptors. This trend is enhanced, not unnaturally, if the innovator feels unappreciated (lacking 'colleague-empathy' – Thomson, 1985). It is quite in accordance with Adaption–Innovation theory that the subset most likely to state they intend to leave their job are adaptors who feel their colleagues 'do not appreciate their problems' (Thomson, 1985). This finding has an important bearing on the understanding of organization climate (see Chapter 4) and on the mechanism of how new intakes, through turnover, show KAI means that steadily approximate that of the established group.

With guidance the layman is more perceptive than he is often given credit for. Keller and Holland (1979) report that peer and superior ratings of individual colleagues' innovativeness (as defined by them) correlate 0.40 with KAI scores. Kirton and McCarthy (1985) had a different approach. KAI scores were obtained from course members, who were then given a short lecture describing the theory and some notion of the way KAI scores distributed in general. Where the course members had little experience of working with each other, group estimates of individuals correlated 0.37 with actual scores. Where their experience was greater (two days of working closely together), the correlation rose to 0.84. Individual estimates of their own scores correlated 0.79 with actual KAI scores. These may be useful findings in the practical task of getting people to tolerate each other in mixed teams. At least they can grasp the main issues and make good working estimates of each other – a foundation to an understanding that needs to underlie tolerance.

GROUP DIFFERENCES IN
ADAPTION–INNOVATION

The general population samples (from eight countries) have yielded data on psycho-social variables. Correlations between KAI and occupational status, level of education, age and sex have been repeatedly reported as less than 0.2, a magnitude that can be statistically significant but nevertheless accounts for little of the variance. The most steady and persistent of these small variations is that females tend, on average, to be more adaptive than males (see Table 11). Subsets of women in occupations return means either close to the general female mean or well away from it, as predictably as do variations in male occupationally derived subsets. Numerous studies have investigated the extent to which some other clearly identifiable groups differ (or not) in their mean scores from the

Table 11 Breakdown of scores by psycho-social variables

KAI scores	Sex		Age					
			Females			Males		
	Males	Females	-30	30–44	45+	-30	30–44	45+
84 and less	67	97	31	23	43	22	18	29
85–108	143	101	37	34	30	42	49	49
109 and more	80	44	26	12	6	35	25	21
N:	290	242	94	69	79	99	92	99
Mean:	98.12	90.84	93.83	92.67	85.94	101.39	98.76	94.20
s.d.:	16.75	17.82	19.15	17.99	15.12	17.32	15.60	16.52

KAI scores	Occupational status[1]			Educational level[2]							
				O-level and less[4]		About A-level[5]		Degree			
	Professional	Skilled	Unskilled	Male	Female	Male	Female	Male	Female	Housewife[3]	Student
84 and less	56	60	27	30	61	20	19	5	7	11	12
85–108	79	88	28	52	51	30	31	10	14	9	39
109 and more	52	41	6	19	21	28	10	13	4	3	22
N:	187	189	61	101	133	78	60	28	25	23	73
Mean:	96.5	94.5	87.4	94.51	88.78	101.36	92.92	100.97	95.00		
s.d.:	18.5	17.5	14.1	18.22	17.95	15.87	17.86	16.10	16.50		

Notes:

1 In the unskilled group 40 are 45 years old or more; only 16 are men

2 Less students and 34 managers for whom no reliable data are available

3 Only women who gave no other indication and for whom husband's status is not known

4 Examination taken about 16

5 Examination taken at about 18

population mean, the extent to which they differ (if they do) from each other, and how these variations correspond to what could be deduced from A–I theory. Before examining the results of these enquiries, which deal only with the *mean scores* of the groups being studied, it is important to point out that there was always a wide variation among the scores of individuals *within* relatively homogeneous groups. These differences often ranged from around 70 to around 120. (The widest ranges obtained from large general population samples are from 45 to 146. The size of the range of smaller groups is roughly proportionally related to size of sample.) This finding has important implications for the understanding of change against the background of group differences at different levels in an organization, or between departments, or between specific occupational roles.

A second critical set of findings that underlies all the cognitive style differences, their effects and implications of subsets at work is that individual competency in general is not related to KAI scores – (see Chapter 5). It should follow from this, and it does, that occupational status in general is not related. There is no built-in permanent advantage to being either adaptive or innovative that holds over time and any situation. Of course, specific circumstances can alter the general pattern. For instance, Keller and Holland (1978a) report that, in their study, innovators tended to reach higher organizational levels (r = 0.27) and had higher education (r = 0.34) than adaptors. The setting for this study was, however, an R&D establishment, where the researchers tend to be innovative, highly educated and fill the highest posts. The administrators tend to be adaptive, averagely educated and fill few top posts. There are different patterns also among junior staff, technicians and clerks. In general, then, the KAI is evenly distributed and variations should be predictable.

It has been shown that when groups of different nationalities share a broadly similar culture, their A–I mean scores show very little variation. Samples from Britain (Kirton, 1976; 1980; 1987a), the USA (Keller and Holland, 1 978b; Goldsmith, 1985), Canada (Kirton, 1980), New Zealand (Kirton, 1978a), Italy (Prato Previde, 1984) and Mexico (Keller, 1984)[1] have produced remarkably similar mean scores.

A sample of occidental managers (all English-speaking) from Singapore and Malaysia had a mean of 97.6, close to that of their Western counterparts (Thompson, 1980). Two samples of UK managers showed an average mean of 97.0 while the general population sample for the UK had a mean of 95.3, 50 per cent of whom were women. The male mean is near to 98. In *general* (undifferentiated for specialism) management samples, in which males predominate, (five studies in four countries, $N = 471$) the average is 98.02. Information drawn from the validation samples of the Slovak (including some Czech), French and Dutch language translations suggests that the manager means from these countries, which included Canadian and Belgium samples, are close to 97, in each case (see manual supplements).

A hypothesis derived from Adaption–Innovation theory (Kirton, 1978c) suggests that where clear boundaries exist in a culture pattern, in the form of expectations that impose a limit on the behaviour of the individuals in that culture, then those people who show by their actions that they are prepared to cross those boundaries are more likely to be shown to be innovative. The more boundaries involved, and the more rigidly they are held in the society concerned, the higher the innovative score will be of those who cross.[2]

In the Thomson (1980) study, managers in Western-owned companies in Singapore were higher in innovativeness than those working in locally owned companies. The latter scored higher than comparable people working in the middle ranks of the Civil Service, who were in turn the most adaptive of the three groups. From a sample of Indian and Iranian managers it was shown (Dewan, 1982) that entrepreneurs had more innovative scores than comparable other managers (means of 97.9 compared with 90.5), and that both groups scored much higher than government officers whose mean KAI score was as adaptive as 77.2.

Indian women entrepreneurial managers were found to be even more innovative than their male counterparts. They had had to cross two boundaries: first by breaking with tradition in adopting a role conventionally reserved for the male, and second by moving even further into the world of risk taking in which only the more adventurous males would be expected to operate. Similarly, McCarthy (1993) found that British women engineering managers were significantly more innovative in cognitive style than women in the general population. They had also had to cross two boundaries: first, by entering an occupational area, which even within Western culture, is still largely male dominated; and second, they had obtained management status within that profession. By contrast, the KAI mean of female personnel managers showed the same difference from that of females in the general population as male personnel managers did from males in the general population. Foxall (1986b) also found that female MBA students (on the highly selective course at Cranfield School of Management, UK) scored further from the female general population mean than did the male students from the male population mean.

DIFFERENCES BETWEEN OCCUPATIONAL
GROUPS AND WITHIN ORGANIZATIONS

From among the general British population samples used in the original KAI study, 88 managers were identified. The mean score of this group was 97.1, s.d. = 16.9 (Kirton, 1987a). This was almost identical to the results for Italian managers (Prato Previde, 1984). Different occupation groups yield means on either side of this score if they are both select and homogeneous, but reveal means close to the mean if the groups are non-select and heterogeneous. For instance, three samples of apprentices and their teachers yielded: mean = 82.4, s.d. = 7.1, N = 22 (Mathews, unpub.); mean = 88.4, s.d. = 10.6, N = 50 (Flegg, unpub.); and mean = 84.12, s.d. - 10.25, N = 437 (Flegg, unpub.). This compares with R&D personnel with a mean of 100.9, s.d. = 14.3, N = 256 (Keller and Holland, 1978a) and a mean = 104.2, s.d. = 13.2, N = 90 (Davies, unpub.). These data are collated in Kirton and Pender (1982).

A more heterogeneous group (Ettlie and O'Keefe, 1982) of 123 American undergraduate business students yielded a mean score of 98.1, s.d. = 14.21. Kirton (1980) reported a further British sample of 79 managers yielding a mean of 96.9, s.d. = 15.27, and a small group of engineers (unspecified as to specialization) in a British pharmaceutical company with a mean of 97.3 covering a wide range of individual scores. Three samples of American teachers are available. The first (Pulvino, 1979) N = 430 yielded a mean of 95, s.d. = 13. The second sample of N = 202 American teachers (Dershimer, 1980) also showed a mean of the same magnitude 97.0, s.d. = 14.0. The third sample of 119 American teachers (Jorde, 1984) showed a mean of 95.5, s.d. = 13.8. Finally, a fourth sample of 182 British teachers (Kirton et al., 1991), also showed a mean of similar magnitude at 94.5, s.d. = 18.0.

In all these results the pattern to be looked for is that where the group has an occupation or tasks in which adaptors and innovators can do equally well (e.g., engineers in general, managers in general, teachers in general), the samples should have mean scores approximate to those in the general population. Where the group tasks are more structured (e.g., apprentices, production, accounting, etc.), the mean should locate towards the more adaptive end of the scale. For less structured tasks (e.g., most marketing, personnel. or finance), it will be placed towards the innovative pole. Other factors also operate, cumulatively or subtractively, e.g., whether the company as a whole is oriented in a particular direction, as in Miles and Snow's defender $v.$ prospector companies (unpublished correspondence with Snow). [3] Whether or not a group has

58

selected itself for general management courses or has been sent to such courses reflects a certain systematic degree of initiative.

Further evidence of the relationship between professional and vocational categories and Adaption–Innovation scores comes from a dissertation by Holland (1987), which suggested bank employees were inclined to be adaptors, with a mean of 90, s.d. = 19.5. (N = 47). Gryskiewicz et al. (1987) supported Holland's findings in that their US banking staff (N = 128) returned a mean of 91, s.d. = 14. Hayward and Everett (1983) showed the same to be true of local government employees, whose mean was 78.9 (N = 52), s.d. = 12.

These studies also prompt the hypothesis that the mean KAI score of the established members of an organization reflect its climate. Both Holland (1987) and Hayward and Everett (1983) showed that groups of new recruits had mean scores that differed significantly from the mean of the established group they were joining. After a lapse of time (3 years and 5 years respectively), there was a considerable narrowing of the gap (see Chapter 4), produced entirely as a result of staff turnover. Gryskiewicz et al.'s study also included a sample (N = 78) of trainees whose mean was a half s d. higher (97, s.d. = 14) than that of their established colleagues. It appears that all the institutions involved in these studies recruited staff whose mean reflected (initially) that of the general population from which they came. Work by Holland et al. (1991) showed that not all novice groups' means differ from those of the established members. Those that do not differ, also continue not to differ after some years; only those that start by differing shift, as a result of turnover, and do so towards the mean of the established members. Flegg (unpub.) found that the Rule/Group Conformity (R trait) score was a good predictor of apprentices' success in final training results, many of them based on instructor opinion.

Further light on the relationship between individuals and organizations in terms of KAI scores was provided by the hypothesis that managers who work in a particularly stable environment will tend to be adaptive, while the mean scores of those whose environment could be described as turbulent tend towards innovation (Kirton, 1980). As noted earlier, this hypothesis was supported by the work of Thomson (1980), which showed that a sample of English-speaking, ethnic Chinese, middle-ranking civil servants in Singapore was markedly oriented towards adaption, with a mean of 89.0; whereas a sample of local (Chinese) managers in multinational companies in the same country was just as markedly inclined to innovation, with a mean of 107.0. Managers, with the same background in local industry (98.0) were located in between.

DIFFERENCES WITHIN ORGANIZATIONS

It is unlikely, as well as undesirable, that any organization is so monolithic in its structure and so undifferentiated in the demands it makes on its personnel, that it produces a total uniformity of cognitive style. This was illustrated by a study (Kirton, 1980) that showed that adaptors were more at home in those departments of a company that needed to concentrate on problems emanating from within their own department (e.g., production). Innovators, on the other hand, tended to be found in greater numbers in departments whose problems arose from outside the department (e.g., sales, progress chasing).

A study by Keller and Holland (1978a) in American research and development departments found that adaptors and innovators had different roles in the sphere of internal communications. Adaptors were more valued for their knowledge of company procedures, and innovators were more valued when the information to be communicated was of an up-to-date technological nature, the source of much of it emanating from outside the company e.g., universities.

Kirton (1980) made a study of members of management training courses, differentiating between those who had selected themselves to go into the course concerned, and those who had been sent in pursuance of their company's training policy. Members of three different courses were tested: one self-selected group of British managers, one company-selected group of British managers, and one self-selected group of Canadian managers. The results showed that the company-selected managers yielded a mean of 96.9 ($N = 79$), s.d. = 15.27, which is close to that of samples of managers in general (97.9, $N = 559$). Managers who had nominated themselves to go on the course were, as KAI theory would predict, more inclined to be innovators, the British sample returning a mean of 103.2 ($N = 81$) s.d. =15.09 and the Canadian managers yielding a mean of 113.4 ($N = 64$), s.d. = 16.20. (This course seemed particularly attractive to innovators – see Kirton, 1980.)

The Canadian (innovatively inclined) group could be further divided according to their job titles into those who worked in adaptor-oriented departments (e.g., line management) and those from the more innovator-oriented departments (e.g., personnel). The latter group was found to be significantly more innovative than the former, with a mean of 116.4 compared with a mean of 100.1. (Since all members of the group were self-selected, it is to be expected that the mean for the whole group would be higher than for the general population, i.e., more innovative.) These findings led to a larger study (Kirton and Pender, 1982) in which the scores

60

of 2,375 subjects collected in various investigations were analysed with reference to the different occupational types represented and varying degrees of self-selection to courses. Occupations involving a narrow range of acceptable procedures, rigid training and a closely structured working environment included engineering instructors and engineering apprentices, with a mean of 83 ($N = 437$), s.d. = 10.18. Those with more flexible and widely ranging procedures were represented by research and development personnel, who yielded a mean of 102 ($N = 346$), s.d. = 13. The differences were large, statistically significant, and in the expected direction.

Even within the narrow boundaries of a single job there can be found differences in cognitive style between subgroups of employees whose functions are specialized. For example, a study now in progress suggests that such a difference exists among quality control workers in a local government research unit. One subgroup is engaged in the vital task of monitoring (an essentially in-unit activity), while another has the task of solving anomalies that are thrown up in the system from time to time (involving in the process several units in the organization). The first of these quality control subgroups (monitors) shows a clear inclination towards adaption. The second group shows a mean score towards the innovative end of the scale. Gul's work (1986) also supports these findings. Gul's sample of 63 final year undergraduates in accountancy at Wollongong, Australia (mean age 21, range 20–45) showed a more adaptive mean than that expected from a general population. Twenty-four scored over 96 (innovative) and 39 below (adaptive). Although the total sample was small, the innovators differed significantly from the adaptors in their preference for financial management topics rather than accounting and auditing (and vice versa). This group also preferred as career choices industry and commerce rather than chartered accountancy and government, and they were more interested in the broader general subjects in their course.

Kirton (1980) in a minute sample found a difference within accounting between cost accountants and finance executives; Gryskiewicz *et al.*'s (1987) finding was more solidly based. Not only was their sample of established bank staff more adaptively inclined than their trainees, both other samples differed significantly from them. Vice-presidents ($N = 36$) yielded a mean of 105, s.d. = 16, and 34 'Strategic and Business Planners, Financial Analysts' yielded a mean of 110, s.d. = 15. Foxall (1986a) was also able to distinguish adaptors and innovators within single occupational/professional categories in a sample of mid-career MBA students. Those engineers who were concerned with planning and designing construction work could be differentiated from other engineers, similarly qualified in formal terms, who were predominantly concerned with the maintenance of systems. Similarly, general managers could be divided into those who were concerned with the direction of the whole organization, including its external relationships, and those who administered internal systems. Financial and cost accounts also divided along these lines, but production and marketing managers could not be so separated, principally because of the small samples of each involved. The production managers were nevertheless classified as internally and adaptively oriented, whilst the marketing managers were classified as externally and innovatively oriented. Female teachers were found, generally, to be slightly but significantly more adaptive than their male colleagues, just as women generally are on average more adaptive than men. Arts teachers, both male and female, were more innovative than science teachers, particularly males teaching maths and physics (Kirton *et al.* 1991). All teachers were more inclined to the streaming/tracking strategy when asked in an academic achievement context than when asked in a social development context. Adaptors favoured this procedure in general, so they were the group most in favour in an academic achievement context and innovators were the group most against in a social context.

Findings of the kind reported in this section show that different roles in a working organization, and even differences of function within one identifiable job, are more likely, on balance to be carried out by either innovators or adaptors. Practical use of evidence along these lines could lead to the better matching of man to job, more controlled balance within teams, and in the long term, to better integration of the specific assets of innovators and adaptors within a company. In terms of research strategy these studies show that as more and more of the organizational influences are controlled by comparing units in the firms, or job functions in one unit, the Adaption–Innovation theory can be shown to express itself in terms of specific job demands. There would be dangers, however, if companies attempted to produce units that were wholly staffed by high adaptors or innovators, as will be explained in the section below on 'Agents for Change'.

ADOPTION OF NEW PRODUCTS AND IDEAS

One obvious area where a measure of Adaption–Innovation might be expected to have validity is in the prediction of the adoption of new products and ideas. The process of the diffusion of a technological novelty throughout an economic sector has been intensely studied over the past thirty years. The classic review of this work is by Rogers and Shoemaker (1971), who derive over a hundred empirical generalizations from over a thousand studies.

Diffusion generally is described in terms of a five-stage model through which an adoption tendency within the individual develops over time from product awareness to product adoption. There is also substantial evidence for a typology based on differences in adoption tendency among individuals in the population relevant to the new products. Adopters may be innovators, early adopters, early majority and majority (or laggards) (Zaltman, 1965).

The connection between Adaption–Innovation theory and the adoption models is that the personality characteristic, 'innovativeness', is attributed to those types who adopt relatively early in the diffusion process (Rogers and Shoemaker, 1971). Three studies have attempted to relate KAI scores to the adoption of a specific 'innovation' (Dershimer, 1980; Jorde, 1984; Mudd and McGrath, 1988). All three involved the adoption of classroom computing in the educational sector.

Dershimer (1980) found no significant difference among mean KAI scores of teachers classified as being 'more', 'less', or 'not inclined' to adopt computing in junior high or senior high classes. Where she did find a significant difference in mean KAI scores (elementary school teachers), the means were curvilinearly related to adoption inclination: more inclined = 100.8; less inclined = 92.2; not inclined = 94.7. In other words the Dershimer data (1980) were only partially consistent with the expectation that the adoption of this specific was related to innovativeness as measured by the KAI. Jorde's results (1984) were more promising. Despite the fact that KAI scores did not enter into the multiple regression equations predicting two academic uses of computing, the zero order correlations were significant: administrative uses ($r = 0.45$); instructional uses ($r = 0.46$), but small.

Mudd and McGrath (1988) showed that mean KAI scores of high frequency adopters (5–8 adoptions) of academic innovations (including computing) at the college instructor level had significantly higher mean KAI scores (104.7) than did low (1–4 adoptions) frequency adopters (95.7). Once again, the general belief of the marketing field is challenged by the repeated appearance of these curvilinear results, which are explored and explained fully by Foxall in Chapter 6. Before the benefit of these additional data, Mudd and McGrath interpreted their findings on the adoption of ideas in terms of the Midgley and Dowling (1978) adoption model, which states that the trait, innovativeness, is less likely to express itself at the level of a specific adoption than of the more abstract level of a range of related adoption targets (product classes, e.g., kitchen appliances, or a group of product classes, e.g., household furnishings). This difference could be explained by the supposition that the adoption of any *one* notion is heavily influenced by factors other than cognitive style. The latter factor emerges only as significant in a pattern of adoptions: a finding reinforced by the work of Foxall and Haskins (1986; 1987) on consumer buying of new food products and the subject of Chapter 6. What is of great interest are the suggestions in it that (a) 'new' is attractive to both adaptors and innovators, but not in the same way and (b) that systematic buying, or not buying, of any kind of product is more likely to be attributable to adaptors than innovators; a linear relationship now, therefore, cannot be assumed.

Generally, these early returns on the validity of the KAI in predicting adoption behaviour (idea or artefact) are encouraging. They are especially relevant to managerial concerns in marketing and product development. This latter is viewed as an increasingly urgent issue in the more basic question of productivity economic development. The contribution of Adaption–Innovation theory's tight terminology and the findings based on its measure to the issues are explored further in Chapter 6.

AGENTS FOR CHANGE

It has already been established that while the mean adaptor–innovator score may vary considerably from one group to another, wide variations between individuals within a group remain. This must mean that many individuals find themselves part of a group whose mean score differs markedly from their own. Research reveals there are three explanations why people find themselves in such a group.

1 They are there because they are temporary members of the group in transit, for example, for the duration of a training scheme.
2 They got there for a variety of reasons but are now trapped and unhappy; they look for ways to move out of the group (Hayward and Everett, 1983).
3 Once in the group, for whatever reason, they have developed for themselves a specific role within the group which they find satisfying and which the group finds acceptable (Rickards and Moger, 1994).

Even conditions 2 and 3 need not be permanent, for if individuals stay in the group, changes in the group's precise function, or climate of opinion, or a change of boss, may bring about a shift in the group's orientation. If this happens, individuals find themselves moving from one of these categories to another, including from 'fitting' to 'no longer fitting' and vice versa.

The consequences of 'not fitting' are now being explored in current research by, for example, Hayward and Everett, 1983; Lindsay, 1985; Clapp and de Ciantis, 1987; Thomson, 1985; Kirton and McCarthy, 1988 (see Chapter 4). McCarthy (1988), in a study of women managers, found that those women who had a 'cognitive gap' greater than one standard deviation between themselves and a self-reported 'typical colleague' reported a greater number of work pressures (taken from an inventory by Davidson, 1982) than women who had good 'cognitive fit'. It is not clear whether these women would fall into category 2 or 3 above, or even both. The findings of Thomson (1985), however, provide a clearer picture. She found 'organizational fit' to be the most important single factor (accounting for 15 per cent of the variance) in a study of Singapore executives' attitudes to leaving their jobs.

The situation (in category 3 above) in which the individual has developed a satisfying role in the group deserves closer examination here, since it has important implications and practical applications in the field of A–I theory. The following analysis will need to be in speculative terms until the completion of further research. At present, three types of agents for changes are assumed:

1 All people as individuals are capable of being agents for change, i.e., they could effect changes as individuals unrelated to any other person.
2 Within groups such agents for change may operate in accordance with that group's prevailing cognitive style mode or
3 they may operate in contrast to it.

These classifications respectively can be dubbed AC1, AC2 or AC3; such that every person (in a group) will be both an AC1 and *either* an AC2 *or* AC3 depending on the particular group A–I orientation. Shifts of individuals from group to group or shifts of a group's orientation will not affect AC1 classification, of course, but may shift the individual from AC2 to AC3 or vice versa (see Figure 3).

The individual in the AC3 mode who can successfully accept and be accepted by a working environment whose cognitive style is markedly different from his own must have particular characteristics which enable him to survive. It is those characteristics which make him not just a potential agent for change, but a successful member of the group, given the contrasting orientation of that group. If successful, he can also act as a natural 'bridge' between the core of the orientation group and those

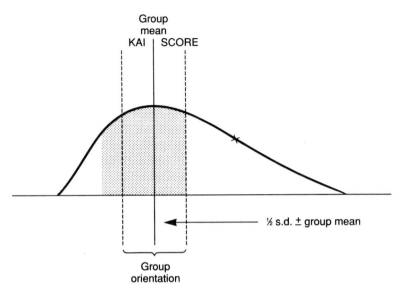

Figure 3 Agents for change

Notes
1   The figure above depicts the distribution of a group, with a mean displaced from that of a general population sample in the direction of *either* adaption or innovation.
2   As shown from research, the range is unlikely to be greatly affected by that displacement.
3   Everyone, as an individual, is a potential agent for change (Type: AC1).
4   Everyone, as a member of a group, is one of two kinds of potential agents for change: (a) The shaded area contains those who are potential agents for change within the group's prevailing orientation, either adaptive or innovative (Type: AC2); (b) The unshaded area contains those who are potential agents for change of a sort outside the group's prevailing orientation (Type: AC3).
5   The X marks one of a number of likely positions for a *successful* agent for change type 3. He or she is far enough from the group orientation to be usefully different but near enough to be able to overcome communication/acceptance problems with the group, given the minimum conditions set out in the text.

located even further away from the group mode. The 'bridger' acts as a mediator in facilitating recognition of the ideas and work patterns of the 'further outers' who might not be as accepted by the group owing to the relative extremity of his or her cognitive style.

To be successful as an AC3, the individual must first have the professional or technical knowledge and skills that will enable him to be recognized by others in the group as a valuable group member at times when major changes are not envisaged. Second, he[4] must also be able to gain and maintain the ongoing respect of his colleagues and his superiors, and thus have the necessary status for his ideas to be recognized and taken seriously. This is not an easy task (Lindsay, 1985). Third, he will need the capacity and the techniques for influencing others, whether by dominance of personality, or persuasiveness, or other leadership characteristics that will make it possible to see that his proposals are carried through.

If this AC3 can hold his place in the group on a day-to-day basis, his style will add a significant resource to the group. He will even have a powerful advantage over his colleagues. This advantage exists because: (a) he will more easily be able to carry out tasks that they find more difficult (in accordance with basic A–I theory); and (b) he will be more likely to anticipate events that others may not foresee since their particular cognitive style may mean that they are not directing their thoughts in that direction.

Like any member of a minority (temporary or permanent), he may have to possess more technical and interpersonal skills, etc. than a counterpart in the majority (AC2 group). The agent for change must therefore be competent, respected and influential. His success in using these assets may be made more easy for him by being selected for, or selecting himself for, a working role within the unit that is more compatible with his own cognitive style than with some other tasks. In the conventional way, he will be seen as supportive of the main function of the group. At a point of crisis or upon the occurrence of some 'precipitating event', this individual can become a potential leader towards change, particularly if he has foreseen and prepared for the critical event. In taking advantage of this position, his personal qualities will come into play. For full capitalization of the new possibilities, management would need to be aware of the dynamics of the situation to understand and support the processes of change that have occurred. Clearly, it would be in the interests of management to facilitate the development of such positive responses to change. There are a number of obvious ways management are doing this; through increasing their own insight, monitoring policies for undesirable restrictions, personal development and some skilled personal intervention. For this latter purpose both individual and group counselling, also based on A–I theory, can play a positive part. Lindsay (1985) reported an incident where an AC3 found himself rejected by his work group following such a situation. In that case Lindsay puts forward the notion that increased awareness of group differences in the general A–I context increased tolerance of both parties to each other.

It must be emphasized that *the agent for change may be either an innovator or an adaptor.* In a predominantly innovator group, a challenging AC3 will be an adaptor, and vice versa. This discovery overthrows traditional assumptions that heralding and initiating change is the prerogative of the type of person to whom the term innovator is here applied. A precipitating event may require either an innovative or an adaptive solution. Whether it is generally expected or not depends on the original orientation of the group and of the nature of its task. An example of an adaptor as an agent for change in a team of innovators is provided by the case in which the precipitating event takes the form of a bank's refusal to extend credit to support further new enterprise in a company that has cash-flow problems. At this point the adaptor, who has been anticipating the event for months, is at hand with facts, figures and a contingency plan neatly worked out. He becomes a potential agent for change. His work can be transformed into action if he has the personal qualities of competence, status and ability to influence others; the others have need to recognize his value also, before the precipitating event becomes terminal. As part of this thought a number of industrial companies are beginning to explore Adaption–Innovation with the aim of increasing the flow of ideas within their departments and devising ways of becoming more sensitive to them.

COPING BEHAVIOUR

The discussion on bridgers and those for whom they provide a bridge, makes the assumption that cognitive style preference is well entrenched in the personality of these adults. The argument is that such preference is resistant to change (see Kirton, 1987a, Chapter 1 of this volume). Man's capacity to learn and to alter behaviour to fit circumstance, however, is high. Van der Molen (Chapter 7) points to the constant trade-off, in social animals, needed between individuals' desire for group membership and individuals' other desires, which could conflict. Learning to manage this conflict begins at birth; so do learning skills, perforce within one's capacity but not always within one's preferred domains. For 'trade-off' to be successful it is, then, a basic assumption that the individual can make such changes to behaviour (in non-preferred ways – i.e., effect coping behaviour) as an accommodation between need (of the group or situation) and preference. The concept of coping behaviour is described in Chapter 1.

In the previous section three situations were identified when the individual may find himself in a group whose cognitive style is markedly different from his own. Whilst in each of them the individual is required to exercise some degree of coping behaviour, clearly the individual who is 'trapped and unhappy' is required to make the largest accommodation between his own preference and the group consensus. Without the power, or perhaps the ability, to identify a role which, with the minimum of coping behaviour, secures his acceptance in the group, he is in the position of having to attempt an excessive degree of coping behaviour beyond his power to sustain. The resultant stress may well be avoided if effective training and counselling is available. The validity of KAI as a survey-feedback instrument in such situations has been demonstrated most recently by Rickards (1990) in using KAI to explore causes of conflict and securing the recognition that 'the greatest need the group has is for tolerance of individual differences'. The identification and recognition of mismatch between individuals and the group is, however, only the first step.

The consequent training must begin by increasing the awareness of the individual and the group about the cognitive style dimension and its importance in organizations. During that process the individual's need for training skills is likely to become apparent; some innovators may need training in social skills, for example, or adaptors may need training in techniques of extending the boundaries which they impose on their generation of ideas. Such training need not always be formal: the opportunity to serve on working parties or undertake special assignments, etc. can give individuals the opportunity to develop their skills, secure a greater recognition among their peers, and enhance their contribution to the organization.

TEAM WORK

Much of the foregoing discussion has dealt with work groups whose mean A–I scores diverge to some extent from the population mean. It seems likely that the greater the extent of this divergence, the more dramatic the precipitating event would have to be to move the whole group's orientation back towards the population centre. For, as suggested above, a change in group orientation based on collective individual coping behaviour would be limited and short-lived unless turnover also played a decisive role. The effects of such an orientation shift on the group and the agent for change may be drastic. This raises the issue of whether an 'ideal' team should always be balanced in A–I terms. Consultancy has not found this a likely or even a desirable condition. Teams, to carry out their tasks successfully, need to have skewed A–I means, often on a permanent basis. From time to time there may also need to be shifts to meet current needs. When this happens the temporary disequilibrium from their usual distribution may be precisely what is required to meet the demands of sudden change and movement forwards from that crisis. Recognition of the factors involved and appreciation of the value of flexibility in such a situation is a key task of management to which this theory may make a contribution. This difficult task is made no easier by the fact that every person involved is part of the problem; a problem that he will view and try to resolve per media of his own preferred cognitive style.

Current research and consultancy are suggesting intriguing new lines of approach in team management. Within, for instance, an R&D milieu, knowledge of the A–I theory is being seen as leading first to more insight, then to more tolerance in teams containing individuals with diverse cognitive styles; the greater cohesion is exhibited as more mutual collaboration. These experiences are leading to other changes in management viewpoints. It is being thought useful to take into account, in team management, the notion that the 'purer' 'R' environment requires high (but not always exclusively higher) innovative orientation, with all its attendant disadvantages. It also follows that projects that start at 'R' should progress towards 'purer' 'D', on through such interface departments as production engineering/planning and then to production itself. During this progress, changing needs should shift orientation steadily towards the adaption mode, which can only be realized by shifts in personnel. Findings such as those of Keller (1986) demonstrate the vital role of group cohesion in R&D success; the significant relationship between innovativeness and project quality but not success in budget/schedule performance; between product quality for pure and applied research projects, but not for development and technical service projects. For counselling, the implications are that management needs openly to plan shifts in personnel as a reward for a group's success. If they do not do this, then moves, when they do happen, will be late and seen as both forced and as 'punishment' for not being adaptive enough to meet the approaching, very different needs of production.

In a wider context, it is hoped that the A–I theory will offer an insight into the interactions between the individual, the organization and the processes of change (See Schroder, Chapter 5 this volume). By using the theory as an additional resource when forward planning, it may be possible to foresee the effect of changes brought about by extraneous factors and to control the actual process of change and its ramifications within the organization. To the extent that imbalance and confusion can be minimized, and cyclic catastrophe avoided (see van der Molen, Chapter 7 of this volume) the beneficial and progressive aspects of change can be enhanced.

The penalties, on the other hand, for being caught in an inappropriate mode can be high. History, as well as contemporary events, shows that no institution is so powerful it can avoid drastic change or total collapse if persistently misdirected. This will be true even if it is also efficient. Adaption–Innovation theory has been only too easily related, by van der Molen, to catastrophe theory. The liability of one preferred mode persisting over the other in the teeth of a hostile outer setting is so easy to find in practice. Endemic as van der Molen finds these trends may be in humans, the capacity for individuals to learn and embody that learning into forward planning and management leaves, in the author's view, our fate in our hands rather than in our genes.

NOTES

1 This sample consisted of managers in close touch with US management colleagues, possibly, in Keller's view, reducing the effect of national cultural differences.
2 A number of studies, as will be seen from data quoted in this section, suggest that groups crossing a clear, distinguishable 'boundary' have a group average mean some ½ s.d. or about 8–9 KAI points different from otherwise comparable groups.
3 Their three defender companies had adaptor chief executives, the rest of the senior management being adaptor inclined but with variations related to function. The obverse in each detail was true for the prospector companies.
4 The reader is reminded that in this text for he, him, his, read also she, her, hers. Such other differences as gender are also additional resources for the group if that group can make proper use of them.

4

COGNITIVE STYLE IN ORGANIZATIONAL CLIMATE

M.J. Kirton and S.M. de Ciantis

INTRODUCTION

Much attention has been generated since the first edition of this chapter on the relationship between cognitive style and organizational climate. It will be our job here to highlight some of those findings that help in pointing the way forward in this important domain of person–environment interaction in determining organizational behaviour. Both concepts have been widely described as 'intervening variables', each operating at different levels of analysis. At the 'macro' level of analysis, climate has been seen as an intervening variable operating between the larger organizational unit and the behaviour of the individuals within it. At the 'micro' level, cognitive climate is the intervening variable. It is defined as the group's mode of preferred cognitive style held by the consensus subset (figure 3; Chapter 3). Preferred style is sharply distinguished from actual behaviour; the former is highly stable, the latter highly flexible and readily modified to meet situational demands and pressures through the temporary use of coping behaviour. Given that both of these 'intervening' constructs also contain a common person (behaviour)-environment feature, it seems fruitful to explore and understand fully their relationship to one another.

There are three possible relationships that can be expected between cognitive style and different forms of climate:

1 That, following the line above, cognitive climate (Kirton and McCarthy, 1988), the aggregate of individual cognitive styles, becomes cumulative and operational at a 'macro' level of analysis, forms a part of the broader *organizational* climate. The cognitive climate, defined largely by the consensus subset, once established, becomes an objective aspect of organizational reality, made manifest by the group within which the individual operates, thereby directly impinging upon his

or her behaviour. Such a position has implications for such issues as person–environment cognitive 'fit', recruitment and turnover, pressure and coping behaviour, interpersonal conflict and clash. This aspect of the relationship between cognitive style and *organizational* climate has been well reviewed in the first edition of this chapter and is retained in full below. Note that the consensus group is defined as (roughly) 40 per cent of the group located one half standard deviation on either side of the mean.

2 That when the climate variables are a relatively objective assessment of the *level* at which the climate operates, then the relationship with cognitive style is insignificant. An example of this is Clapp's (1991) measure of the extent to which organization members are encouraged to partake in changes being undertaken by the organization – 'how much' (level) rather than in what style. Similarly, Isaksen and Kaufmann (1990) have also discovered, that in Ekvall and Waldenström-Lindbald's (1983) Creative Climate Questionnaire (CCQ), eight (*viz.*, freedom, dynamism, trust, idea time, play/humour, idea support, debates, risk taking) of the ten dimensions are indicative of level, which like Clapp's measure have negligible expected correlations with KAI.

3 That there are different classes of variables relating to the way individuals perceive and subsequently react, within their subjective, '*psychological* climate' (James and Jones, 1974). An earlier study by Kirton (1980) found that adaptors and innovators have different perceptions (*psychological* climates) of the same environment as to whether it was more (as in the case of adaptors) or less turbulent (as measured by Heller's Turbulence and Uncertainty Questionnaire, 1976). Clapp and Kirton (1994) have speculated that the remaining two Ekvall variables, labelled conflict and challenge, which Isaksen and Kaufmann (1990) found correlated, albeit weakly, with KAI, may be in this third group. Because of their characteristic *psychological* climate, innovators are more likely to see incoming problems as a source of personal conflict; whereas adaptors are more likely to see them as a challenge to the group which requires group action to resolve. Clapp and Kirton (1994) have suggested that it might be possible to combine these two latter Ekvall variables into a single, bipolar, psychological climate-style type measure. If this is found to be possible, then the stronger, more reliable bipolar factor might well yield a stronger correlation, and the subsequent interpretation of this area might be somewhat easier to make.

So, to what extent does cognitive style in itself contribute to the formation of a 'cognitive climate'? Are climate variables independent of cognitive style, representing levels of constructs which can be approached through a range of styles? Does an individual's cognitive style preference affect the perception of the environment, thereby constituting individually subjective *psychological* climates, as distinct from *organizational* climate as an equally shared objective organizational reality? But are these three interpretations that mutually exclusive? These are the key questions we hope to cast some more light upon in this chapter.

THE INDIVIDUAL AND THE CONSENSUS GROUP

Organizational climate is one concept in a succession of interrelated layers of concepts with, at the outer layer (Payne and Pugh, 1973), the wider economic and cultural environment and, at the innermost, the individual who contributes to and is influenced by the whole system. For Payne and Pugh (see Figure 4), the economic-cum-cultural concept is composed of the economic, political and (wider) social macro-systems. These, in turn interact with succeeding layers of concept clusters of which organizational climate is one; others are organizational context, organizational structure, the work group and the individual. The economic system, to take one example, may directly stimulate the development of a technology; technology, an element in organizational context, may strongly influence the type of authority system chosen (Woodward, 1965).

The social system, to take a second example, influences individuals' contributions to the group's belief system, one element of which could be a notion of 'progressiveness', which in turn could encourage those individuals, especially those who are leaders, to experiment with alternative forms of authority systems (Burns and Stalker, 1961). All the while, political concepts in Payne and Pugh's wider society may incline individuals to value one authority system over another. Each of these variables, then, can interact directly with another, act indirectly through others, or be itself an intervening variable.

All the systems in Payne and Pugh's model are manmade and, therefore, individuals must be the critical elements within them. No explanatory theory should underestimate the power of these systems to affect individuals, or the intractable nature of some variables which, by being beyond man's gift to manipulate them at will – say, that iron is malleable on heating – also have powerful effects. However, it is the individuals' needs that spur their creativity to achieve the technology, develop the organization, and engender the ways of collaborating that eventually provide the community with the desired iron artefacts.

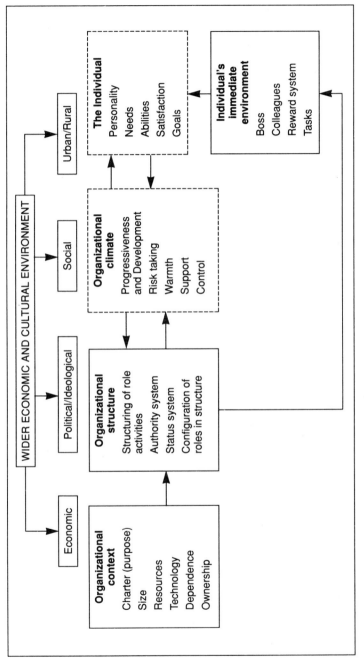

Figure 4 Major influences on organizational structure and climate
Source. Reprinted by permission of Professor Roy Payne and John Wiley & Sons Inc.

If it is accepted that the individual is the all-pervasive influence, we contend then, the range of characteristic cognitive styles of individuals' creativity, problem solving and decision making is of especial relevance, and so is a primary source of influence on all the factors in Payne and Pugh's model. Once the systems exist, the individual may, alone, have little impact on the larger, more stable elements, as it is also true that 'the organisational setting limits and influences people's behaviour' (ibid.). Our view is that the whole range of factors needs to be considered to understand 'climate', but here we concentrate on the influence of people's cognitive style and its aggregation into cognitive climate.

In theory, there are three obvious subsets of interest:

1 the leaders (individual × power);
2 the consensus group (individual × number); and
3 the individual whose contribution is seen as immediately needed (individual × situation).

In this chapter the emphasis is on the consensus group.

The individual's cognitive style and its role in organizational climate lie implicit in the literature. More explicitly, in a recent review of organizational behaviour, Schneider (1985: 589) notes: 'a development in leadership and management has been a renewed focus on traits as correlates of effectiveness. The newer efforts focus on cognitive complexity or cognitive style . . . defined as the way people process and evaluate information.' Although a rather narrow view of cognitive style, it is not in discord with the wider view expressed in these chapters.

The interest in cognitive style for recent writers has been the notion that 'people may be more satisfied and effective if they are working in conditions that are most compatible with their cognitive (personality) style' (Goodenough, 1985). One such key area of compatibility for Goodenough is between the problem-solving style and the job characteristics produced by the technology of the work processes being performed. Technology has been defined as the array of techniques employed by an organization and its sub-units to transform inputs into outputs (Perrow, 1967; Hunt, 1970). It has been related to variables at both the organizational (Woodward, 1965; Hickson et al., 1969; Mohr, 1971) and individual (Trist and Bamforth, 1951; Cooper and Foster, 1971), levels of analysis. These sociotechnical theorists have argued that technology affects individual behaviour. This link may, however, best be seen as mediated through function differences (e.g., production or marketing) or differences in organizational structure. For the former, this is because different functional specializations employ different technologies in achieving work goals, which in turn are reflected in differences of job characteristics. For example, Forbes (1975) analysed various functional specializations and placed them on a continuum representative of the degree to which technology related to varying degrees of uncertainty. Having done so, the use of formal rules and authority was demonstrated to decrease from finance/accounting, through production, engineering, marketing/sales, to personnel/training, thus providing some support for its validity. So, it seems clear in our view, that job characteristics represent crucial variables in linking technology with individual behaviour.

Perrow (1967) has little to say on function as an intervening variable but identifies aspects of technology (routine versus non-routine) that result in organizational structures such as those described by Burns and Stalker (1961) as 'mechanistic' or 'organic'. Similarly, Pierce (1984) found that in pre-programmed (lower degree of freedom/system controlled) technologies, employees perceived their jobs as routine (simple) as opposed to non-routine (complex). Other research has generally focused on changes to or from batch, mass or process technologies and the effects of such changes on job characteristics (Billings et al., 1977). Woodward (1965) found that in batch production technologies, decision making was more likely to be directive, but that in continuous processing technologies, there was a higher degree of participation. The empirical studies suggest that one way or another it is reasonable to suppose that there is a link between technology and job characteristics.

Whether or not function is seen as an intervening concept, this link has received less direct attention than it deserves (see Slocum and Sims, 1980 for review). However, the relationship between job characteristics and individual behaviour has been more extensively researched. Much of this work investigating job characteristics has focused on such variables as task variety (Cooper and Foster, 1971) as a determinant of employee motivation, satisfaction and performance (Hackman and Lawler, 1971; Brief and Aldag, 1975). Much of this 'motivational' research has occurred in the context of the development of the job characteristics model of task design (Hackman and Oldham, 1975; 1976; Roberts and Glick, 1981; Kiggundu, 1983). Other dimensions of individual behaviour affected by job characteristics have also been explored, for instance, Hannaway (1985) found initiating and search behaviour to be influenced by the degree of task certainty. Examples of studies involving organizational process and behaviour are, for performance, Lawler et al. (1973) and for job satisfaction, Schneider and Snyder (1975).

All these empirical studies offer some support to the contention that relationships exist between the variables of technology, organizational process, function, job characteristics and individual behaviour. Such relationships in turn lend support to the initial view that elements of such 'macro'-variables conglomerate into what is generally described in the literature as organizational climate; which is also assumed to impinge directly upon individual behaviour.

Authors have not overlooked the power of individuals to impose a group-derived consensus on the interpretations of all the above variables; the individuals in the group thereby helping to create their own collective interpretation of organizational climate. As has already been remarked, Goodenough (1985) introduces as a core concept in this social variable the concept of cognitive style. We support this view on the grounds that, since institutions do not think, act, impinge etc., in the end it is people who, whether as individuals or as individuals through groups, and (finally) through structure, determine the organizational climate. The cognitive style concept is therefore, increasingly being seen as another critical intervening variable in work performance (Robey and Taggart, 1981; Robertson, I.T., 1985).

The central argument of this chapter is that part of the overall organizational climate stems from a consensus group sharing a very similar cognitive style, i.e., within one-half a standard deviation around the mean of the work group as measured by KAI (Kirton, 1984; see also Chapter 3). The implication of this is that through their cognitive style, individuals interpret the conglomerate of variables just described. This may involve, for example, emphasizing certain job characteristics and delegating others less attuned to the prevailing cognitive style preference to other people, e.g., subordinates. It is therefore assumed that the viewpoint of the 'consensus group' plays a key role in the interpretation of the job characteristics, the degree and direction of change within the company, and the extent of tolerance of alternative viewpoints within the group. It is this shared problem-solving style which constitutes the 'cognitive climate' within what is generally understood as organizational climate. The KAI data available will now be reviewed to test that, by implication, this consensus group exists and manifestly acts as a pressure upon individual organizational members.

EVIDENCE FROM OCCUPATIONAL GROUPS

The findings of numerous studies (see Chapter 3) suggest that subsets of the general population yield KAI scores that distribute widely but with slightly skewed distributions. The obvious assumption is that those grouped round the mean constitute the orientating preferred style mode. If this is so, then this consensus or aggregate of preference should contribute to the larger organizational climate, and ought, therefore, to have measurable effects on the individual, especially those who have different ways of approaching a problem and a different concomitant 'personality package' (Kirton and de Ciantis, 1986) which is associated with the preferred working style. Thus, a person with an innovative style will be more willing to take risks and disagree with the existing consensus if the consensus group is adaptive. This may be a source of irritation to people with the more adaptive style, who are, in this case, concerned with making manifest creative action whilst maintaining that consensus. Conversely, adaptors may irritate an innovatively orientated group by having in the majority view, for instance, excessive caution or need for order. As cognitive style is considered to be stable (Messick, 1976; Goldstein and Blackman, 1981; see Chapters 1 and 2) and thus not readily altered by training (Kagan and Kogan, 1970), the situation of individuals who find themselves in a cognitive climate that does not match their own needs to be explored. In Chapter 3 such situations are identified as occurring when individuals may:

1 be temporary members, possibly under training and can look forward to an early release;
2 have found or created a niche which suits them and developed a particular role identity acceptable to the group;
3 be exercising coping behaviour in order to remain within the group. The effect on the individual will depend on the amount and duration of coping behaviour necessary and his own personality and motivation. Inevitably there will be stress in some cases great enough to compel him to leave the group (e.g., Thomson, 1985).

At least by implication, it is assumed that group cognitive style consensus or cognitive climate is part of the wider organizational climate. Another element in the assumption is that cognitive climate impinges on individuals as do other elements of organizational climate. Tests of this last assumption can be that:

1 Groups of similar homogeneity (i.e., specific occupational groups) will have similar and expected distribution scores on KAI.
2 (a) Groups will either recruit those who will show collectively a similar mean and range, (e.g., Gul, 1986) or
   (b) the new entrant group will, over a short period of time, conform to the establishment group's mean and range. This comes about

by turnover, not as a result of individual change in cognitive style, which is regarded as stable (e.g., Holland *et al.*, 1991).

3 The group's members may personalize differences of style outlook between themselves and those not in cognitive fit, and exert pressure on the latter to leave (e.g., Lindsay, 1985).

4 A group member, in wide 'misfit', who is not under undue stress, will have earned the group's respect and tolerance to be different by providing a service 'fitting' to such individual but not to the (their) group (e.g., Rickards and Moger, 1994).

There is already considerable evidence (see Chapter 3) that occupational groups not only tend to have skewed, though still wide KAI distributions, but that the direction of their mean displacements are expected according to whether the demands of the job in the researcher's view are more suited to an adaptive or innovative style (e.g., Foxall, 1986b).

Groups such as bankers, accountants and those involved in production, who are largely required to work in a system within which the answers to problems can be found, tend to be adaptive (Kirton, 1980; Thomson, 1980; Kirton and Pender, 1982; Hayward and Everett, 1983; Holland, 1987; Foxall, 1986a; Gryskiewicz *et al.*, 1987; Gul, 1986). Conversely, the group mean tends to be innovative where employees are required to work in an environment that embodies more than one system (e.g., Quality Control can consist of monitoring and negotiating) or to act as an interface between systems (e.g., Finance must operate within both the company paradigms and relevant outside financial institutions' paradigms). Hence, research has shown employees in R&D, planning, personnel and marketing to be on the innovative side of the general population mean (Keller and Holland, 1978b; Kirton, 1980; Thomson, 1980; Kirton and Pender, 1982; Foxall, 1986a; Gryskiewicz *et al.*, 1987; Lowe and Taylor, 1986). Other groups can be readily shown to contain subsets, of differing orientations within them (e.g., 'engineers' containing production engineers, R&D engineers, etc.). More recent work shows that even the skewed groups may be composed of such distinct different subsets (Foxall, 1986b; Gryskiewicz *et al.*, 1987; Gul, 1986).

These studies lend substantial support to the first of the hypotheses that well-defined subsets will have relevant KAI means. Work by a number of researchers is still in progress testing the other hypotheses. From the studies already carried out, however, a picture is emerging that gives support to most of these and illustrates the problems that can arise when individuals find themselves working in an 'alien' cognitive climate.

RECRUITMENT AND TURNOVER

Hayward and Everett (1983) administered the KAI to employees in a local authority setting and found that new recruits were mildly innovative. However, the staff who had been in post for, on average, five years or more were shown to be a more homogeneously adaptive group. This is unlikely to be explained solely by an age effect, as the largest correlation so far found (see Kirton, 1987a) between KAI and age is small ($r = -0.19$). It could be argued, of course, that earlier recruits had changed their cognitive style in order to accommodate to the prevailing climate (see Chapter 1 for the argument on the stability of KAI scores). Hayward and Everett (1983), however, noted that the resignation pattern at the end of their study (a period of nearly three years) was disproportionately innovative when the overall cognitive climate was adaptive.

The difference in the mean of the entrant group from that of the mean of established members of a particular occupational group was also noted by Holland (1987). He found a significant difference ($t = 2.0$, $p = <0.05$) between 51 established bankers (mean 91.2, s.d. 17.3) and 40 bank trainees (mean 97.8, s.d. 18.9). These results are in line with those obtained on American bankers (Gryskiewicz et al., 1987). Bank trainees ($n = 78$) in this study had a mean of 97 (s.d. 14) whereas branch managers ($n = 128$) yielded a mean of 91 (s.d. 13.5) ($t = 2.6$, $p = <0.01$). Results of some work (Holland et al., 1991) in a pharmaceutical company adds further general support, but suggests that recruitment policy can, on occasion, produce new entrants' group means little different from that of the mean of the people they are joining. Flegg (in a private communication) reported that a consultancy-research programme he

Table 12 Mean scores by length of service and resignations[1]

| | Number of years' service | | |
	Novices <5 years	Established >5 years	Total
Total sample of local government employees	107.1 (18)	78.3 (49)	(67)
Subset leaving at end of study	121.4 (6)[2]	None	(6)

Notes:
1 s.d.s are not available.
2 Mean of those <5 years' service remaining in post was 99.9.
Source: Printed by kind permission of Dr Hayward; see also Kirton and McCarthy, 1988

undertook on over 400 apprentices in a training department of a multi-national company showed that the best predictor by a small fraction, among many other variables used, of whether individuals would eventually pass, was their score on the R factor score of KAI. The more adaptive were more likely to succeed in this adaptive environment.

Clues are beginning to accumulate on how the cognitive climate facilitates these changes in group composition. A study by Thomson (1985), for instance, sheds light on possible reasons why the 'cognitive deviant' may be unhappy and want to leave the organization. Her study included Singaporean (ethnic Chinese, English-speaking) executives working in Western multinational companies and in local companies as well as middle-ranking Singaporean Civil Servants. She hypothesized that those individuals who found themselves in organizational fit would be less likely to express the intention to leave their job than the individuals who were not in organizational fit.

The measure of fit in this study was based on a classification of organizations as adaptive or innovative according to whether the (ethnic Chinese) managers had to cross a cultural boundary or not (Kirton, 1978c) to belong to the organization. This crudely equated local industry and the Civil Service with adaption orientation and multinational companies with innovative orientation. Support for this classification was found in an earlier study (Thomson, 1980) in which local (Chinese) managers working in Western-owned companies were found to be significantly more innovative than compatriot managers within the Civil Service; others in local industry being located roughly in the middle.

In the study, originated in an attempt to understand the very high turnover rate that was then a general feature of Singapore, it was found that from the total sample of over 600 managers, of those innovators located in multinational companies (and therefore assumed by her, following the earlier works, to be in organizational fit), 46.5 per cent reported an intention to leave compared with 53.6 per cent in organizational non-fit (Chi^2 4.1, $p = <0.05$). Similarly, 48 per cent of adaptors assumed to be in organizational fit reported this intention compared with 60.3 per cent of adaptors in non-fit (Chi^2 6.8, $p = <0.01$).

Interestingly, this suggests that adaptors in non-fit situations may be under more pressure than corresponding innovators – a finding easily understood in terms of the Adaption–Innovation theory. Adaptors are concerned with being in tune with consensus; innovators are not always sure what any particular consensus currently is. Adaptors are, therefore, more likely to feel the discomfort of not fitting. Thomson also tested the relationship between organizational fit and 'problem empathy' by asking respondents to report whether they found that other people in the organization approached problems in the same way as themselves. She found that being in organizational fit was associated with feeling that others in the same organization empathized with the individual's problems. Furthermore, having the intention to stay in one's current job (see Table 13) was also associated with this feeling of problem empathy or the lack of it.

Table 13 Problem empathy, organizational fit and intention to stay

		With problem empathy %	Without problem empathy %
A	In organizational fit	61	39
	Not in organizational fit	30	70
B	Intention to leave	26	74
	Intention to stay	60	40

Note: Significant differences in both A (X^2 48.2) and B (X^2 79.6) $p = <0.0001$.
Source: Printed by kind permission of Dr Thomson

One remarkable aspect of Thomson's second study is the crudity of some of the hypotheses based on her first study. 'Organizational fit' lumps together all Chinese managers in multinationals with a KAI score of 96 or more. The other contrasting categories are equally simply defined. Her measure of 'empathy' depends on a single question. It must be a reflection of the validity of the underlying notions that significant meaningful results were obtained. A replication study using more refined measures should yield interesting data. Such a study might now generate a measure of 'climate discrepancy'. This notion, advocated by Payne and Pugh (1973), could now be based on the individual's distance from the consensus mean. The way to quantify the contribution to the consensus, of a group's leader when not located on the group mean, is a study in itself.

PRESSURES: COPING AND CLASHING

It is likely that it is the individual's sub-climate, that is their immediate working group within the overall organization, which is the crucial factor in determining whether cognitive misfit will occur. McCarthy 1993 examines fit at this micro-level. This study involves asking a sample of women managers to rate themselves and a 'typical colleague' on the KAI.

Previous research has shown that individuals can make accurate assessments of others with regard to their KAI score when there is a history of a working relationship (Kirton and McCarthy, 1985). Results from this study show that those women managers who had a cognitive gap equal to or more than one standard deviation between themselves and their colleague, reported significantly more work pressures (total number, not type or degree, from a list in Davidson, 1982) than managers who had closer cognitive fit (see Table 14).

Table 14 Mean work pressure scores of female managers

	N	M	*s.d.*
Cognitive gap sample	38	142.9	35.8
Cognitive fit sample	40	121.4	33.1

Note: Difference between means (one-tailed) $t = 2.76$, $p = <0.005$
Source: McCarthy, 1993

The direction of the gap (i.e., whether the woman is more innovative or adaptive than her colleague) may of course influence the *type* of pressures reported, but it is the gap *per se* which seems to determine the amount of pressure. Whether these pressures could be objectively measured as distinct from subjectively reported is not clear. Kirton (1980), using a modified version of Heller's (1976) turbulence and uncertainty questionnaire, found that innovators reported more turbulence at work than did adaptors. Just how much of the variance found could be accounted for by:

1 differences not attributable to individual variation;
2 innovators gravitating to turbulent environments (and vice versa); or
3 innovators engendering turbulence (and vice versa)

has as yet not been studied.

Even gaps of one standard deviation may be tolerated if the individual is able to employ effective coping behaviour, as part, perhaps, of securing themselves a niche. One study in progress, which suggests that people do accommodate their behaviour but not their preference to the prevailing cognitive climate, compared self-reported cognitive style on the KAI with colleagues' ratings of perceived behaviour based on the same scale (Clapp and de Ciantis, 1987). These two sets of scores both yielded high internal reliabilities and, with a rank order correlation of 0.72, were found significantly related. However, there was an average difference of half a standard deviation (towards adaption) between a person's self-estimate and the rating of perceived behaviour given by the colleagues. This suggests that the organizational climate was inducing an outwardly noticeable accommodation by the individual towards its prevailing ethos.

Six of an intensely studied sub-sample ($n = 23$) showed a gap of as much as one whole standard deviation or somewhat more between self-style and reported behaviour. One of these was a male who had recently moved into a job very different to that to which he was accustomed, and the other five were among the six women (of a total of 12) with the more innovative scores. The individuals in this study had all been working together for a minimum of three years, which would suggest that the majority were able to cope with the pressures that had arisen from this requirement to behave more adaptively. As such, they have seemed able to make a successful accommodation, within these limits, between their personal style and the demands of the cognitive climate over a long period of time, but the study did not include any estimate of personal cost (e.g., in terms of reported stress). Further work in this field is, therefore, surely needed.

INTERPERSONAL CLASHES

A number of anecdotal cases describing individual and group difficulties as a result of large cognitive gaps are informally reported by practitioners (trainers and consultants) with some empirical published support provided by McHale and Flegg (1985; 1986). There is one detailed study by Lindsay (1985), however, which is of particular interest as it describes a team that did not reach the inferred successful accommodation reported by Clapp and de Ciantis.

Lindsay reports that he was asked to provide a counselling service in a small department of an international oil company which was experiencing a conflict concerning perceived effectiveness between two departmental managers and their senior analyst. The former stated that they expected their staff to be 'creative, dynamic, thorough and self-sufficient'. In addition, staff were expected to initiate work and see it through to completion within reasonable deadlines. They had to establish credibility with other managers in client companies. An important requirement, however, was for their work to be seen to tie in directly to the business plan and not contradict the prevailing 'business' climate. In nearly every aspect, the departmental managers felt the analyst to be lacking.

Lindsay found that whilst the analyst's outline of his own job was in broad agreement with that shared by the departmental manager and his deputy, he felt that his managers and clients were 'short-sighted' in that they didn't perceive the pattern of business in the future. The people involved, therefore, had different perceptions as to what direction the business should take. Lindsay then noted that there were marked differences in cognitive style as measured by the KAI, with the managers averaging 86 and the analyst 117. Based on general population norms, this meant a gap of nearly two standard deviations.

Counselling sessions were arranged with the analyst to devise a personal development plan that would enable him to function better in the department. However, the absence of the most senior manager eventually resulted in a blow-up between his deputy and the analyst which led to the analyst's decision to seek new employment. What this study shows is the reality of the climate pressure on the cognitive deviant as could be predicted from the 'person–environment fit' model (French *et al.*, 1974). This is one of the stress-generating forces on individuals, which by the subsequent turnover maintains the established group's mean cognitive style. It can be inferred from Clapp and de Ciantis's study not only that many groups contain wide ranges of style but also that, in some groups, not all the less-fitting members are necessarily so stressed as to be unhappy or ineffective. For all of us, it must be added, 'coping behaviour', as here made manifest in the difference between self-score and self-as-perceived by others score, is an important, ever-present factor in our social life.

From the work carried out to date, therefore, the size of the cognitive gap seems to be important in determining whether the individual will survive easily within the organization. Anecdotal reports suggest that the half standard deviation gap is often recognizable and generally not a problem; more than one standard deviation causes difficulties in integration and begins to raise noticeable problems of communication and strains on goodwill. Further research is required to examine these observations in detail.

CONCLUSION

To conclude, we have contended that cognitive climate is a basic and pervasive factor among those that determine organizational climate in the Payne and Pugh model (Figure 4). Cognitive climate is defined as the aggregation of individual cognitive style, particularly of those clustered closely around the mean – altering as consensus alters, influencing individual behaviour and where there is disparity, creating stress.

The use of the KAI as a measure of cognitive style has demonstrated the importance of taking into account this interaction between the cognitive climate of the group and the cognitive styles of the individuals who make it up. For example, a woman engineer is still today very much in the minority and so is likely to have a higher innovative score and to have as an innovator, for example, more feminist views than the female norm. Introduced into R&D, she may well find many of the males also innovative and the group, for more than one reason, 'permeable'. Introduced into maintenance, she would be likely to find the group to be all male, more adaptive than most men and women, more cohesive, and probably less willing to accept either a woman or an innovator (or any person different from the prevailing norm) – a clear challenge to the group, to her, and to the company.

As with all social groups (see Chapter 3), difference from consensus can all too readily be seen as a fault or as incapacity.

Traditionally, selection and training have been seen as two methods of improving 'man–job' fit (Rodger and Cavanagh, 1962). The emphasis in selection, not unnaturally, is generally on specific job characteristics rather than on such dimensions as work group climate (Schneider, 1983). However, the findings reported in this chapter suggest using KAI as a measure, since identification of a person's preferred way of working would be a very useful addition to the selection process (whether recruitment or teambuilding), bearing in mind that for any group the desirable cognitive style balance within it to deal with today's problems may not be the same tomorrow. Cognitive style can be considered as a useful concept to take into account not only when forming teams, but also in their subsequent fruitful cohesion (Keller, 1986), where teams need to generate, explore and capitalize on initial differences of opinion, aim and style without allowing them to become permanently and unproductively divisive. Individuals, therefore, need to acquire insight and generate tolerance into others' different cognitive styles, thereby, paving the way to better collaboration in more heterogeneous groups.

The literature already reflects these views. For instance, the three extracts below from Goodenough (1985) can easily be accommodated into the cognitive climate notion and be expanded by what has already been written here into useful points for consideration by managers.

> . . . the requirements of a specific problem may be more conducive to the deployment of a particular style.
>
> Thus stable individual differences in the preferred way of working may make the resolution of some problems easier than others.

It pays to keep rethinking the best use of people available against both stable and changing elements of demand. It pays to ensure those in the group who locate outside the consensus group are well used to everyone's satisfaction.

. . . business environments may force people to work in a way which is more or less effective for them, that is in a way which fits or could be counter to their preferred style.

Thus, if there is more than one way of doing the same job and/or a team is involved, effectiveness might be improved by allowing people to work in the way they prefer, as often as possible.

. . . in the purer social context, is the issue of compatibility matching among people.

Thus, two people may be equally effective, but clash because they have very different ways of working; or, by way of a corollary, where matching lessens then tolerance needs to increase. Training departments can have a significant role in engendering insight and teaching a wide range of coping skills and strategy, but eschewing forlorn, undesirable attempts to bring about permanent change to personal style.

What can be concluded from the above discussion is that the identification of a cognitive climate within the wider organizational climate has useful implications for the leader and manager who is attempting to build effective teams. Even though some problem areas may be more conducive to the deployment of a particular style, it is unlikely that best results will be obtained by trying to build a totally homogeneous team. As O'Toole (1979) points out, a certain amount of healthy conflict may be the source of useful change in organizations. Furthermore, an organization's goals are likely to change over time, so that the requirements for a particular style of problem solving will also fluctuate. People whose scores are well off the group's mean, but who are respected and integrated, make ready-made foci for shifts in cognitive climate, in ways that might be more acceptable and with more continuity than abrupt changes imposed from outside the group (see 'Agents for change' (Kirton, 1987a); Chapter 3). In short, the challenge is to create the right balance and foster tolerance amongst team members who may have very different cognitive styles and, when needed, to make the necessary alterations, by rebalancing teams as circumstances alter, while retaining team understanding and willing co-operation.

CURRENT POSITION AND FUTURE DIRECTIONS

As in the field of cognition, studies of organizational climate have also been plagued by a failing to distinguish between level (what is done) and style (how it is done). This problem with terminology, particularly in relation to 'creativity' and 'innovation' and the meanings attributed to them, is explored not only in Chapter 1, but even more fully in Chapter 6 in the marketing domain. For instance, Isaksen and Kaufmann (1990) did not make use of this distinction fully when exploring the relationship between Adaption–Innovation and Climate using the Creative Climate Questionnaire (CCQ), (Ekvall and Waldenström-Lindbald 1983). This measure, overall, was designed to differentiate between organizations characterized along a summated dimension ranging from 'stagnation' to 'innovation', where organizations oriented towards the former are less commercially successful and 'less creative' than the latter. Here, as argued by Clapp and Kirton (1994), lies a conflation of the variables of level, style and effectiveness. Stagnation is clearly an aspect of level (low) and 'innovation' is clearly (by definition) style: 'doing things differently' as opposed to 'doing things better'. 'Doing things better' is clearly not synonymous with 'stagnation', which is not doing things at all. Likewise, 'innovation' is neither successful nor appropriate in every situation; so to place these as the low/high ends of an effectiveness dimension is clearly erroneous.

Stagnation might best be seen as opposed not to style (innovation), but rather to high activity (level). The term 'dynamism', often used in the climate literature, might well provide a useful label for the latter (indeed, one of Ekvall's ten CCQ subdimensions is labelled dynamism/liveliness and, as expected, is unrelated to KAI (Isaksen and Kaufmann, 1990). At this point we can separate low (stagnation when inappropriately low)–high activity (or dynamism when appropriately high) level from another type of effectiveness where the appropriate style (e.g., adaption or innovation) needs to be used in relation to the situation at hand. The underlying willingness to shift is often called rigidity–flexibility (e.g., Reddin, 1970) or creative motive (Amabile, 1983). We can agree with Ekvall and Waldenström-Lindbald that the very term 'stagnation' is pejorative, in that it implies too low a level for the needs of a particular situation. In the same way, too high a level of activity for the situation at hand may be wasteful to the point of being 'chaotic'. Ekvall's generic use of the term 'innovation' is causing a problem, just as Foxall (Chapter 6 of this volume) finds it does in the field of consumer behaviour. The more semantically correct term, when in appropriately high quantities, 'dynamism', gives less problems when identifying the appropriate *level* needed to resolve the novelty in hand.

Thus, climate may be construed in both level and style terms, each of which must be operating at the appropriate amount and orientation to be effective, in any given situation, at a given time. Appropriate flexibility then becomes a key variable in maintaining a healthy organization. This has particularly relevant implications for strategic leadership in the maintenance of high-performing organizations during the ongoing developmental stages of the organizational life-cycle, whereby what level and style is more appropriate is likely to change in accord with organizations' requirements (Vicere, 1992). Further, climate may be construed both at the individual level of analysis, where the cognitive climate will result in an individual's state of 'fit or non-fit' within the group. The pressure exerted by cognitive climate, as with any other kind of climate, will be felt more by those in 'non-fit' than those in 'fit'. In fact, because of individual psychological climate, those in non-fit will perceive the climate differently from those in fit. At the organizational level, parts of the organization, be it a division, sector, unit, etc., will be at a greater or lesser degree of accord with the larger system of which it is a part, up to the level of culture. Clashes between groups, be they on the same level, or in hierarchical relationship, can reach such degree of conflict as to affect the performance of at least one, probably both, and even others closely involved with either. This parallels the conflicts earlier noted between individuals (see Chapter 3). However, such conflicts between groups are no more inevitable, if just as likely, as conflicts between people. As with people, groups that differ in cognitive mode but that also can work together harmoniously, have between them a wider range of problem-solving resource and are therefore liable, in the long run, to be more successful. It is obvious that managing diversity is more difficult than managing homogeneity, but the rewards are potentially higher.

5

MANAGERIAL COMPETENCE AND STYLE

H.M. Schroder

Each year most organizations allocate considerable funds to train or develop managers, presumably because of the expectation that such training will produce improved organizational effectiveness in such areas as productivity, quality and climate. This strategy makes several assumptions. First, that not only will the training change the behaviour of the manager, but that this change will be associated with improved performance of the manager's organization. In addition, most training/ development programmes assume that skills learnt are expressed in similar ways by all managers, such that all managers with these skills make a common contribution to the organization. In most cases, these assumptions either have no foundation or are erroneous.

In order to improve the implementation and effectiveness of current Human Resource Development strategies, it will be necessary to:

1 identify *competencies* which, when possessed by managers, consistently produce a significant improvement in the performance of their organizations (when compared to the performance of organizations managed by persons who do not possess these competencies); and

2 identify variables that affect ways the various competencies are expressed by managers in organizational contexts. The significant point here is that competencies are integrated into the manager's more basic personality structure, so that two managers who possess the same level of a given competency may use the competency differently. These more enduring differences in the style of the expression of competencies generate different reactions from others (e.g., from subordinates or supervisors) and are associated with making different contributions to the organization.

That is, the measurement and development of managerial performance are improved when both competence and style are taken into consideration. This chapter will deal with the way adaptive–innovative style and theory (Kirton, 1976; 1987a) impact on the expression of managerial competence in the management of organizations. The studies will be organized around the following headings.

1 Managerial competencies: their identification, definition and measurement.
2 Kirton Adaption–Innovation Style: its identification, definition and measurement.
3 The relationship between managerial competence and style. This study confirms the independence of the two variables, indicating that both must be taken into account in understanding organizational behaviour.
4 Style and the expression of competencies. This study confirms that style differences affect the way competencies are expressed, not the quality of the performance. These differences in expression have important short- and long-term implications for the effectiveness of any organization.
5 Implications of this research for competency style and organizational performance.

MANAGERIAL COMPETENCIES

This study is based on middle-level managers from 'for profit' organizations who paid a fee to participate in an assessment/development programme. The assessment of eleven competencies was made using an assessment centre methodology, by highly trained, multiple assessors across multiple simulated situations (exercises). Four behavioural simulations were used: an in-basket exercise; a fact-finding analytic exercise; and two group exercises – one competitive with fixed roles and one co-operative with no fixed roles.[1]

The assessment schedule covered testing and the administration of the simulated exercises requiring a period of twelve hours over one and a half days. This was followed by individual feedback and follow-up development.

Identification of the competencies

Eleven different competencies were assessed in each of the four behavioural exercises. The assessors arrived at an overall rating for each competency using definitions and behavioural indicators in the Competency Manual (Schroder, 1985).

The competencies were selected on the basis of experimental studies which demonstrated significantly better performance of organizations (or units) whose managers possessed each competency. The identification of the competencies draws heavily on the work of Richard Boyatzis. Boyatzis defines a competency as:

> characteristics that are causally related to effective and/or superior performance in a job. This means that there is evidence that indicates that possession of the characteristic precedes and leads to effective and/or superior performance in that job. In addition to a theoretical prediction as to the causal relationship between a characteristic and job performance, an empirical relationship between the characteristic as an independent variable and job performance as a dependent variable should exist.
>
> (Boyatzis, 1982: 23)

This definition requires that studies using 'external validity' be used to identify competencies. That is, some external criteria of success of the organization such as climate, quality, productivity or satisfaction must be used to classify organizations as low, average or high performing. In this way, studies can demonstrate competencies which differentiate between managers of average and high performing organizations and are associated with superior performance of the organization. Competencies identified by this method must be differentiated from competencies or dimensions that have been identified by job analysis. Typically, job analysis studies do not use external criteria of 'superior performance' in a job. Job analysis is based on content validity, namely, interview and questionnaire data referring to 'what managers do when they do the job well'. Characteristics or dimensions identified by this method may not differentiate between managers of average and superior performing organizations.

Following Boyatzis, the competencies identified in this study are to be differentiated from threshold competencies, which are not discussed in this chapter or used in this research. Again, according to Boyatzis:

> A threshold competency is a person's generic knowledge, motive, trait, self-image, social role, or skill which is essential to performing a job, but is not causally related to superior job performance. For example, speaking the native language of one's subordinates would be considered a threshold competency. On the other hand, those characteristics that differentiate superior performance from average and poor performance are competencies.
>
> (Boyatzis, 1982: 23)

Four major sources of research were used as the basis for selecting the competencies used in this study and selected for managerial assessment and development programmes in the Center for Organizational Effectiveness. These are Boyatzis (1982), Huff *et al.* (1982), Streufert and Swezey (1986), and reliability and validity studies of assessment centre measures (Schroder and Croghan, 1984).

Boyatzis used a number of studies across different organizations such as service, financial and manufacturing. He found several competencies which consistently differentiated between managers of average and high performing organizations. In general, the same competencies were found to differentiate across the managers of different organizations, but some competencies are unique for first-line managers, middle-level managers and chief executive officers. This indicates that managerial competencies which are based on external validity studies are the same for managers of public and private organizations and for the managers of service, financial, manufacturing and retail organizations, but differ across different levels of management in all organizations. These competencies are shown in Table 15.

The Florida Council on Educational Management study by Huff *et al.* (1982) used school principals. (Educational organizations were not used in the Boyatzis studies.) High and average performing schools were identified using student skills in mathematics and communication while partialling out the effects of non-academic factors such as education and socio-economic status of parents. The study found that certain competencies significantly differentiated between the principals of average and high performing schools based on the external criteria of student performance in mathematics and verbal skill tests. These competencies are also listed in Table 15.

The last column in Table 15 lists the competencies used in this study. They are based on the studies reported above and supporting evidence from other studies. A series of experimental studies (Schroder *et al.*, 1969; Streufert and Swezey, 1986) focusing on the relationship between cognitive competencies and performance in individual and group situations is consistent with most of the findings reported above. The combined evidence supports the identification of four cognitive competencies: information search, concept formation, interpersonal search and conceptual flexibility. The evidence from the Boyatzis and Florida Council studies are supported by a number of validity studies of dimensions measured in assessment centres, for example, Bray *et al.* (1974), Hinrichs (1978), Sackett and Dreher (1982), and Thornton and Byham (1982). The combined evidence supported

Table 15 Managerial competencies schemata using external validity criteria

Boyatzis competencies[1]	FCEM competencies[2]	COE competencies[3]
Notes:		
Diagnostic use of concepts	Monitoring	Information search
Conceptualization	Pattern recognition	Concept formation
Logical thought		
Perceptual objectivity	Perceptual objectivity Analytic ability	Conceptual flexibility
		Interpersonal search
Use of socialized power		Managing interaction
Managing group process		
Developing others' accurates self-assessment		Developmental orientation
Concern with impact	Persuasiveness	Impact
Self-confidence		Self-confidence
Oral presentation		Presentation
Proactivity	Sense of control Focused involvement in change	Proactive orientation
Efficiency orientation	Commitment to quality	Achievement orientation

Notes:
1 From the studies reported by Boyatzis (1982)
2 From the Florida Council on Educational Management Study by Huff *et al.* (1982)
3 Competencies based on studies in 1 and 2 above as well as Streufert and Swezey (1986) and other studies on the validity of the assessment centre method. These competencies are used for assessment/development programmes in the Center for Organizational Effectiveness and are the competencies used in this study (see Schroder, 1985)

the identification of the remaining seven competencies used in this study.

Definitions of the competencies

The cognitive competencies provide a manager with the potential to gather and process sufficient relevant information for the understanding of events and for decision making. Information, experiences and feedback must be gathered from a variety of sources, perspectives and means (information search); this information must then be 'processed', linked, sequenced or organized into alternative meanings, concepts or options (concept formation); and then the most relevant or significant but different conceptions must be used simultaneously and integratively in making decisions. In complex situations, events must be viewed from different conceptual positions (perspectives) and related via a comparison of pros and cons of both in decision making (conceptual flexibility).

Motivational competencies provide a manager with the potential to involve and motivate others. The foundation competency in this cluster is interpersonal search, described as understanding the concepts, ideas and perspectives of another (e.g., a subordinate) from the other's point of view. In addition, this cluster also includes the potential to involve others, to facilitate interaction and the participation of others, to work with others as a team and build co-operation between units (managing interaction), and the potential to hold a positive regard for others and provide them (e.g., subordinates) with opportunities to learn through coaching and performance feedback (developmental orientation).

Three competencies provide the manager with the potential to lead. Managers need to be able to develop their own 'stand' or position, to make a decision when required, and be able to justify that decision (self-confidence). They also need to be able to make oral presentations which communicate what is supposed to be communicated in a clear manner using non-verbal, symbolic and graphical aids to reinforce the main points (presentation). Lastly, they need the potential to gain and sustain the attention of others, to influence others via credibility, modelling, self-interest and alliance formation (impact).

A manager's potential to achieve organizational excellence is also based on the achieving competencies. This includes the initiative to take total responsibility to 'make things happen' rather than react; to initiate and implement ideas and strategies (proactive orientation); and to demonstrate a commitment to efficiency and quality by setting challenging goals for self and others, striving to 'improve', and measuring progress in reaching goals (achievement orientation).

Definitions and general behavioural indicators of these competencies are presented in the general manual (Schroder, 1986) and in more specific situational manuals – for individual analytic situations, two-person conference situations, behavioural event interview situations, and group situations (Schroder et al., 1986).

Measurement of competencies

Managers used in this study attended an assessment centre for developmental purposes. They performed in each of the simulated exercises designed to present demands for the competencies identified above. Multiple raters (trained assessors) observed each manager's behaviour and rated each of the competencies using the manuals described above. After the assessors recorded their individual ratings (along with the relevant behavioural indicators for that rating), they met to decide the best (consensus) rating (given the indicators observed): (1) for each competency for each exercise, and (2) for each competency across all exercises. The latter is referred to as an overall competency rating. It is not necessarily an average of the ratings of a competency across the four exercises. Rather, it is the assessors' best estimate of the degree to which the manager possesses the competency. This judgement is subjective when the ratings of a competency vary significantly across exercise settings. Large variations do occur since behaviour is affected by the situation and these exercises were designed to provide wide situational variation.

According to Boyatzis (1982), the higher the motivation associated with a competency, the more it will be expressed across situations. For example, managers with high achievement motivation who also possess the achievement orientation competency would be expected to engage the competency across a broader range of situations than a manager who has learnt the competency but has lower achievement motivation.

More research is needed on the combination of ratings across situations to rate overall level in a competency area. For practical purposes, such a measure may not be useful or, indeed, meaningful. However, for research purposes in this study, we accepted a general rule that weighted ratings of the possession of a competency even in one exercise counts in making the overall rating. This bias was accepted on the basis that demonstration of possession of a competency, even in only one exercise situation, indicated that the manager can use the competency. The fact that it is not engaged in other situations needs to be known for developmental purposes, but it may not be a matter of competence in that area – it may be due to other factors such as 'competition', which reduces the potential to engage that competency for that manager in that situation.

MANAGERIAL STYLE

Some elements of the A–I theory are particularly relevant to this chapter. For a start, it emerged out of studies of the ways in which new ideas were developed and implemented in an organization (Kirton, 1961). According to Kirton (see Chapter 1), adaptive and innovative solutions are equally creative, but in different ways. For solutions, adaptors depend more directly on generally agreed upon paradigms. They are skilled in initiating changes that improve current ways of doing things. Innovators, by contrast, are more likely to reconstruct the problem, to work outside the boundaries of accepted paradigms, and are skilled in initiating change based on different ways of doing things. Adaptors create ideas to improve the efficiency of current practices and methods of operation and tend to incorporate novel ideas into existing models or plans. Innovators create ideas which, if implemented, would change the way things are done. New information or observations are used to generate new methods, policies or procedures. In organizations, high-scoring adaptors and innovators experience difficulty in communicating and collaborating, yet both are needed for the organization to function effectively.

Again, Kirton observes, adaptors contribute stability, order, continuity, co-operation and co-ordination while innovators provide the break with past 'accepted' ideas, the future orientation and uncertainty. In this way, adaptors tend to be perceived by innovators as methodical, sound, dependable, conforming, traditional and practical; and innovators by adaptors as 'rocking the boat', radical, abrasive, impractical and undisciplined. It is also important for this chapter to remember that the range of responses, extending from high adaptability to high innovation, is relatively fixed and stable, and in the general population is normally distributed.

In the past then, we may suppose, most organizations placed greater value on the adaptor while the academic community tended to 'pin the rose' on the innovator. In current organizational environments, characterized by increasing competition and the need for rapid change, excellence can only be achieved by integrating both styles into the culture. Persons falling towards the adaptive end of the continuum are more concerned with improving the effectiveness of the organization through improved performance of the operational paradigm, its people in their current roles, its methods, policies, procedures and rules. People at the innovative end of the continuum are equally concerned with improving the effectiveness of the organization, but differ in their focus on changing the paradigm or proposing ideas that introduce uncertainty (or instability) in the methods, policies, procedures and rules. This difference in style creates communication problems and often power battles between the groups (Kirton, 1984; 1987a).

Until recent times, most organizations operating in relatively stable environmental contexts could function efficiently with their power base and culture anchored in the adaptive strategy. With the advent of accelerated change in technology, people and markets, it is becoming increasingly urgent to integrate the innovative people into planning and operation of the organization. Today, organizations are looking for ways to become innovative, to keep abreast of new ideas in addition to implementing new ideas effectively. To be effective, this will require the integration of innovative change and adaptive efficiency (precise operation of the changed paradigm). In human resource terms, it requires training or building situations so that adaptors and innovators can work together in pursuit of superordinate organizational goals.

RELATIONSHIP BETWEEN MANAGER COMPETENCE AND STYLE

What kind of human resource development programmes will be needed to continue to improve organizational effectiveness through the integration of efficiency and innovation? To a large extent, the answer to this question depends on the nature of this 'cognitive style' variable: Do managers with different styles (Adaption–Innovation) possess different competencies? That is, do these style differences rest upon the outcome of the possession of different patterns of competencies? Or: Do managers with different styles possess the same competencies (and level of competence) but *express* the competencies differently?

According to Kirton (see Chapter 1), level and style are independent. A number of studies support this contention, finding no significant relationships between KAI scores and either measures of intelligence or levels of creativity (Carne and Kirton, 1982; Ettlie and O'Keefe, 1982; Gryskiewicz, 1982; Keller and Holland, 1978a; Goldsmith, 1985; Kirton, 1978a; Kirton and de Ciantis, 1986; Prato Previde, 1984). Despite the importance of these studies, they do not demonstrate the independence of style and managerial competence in the organizational environment. In general, measures of intelligence, creativity and differentiation have not been found to differentiate between levels of managerial performance. Adaption and innovation represent complex differences of significant magnitude in the organizational environment and the problem is to determine if these differences are associated with 'level' variables, which are known to influence the effectiveness of organizational performance. A study of the relationships between the competencies identified above and KAI scores will permit us to generalize beyond generic 'level' variables (such as intelligence) to measures specifically associated with managerial and organizational behaviour.[2]

Procedure and results

As indicated above, methods, manuals and procedures have been developed to measure (rate) the degree to which a manager demonstrates the use of each of the eleven competencies in simulated managerial situations. Correlations between KAI scores and competency ratings of 83 managers based on four simulated exercises are presented in Table 16. This table shows that correlations between KAI scores and assessor ratings of managers' behaviour on 11 competencies are all very low and all except one are not significant. This finding supports the hypothesis that KAI style is basically independent of managerial competence and that in dealing with the measurement and development of managerial performance, both must be taken into account.

Table 16 Correlations with 11 measures of managerial competence

Competency	Correlation
Information search	−0.01
Concept formation	0.22
Conceptual flexibility	0.12
Interpersonal search	0.09
Managing interaction	0.08
Developmental orientation	−0.03
Impact	0.10
Self-confidence	0.13
Presentation	0.10
Proactive orientation	0.05
Achievement orientation	0.18

The independence of level and style

The data reported in this study, as well as other data, consistently show a low but significant relationship between KAI style and competence in the cognitive area (see correlation of 0.22 between concept formation and style in Table 16). Concept formation is defined as forming ideas that become the basis for solutions, using concepts diagnostically, and forming alternative ideas to gather a greater range of information. Does this mean that there is a slight tendency for innovators to form more ideas as a basis for planning and problem solving? This may well be the case, but more research is needed to demonstrate this directly. In problem solving in managerial contexts, adaptors would be expected to develop ideas and then find the common element by letting the ideas emerge in the paradigm so as to reduce differences, reach consensus, and proceed with the steps, organization and co-ordination required for implementation. The innovator would develop ideas inside, at the edge, and perhaps outside the paradigm in use. Even though the number of concepts formed and used diagnostically may be the same, assessors may perceive more concept formation in innovators. This would indicate a slight interaction between style and competence in the cognitive areas due to the definition of the competency. The hypothesis is that adaptors produce just as many creative or pragmatic ideas as innovators, but the ideas of innovators are more salient to the assessors. If this turns out to be the case, it can be overcome by improved scoring manuals and assessor training.

If managerial competence and KAI style are independent variables as the data suggest, then KAI style would appear to be a personality variable, which influences the way managerial competence is expressed (see Chapters 1 and 2; Kirton 1987a; Kirton and de Ciantis, 1986). In order to test this hypothesis in the managerial/organizational context, a series of four parallel experiments were conducted.

STYLE AND THE EXPRESSION OF COMPETENCE

In each of the four experimental settings, all the managers in an operational department were given the KAI Inventory. Then, in consultation with the head of each department, two teams of managers were selected so that they differed as widely as possible on KAI scores and were equal in competence and status. The aim was to select two teams in each department so that other departmental members would perceive them as equal in performance, experience and ability. The four departments will be identified as production, construction, land management and management. The first three were operating departments in a large organization. The management group consisted of managers from a variety of organizations attending a masters programme in management.

Table 17 presents the numbers of managers involved in each total departmental group, and the KAI scores of the team members selected to be as different as possible on the adaptive–innovative style and as equal as possible on managerial status, competence and experience.

101

Table 17 Adaptor and innovator team data

| Department | Total managers in dept. or group | KAI scores | |
		Adaptor team	Innovator team
Production	13	76, 78, 89	107, 115, 123
Construction	17	71, 77, 79	109, 110, 122
Land	18	71, 73, 87	110, 113, 115
Management	11	76, 86, 89	118, 123, 127

Procedure

Each of the departmental groups were assembled at a conference centre by the department head for a four-hour period to attend a programme called 'Management Style'. The purpose of the programme was to improve communication in the department. Before coming to the conference centre, the KAI Inventory had been administered and the adaptor and innovator teams had been selected. In addition, the department head had written out a problem which the teams would work on at the conference. The problem was typical of the current issues facing the department and one that all members would feel to be significant and relevant. The problems were:

Production: 'How can we improve our effectiveness by better anticipating equipment failures?'

Construction: 'In a construction department such as ours, a great amount of time is spent away from the work location, loading and unloading materials, waiting on tools and supplies, equipment breakdowns, rain, talking to clients, and so on. These reduce our productivity and can create a negative customer image. How can we improve our performance in this area?'

Land: 'The company must add substations in its service area in order to continue to provide reliable electric service to our customers. Anticipating growth, a standard substation was planned and zoned in a sparsely populated area ten years ago. Now the area surrounding the one-acre tract is highly developed with single family homes ranging in value from $125,000 to $300,000. At this time (1986), the substation must be constructed in order to meet the anticipated needs. The owners have heard about the construction, have banded together with an attorney in order to prevent construction. List some ideas about how this problem can be solved.'

Management: The managers in this masters programme were asked to make recommendations about how the thesis programme could be improved.

After arriving at the conference centre, the following steps in the procedure were implemented:

1 Introduction to management style/communication by the facilitator. In this ten-minute introduction, style was introduced through athletics and sports, e.g., swimming, golf, dancing. The point was that while styles differ and spectators will differ in liking one style better than another, performance can be the same. The transition to communication was brief, stating that people also possess different styles in communicating and even though the different styles may be associated with equal levels or quality of communication, the styles affect listeners differently.

2 Team 1 (Adaptor Team) and Team 2 (Innovator Team) were identified and asked to move to two different break-out rooms and work on the problem. This is the first time any participant knew that these managers would be working on a problem and no one was aware that they had been selected in any particular way. The teams were selected to be equal in status, experience and competence. A copy of the problem was handed to each team member in the break-out room. An easel with pad and marker pens as well as paper and pencils were provided. Independently, they were instructed to complete the task and return to the conference room to report their recommendations to the group in 30 minutes.

3 The remainder of the group was informed that the two teams were working on the problem independently and would return in 30 minutes to make their recommendations. Their task was to be observers. They were instructed to observe each presentation, to list major characteristics of each (how they went about the task, what they focused on), and to be ready to state any differences observed.

4 One team was selected (by chance) to present to the group first. The other team was given a break in another room and asked not to continue to discuss the problem. After the first team presentation (approximately 7–10 minutes), the second team made their presentation.

5 With the total group of participants assembled, the facilitator went through the following steps:
  (a) A quiet period of 5 minutes was observed during which each participant observer wrote down an adjective or short sentence

describing Team 1, Team 2 and the difference between the two.

(b) Each observer, in turn, was asked to state his or her observations and the facilitator wrote down the exact words on an easel under the three columns.

(c) This is the most significant step. When all observations were recorded, the facilitator asked the group to summarize the observations. Is there a difference in the way the two teams went about this task? Is there a difference in style? This was the exciting part of the programme and to the facilitator the most convincing evidence of the validity of KAI. Supervisors and first-line managers, with no prior experience with this style measure or perhaps psychological measures in general, expressed enthusiasm about their discovery of a difference between the teams. They were impressed with the clarity of the differences, and the facilitator knew how well they matched the theoretical behavioural descriptions of innovators and adaptors. To describe the differences between adaptors and innovators, they used such terms as 'gave more information $v.$ offered a different solution to the public; proceeded topic by topic $v.$ blue-skying; covered the task $v.$ went outside the task; solved the problems we talked about $v.$ brought up new problems'.

At this point, a number of the participants began to question the facilitator about 'how the teams were selected'. In all four programmes, the participants reached the conclusion (on the basis of their observations) that there must have been a selection criteria and that it was probably the 'test' they had taken. This realization did not occur earlier and in each programme was verbalized during step (c).

(d) At this point, the facilitator presented an overhead containing the characteristics of adaptors and innovators (Kirton, 1976). There was no need for the facilitator to explain – the group was fully aware that this overhead table was a formal listing of the observations they had made about the two teams, and observers made many 'humorous' remarks about their colleagues on the teams, for example: 'I always knew you were weird. Smith' or 'It's no wonder I always get into trouble working with you'.

Such remarks were taken up by the facilitator and used to introduce the group to the ways this understanding can improve their communication and team effectiveness.

(i) People with styles different to us may be perceived as being difficult to work with. An overhead presenting the perceptions adaptors have for innovators and vice versa was presented and discussed.

(ii) Different styles are needed, because each style makes a unique and equal contribution to the organization.

The contributions of adaptors and innovators were then presented and discussed.

(e) When the characteristics and contributions of adaptors and innovators were fully discussed and related to Teams 1 and 2 observations, participant scores on the KAI were handed out so that each participant received only his or her own score. Numerical scores were not given. All KAI scores were communicated via an illustration. The presentation of three different scores are illustrated in Figure 5 below.

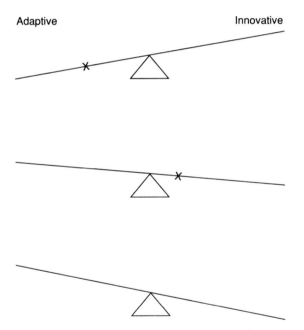

Adaptive   Innovative

Figure 5 Method of presenting scores to participants

(f) A break was taken at this point. This was designed to open up opportunities for participants (who all work together in a department) to share their scores and develop an understanding of how style affects the way they go about doing their work. In all

105

programmes, the participants were eager to share their scores and there was lively discussion about examples from past situations.

(g) In the summary, a series of points was highlighted on how to facilitate team effectiveness by capitalizing on improved working relationships between people with different styles.

Results

The general validity of the Adaption–Innovation theory and its application to organizational behaviour were strongly supported. In all four groups, all 59 managers could easily identify the adaptor and innovator teams, on the basis of the observations written on the easel and after the group reviewed the table of characteristics of adaptors and innovators listed by Kirton (1976). In addition, all observers in each department rated overall performance of the teams as being good and equal, lending informal validity to the independence of level and style.[2]

The observations of the four groups were then analysed on the basis of the competencies. The objective was to explore the hypothesis that style affects not the level but the expression of the competencies. First, all competency relevant observations were identified – that is, observations that indicated the use of one of the 11 competencies. Where similar competencies were used by adaptor and innovator teams working the same problem, any differences in expression could be observed. The data available for these four sets of teams are presented in Table 18.

While these data are incomplete, they strongly indicate that at least in a number of competencies, one's style affects the way competencies are expressed. This is clear in information search, where although the absolute breadth and depth of search (competence) is equal, more categories and sources of information for innovative teams are at the 'edge' or outside the departmental paradigm. In all departments, both teams formed a number of excellent concepts and used concepts diagnostically (competence), but innovator teams developed concepts that were somewhat different from the current operating philosophy. They came up with ideas that may not be radically different, but that would require changes. The adaptor teams formed concepts about the problem and how to improve organization and operations which do not require change in procedures, methods or relationships.

Similar observations hold for all competencies on which comparative data were available:

- **Interpersonal search** Innovators seek less input from people inside the department, but slightly more from people and factors outside;
- **Managing interaction** Adaptor teams involved others in the operations so as to make it work better, innovator teams involved others about solutions or ideas;
- **Developmental orientation** Innovator teams identified ideas about the criteria for development and then designed a changed curriculum to reach these developmental goals, while adaptor teams designed a curriculum to fit the needs of the students within the curriculum paradigm;
- **Impact** Adaptors presented current and historical information so that customers would understand and give their support, innovators came up with ideas about 'advantages' and would 'sell' these to customers along with information to gain their support;
- **Self-confidence** Confidence and decisions were anchored in making the system work better for adaptors and in making the system change for the innovators;
- **Pro-active orientation** Adaptor teams initiated actions associated with task needs, covering all aspects of the problem while innovator teams focused less on task and more on strategic ideas covering only parts of the problem.

In addition, several general differences (which could not be associated with a specific competency) between adaptor and innovator teams were: How to improve on ideas which have been talked about *v.* different ways; more detail, more precise *v.* blue-skying; lesser blow to public *v.* greater blow to public; information to the public *v.* specific recommendations; wanted customer approval *v.* solutions determined by company; shotgun approach (hit all points) *v.* highlighted issues and went to a plan; more cautious, deliberate *v.* more aggressive; 'floor' aspects, the nitty-gritty *v.* planning and ideas.

COMPETENCY, STYLE AND ORGANIZATIONAL PERFORMANCE

Competency and style

Many years ago, Kurt Lewin (1935) described behaviour as a function of the interaction between person and environmental characteristics. More recently, Boyatzis (1982) theorized that organizational effectiveness will be highest when managers possess the competencies to perform the

Table 18 Effects of style on the expression of managerial competencies

Competency	Adaptive teams	Innovative teams
Information search	Sought information from customers on costs, materials overtime, trending.	Gathered information from other industries as well as historical information and observations.
	Identified information to give customers to keep them informed of site location procedures, area requirements, distribution requirements.	Searched for advantages that could be provided to the customer – some well at the fringe of the paradigm, i.e., relatively novel in the organization.
	Gathered much information about what crews could do in periods of equipment breakdown; alternative duties, new duties.	Gathered some information about alternative crew duties. Also sought information on factors outside own group which caused breakdowns, other supervisors, policies, preventive maintenance.
Concept formation	Formed concepts about job functions needed to improve planning, budgeting, safety, dispatch, etc. Concepts about sequence.	Formed concepts about industry-wide problems and how existing information (from monitoring and observation) would be used.
	Concepts focused on the roles of crew members – what jobs were possible and what crew members would do during breakdowns and rain.	Ideas formed about how to prevent breakdowns (involving other groups) as well as some ideas about roles of members.
	Concepts about the topics to be included in existing courses.	Developed concepts about new courses and formats. These ideas were at the fringe of the operating curriculum paradigm.
	Formed concept to proceed by informing customers of all the history and facts and made the assumption that with this input, they would see that the advantages outweighed the negative factors.	Formed concepts (solutions) designed to be positive to the customers. Concepts about advantages to the customers.
Conceptual flexibility	All teams identified both perspectives of each issue and considered both in arriving at decisions.	

Interpersonal search

Sought input from customers, crews, students, etc.

Some input sought from people outside of organizational unit, e.g., other managers, people outside of organization.

Managing interaction

Encourage communication between operations and maintenance to reduce down time of equipment – that is, to become apprised of equipment problems before it breaks down.

Share information between operations, maintenance and planning in order to identify critical problems and develop solutions.

Encourage communication with customers regarding historical information and procedures and policies.

Encourage communication with customers about solutions proposed so as to highlight advantages to them.

Developmental orientation

All teams observed the need for the development of people in the management team exercise.

Development focused on how the thesis programme could be designed to fit the needs of students and their growth.

Development focused on how the thesis programme could affect the development of students – what would it develop? Developmental outcomes were identified and then used as a basis for action.

Impact

All teams demonstrated concern for input in the construction team exercise.

The team presented a series of incremental steps to share the whys, the facts and the history of events with customers so as to gain their support.

Presented ideas or solutions to the customers to show them the advantages of the location of the substation. (This was perceived as 'more risky' by the adaptor team.)

Self-confidence

All teams made and justified required decisions and were confident of success.

Made decisions, which when implemented would improve the analysis and monitoring of equipment and maintenance. Decisions were tied closely to the operation.

Decisions were made about how the planning should be done in the future to increase anticipation of equipment problems.

109

Table 18 continued

Competency	Adaptive teams	Innovative teams
	Made decisions about goals, sequences and steps in presenting information which would lead to acceptance by customers.	Made decisions about specific advantages to be presented to customers.
	Made decisions about what kind of a thesis programme would fit the needs of students and the topics and steps to be included in existing courses.	Made decisions about the core concepts needed if a thesis programme is to be successful. These core concepts would 'stretch' the traditional academic concept.
Presentation	All teams presented clearly and used aids, graphics and questions appropriately.	
Proactive orientation	More emphasis is on the task; covered all aspects of the problem from planning through budgeting, safety, dispatch, overtime, testing.	More emphasis on strategy; emphasis on part of the problem – on how the department was to proceed to plan.
	Initiated actions associated with going to the customer with the history, events and information so that customers would see the value of the location of the substation.	Anticipated all possible forms of opposition from customers, developed solutions showing advantages and benefits.
Achievement orientation	All teams demonstrated emphasis on setting challenging standards and measuring progress toward those standards.	

tasks demanded by their jobs and to cope with the climate of the organization. Managerial tasks may be described in terms of competency demands, that is, the competencies managers will need to perform effectively in that situational context. The results of this study indicate that organizational effectiveness will be highest (a) when managers possess the competencies to perform the tasks demanded by their jobs and the climate of their organization, and (b) when managers possess the appropriate mix of styles to produce the kind of organizational change needed to cope with the business environment.

110

Integration of adaption and innovation

Assuming that competence is equal across the managers of two organizations, Adaptive–Innovative (A–I) style differences of the managers will produce significantly different effects. If organization A possesses greater numbers of adaptive managers and upper-level managers, then managerial competence will be focused on improving the productivity and efficiency of the current paradigm – the current system, markets, methods and procedures. Such an organization may be very efficient and productive, e.g., in controlling cash flow and the cost of information processing, but it may not be preparing itself for the changes needed in the future to meet changing methods, technology, values, competition or markets.

On the other hand, if organization B possesses greater numbers of managers with high levels of innovation, then their competence will be expressed more in terms of exploring ideas at and beyond the boundaries of the current organizational paradigm. Such an organization may be very innovative, in possessing new products, services or methods for instance, but it may not give sufficient attention to such factors as stability, cohesion, continuity, reliability, and as a result efficiency may decrease. In both organizations (A and B), there is a failure to integrate the forces of efficiency and innovation in the organization.

Not long ago, organizations existed in a more stable environment in which values, technology and markets remained relatively constant. Innovation could be slow and incremental. Such organizations can and were managed well by more adaptive, competent managers. In the 1980s, change has accelerated with revolutions in technology, the values of people, and the advent of open competitive international markets. Now innovation must be more radical.

One organizational strategy would be to integrate innovation and efficiency. Competent, innovative managers would be integrated with competent adaptive managers who would work closely together to produce 'efficient innovation'. A different organizational strategy would be followed if we believe that the innovative managers will lose power to the adaptive managers because profits are made by 'doing things better' (Drucker, 1969). This organizational strategy would involve the separation of some of the innovative functions ('skunk words': Peters and Waterman, 1983) from the efficiency functions, namely, reducing the costs and increasing the quality of products and services, which have emerged out of the innovative side.

Strategies will vary widely between these two extremes depending on

111

the business environment and the culture of the organizations. However, even if there is some separation of innovative and efficiency functions, the contributions of both adaptors and innovators are needed in all work groups at all levels in the organization – in departments, projects and in cross-functional groups – to ensure that needed changes in procedures, work design, people and methods are timely and are managed efficiently.

Implications for human resource development

In order to build organizational effectiveness and readiness for change, modern organizations will need to take the following steps:

1 Select and develop competent managers to perform the tasks of a complex organization.
2 Select managers with an appropriate mix of A–I style in order to provide variation in the expression of competencies in the efficiency and innovative modes. Since A–I style appears to be a basic personality characteristic (Kirton, 1987a: Chapters 1 and 2), it would be expected to be quite stable and quite difficult to change. That is, the role of development is not to change a manager's style, rather it is to increase their awareness of their own and others' A–I styles, how it affects communication, and how to cope with others' complementary styles in order to integrate efficiency and innovation.
3 Integrate different A–I styles in organizational functioning.

One of the most important tasks of the modern manager is to integrate the divergent expressions and contributions of managers and other employees with different A–I styles. In the absence of this integrative role, the divergent style groups (particularly the adaptive members) form cohesive norms and set up strong resistances to integration. Managers need to develop considerable competence in such areas as conceptual flexibility and managing interaction in order to identify these different styles and contributions (options); they must also work to build teams of people with complementary styles, to integrate their contributions in organizational performance. This involves multidimensional thinking competencies (Streufert and Swezey, 1986) and managing group process competencies (Boyatzis, 1982). It includes building alliances between moderate style managers (those not showing a strong preference for either the adaptive or innovative style) and those with higher preferences for the A or I style in order to achieve managed change, which is optimally responsive to the strategic environment.

112

NOTES

1 These simulations were developed by H.M. Schroder for use in assessment/development programmes in the Center for Organizational Effectiveness at the University of South Florida.

2 Since this chapter was written, more support has emerged, e.g., Hammerschmidt and Jennings, 1993.

6

CONSUMER INITIATORS: *BOTH* INNOVATORS *AND* ADAPTORS!

G.R. Foxall

INTRODUCTION

Consumer researchers have shown an interest in the first adopters of new products and brands that exceeds their concern for almost any other aspect of purchase and consumption. Both theoretical and practical studies have sought to locate these 'consumer innovators' and to establish the role they play in the creation of markets and the communication of 'innovations' (see Foxall and Goldsmith, 1994). This chapter argues that, for all its popularity among investigators, 'consumer innovativeness' remains a field of enquiry beset by confusion over basic terminology and an inability to come to terms with the weak evidence on which its generalizations about the personality profiles of 'consumer innovators' are based.

The problem of terminology presents a major critical issue, one that hinges around the use of the word 'innovative' and its derivatives. It is not just a matter of too casual use of this word, but a more deeply held misconception, common among students of creativity, including marketing, that innovativeness equals 'new', 'novel', 'exciting', 'modern', and even 'good', 'appropriate' and 'superior'. If only it could be measured well, then how convenient this would be for those who believe that 'innovators', the risk-taking, trend-setters, are the very people who can be expected to buy *any* new product. *It is this very hypothesis that the present chapter examines critically on the basis of empirical evidence as well as a priori argument.*

The chapter begins, using the existing terminology, by summarizing why consumer innovativeness has become a central topic in both new product marketing and the explanation of early adoption. In doing so, it comments on the elusive nature of the personality traits assumed to be associated with consumer innovativeness. Although the conventional terminology is necessarily employed thus far, a solution can now be proposed to the confusion it has engendered. Next, the chapter argues that the personality profiles of early adopters can be usefully investigated by the Kirton Adaption–Innovation Inventory (KAI), which measures both the cognitive/personality styles generally associated with consumer innovativeness and those that are, by implication, diametrically opposite.

Five empirical studies of 'innovative' consumer behaviour which employ the KAI are described. The first three studies concern consumers' early adoption of new food products and brands, i.e., with 'purchase innovativeness'. The last two studies concern consumers' use of personal computers to solve a range of problems, i.e., with 'use innovativeness'. The revolutionary nature of the findings is apparent in that in no case is the consumer behaviour uniquely associated with an innovative personality profile. In the case of new foods, both the *innovators* identified by Kirton's measure and the *adaptors* who exhibit the obverse personality profile are found among both adopter groups. In the case of computer software adoption, while the innovative cognitive style is closely related to 'use innovativeness', this behaviour is fully explicable only if consumer involvement is also taken into consideration.

Finally, the implications of these findings for marketing practice and the explanation of early adoption are discussed and directions for further research are suggested. Foremost among these implications is the need to bring about a change in terminology linked with a comprehensive theory and an appropriate measure.

CONSUMER INNOVATORS IN MARKETING PRACTICE AND CONSUMER THEORY

New product strategy

The marketing literature imputes one or other of two strategies to consumers according to the stage in the product life cycle. The first adopters of new products, who differ socially and economically from later adopters, are portrayed as more involved in the product field and are said to engage in extended problem solving prior to purchase (Howard, 1989). These so-called 'consumer innovators' are socially independent, requiring little or no personal communication before adopting (Midgley, 1977). By contrast, later adopters need other people to 'legitimate' the purchase and use of new products: the product life cycle may have progressed well into its maturity stage before the last of them buy for the first time. Later purchasers are said to be less involved in the product field; by the time they adopt, pre-purchase decision making has become safe and routine.

The expected patterns of behavioural and psychographic difference between early and later adopters form the basis of a strategic prescription for product development according to which marketing mixes should be tailored to the distinctive requirements of successive adopter categories. The resulting temporal market segmentation is described as leading to the profitable development of both new and established products (Baker, 1983; Wind, 1981). If potential initial and later adopters of new products can be identified at appropriate stages of the new product development process, the tailoring can begin that much earlier and be incorporated into the market testing of alternative prototypes.

Non-product elements of the marketing mix, notably persuasive communications, can be directed specifically towards the needs and vulnerabilities of the homogeneously conceived primary market. Numerous attempts have been made to differentiate these adopter categories psychographically, on the basis of links between early adoption and such traits as risk taking, impulsiveness, dominance, inner-directedness, flexibility and venturesomeness, and perception of new product characteristics (Foxall, 1984; Foxall and Goldsmith, 1988; Gatignon and Robertson, 1991; Midgley, 1977; Rogers, 1983).

Personality traits of first adopters

Identification of the personality characteristics of these initial adopters has also excited intellectual curiosity. One of the more sophisticated theoretical quests for the nature of 'the innovative personality' is that of Midgley and Dowling (1978), who draw attention to the situational influences that facilitate or impede early adoption. However, the principal explanatory element in their model is a hypothetical construct, 'innate innovativeness', mediated by product field interest. They argue that, in order to account for different levels of 'actualized innovation' – the single act defined by time elapsed from launch, the adoption of several new products in the same field measured by a cross-sectional method, and the adoption of new products across product fields measured by a generalized cross-sectional method – it is necessary to posit increasingly abstract concepts of 'innovativeness', an abstract personality trait assumed to be possessed in some degree by everybody but actually existing only in the mind of the investigator. The extent of an individual's early adoption is ultimately explained by a reference to his or her degree of innate innovativeness, which is 'a function of (yet to be specified) dimensions of the human personality' (Midgley and Dowling, 1978: 235). Hirschman (1980) speaks similarly of 'inherent' innovativeness and 'inherent' novelty seeking without specifying the traits with which they might be associated.

Both managerial and theoretical views of the personality profiles of these consumers anticipate a relationship between the behaviours of interest and the psychographics of the people who perform them. But empirical confirmation of their expectations has been elusive. The quest for operationally measurable traits of personality related to innovative behaviour has a long history in marketing and consumer psychology but has produced nothing more than a mass of weak, if positive, correlations. The most that can be said is that these weak findings constitute a body of consistent evidence which links innovative behaviour with several cognitive–behavioural traits: category width, flexibility, tolerance of ambiguity, self-esteem, and sensation seeking (Foxall, 1984; Foxall, 1989; Horton, 1979; Midgley, 1977; Mudd, 1990; Rogers, 1983; Schiffman and Kanuk, 1987; see also Goldsmith in Chapter 2). The implication is that if the personality traits that explain actualized innovativeness (and which, by implication, are the 'yet to be specified' dimensions of personality of which innate innovativeness is a function) are to be identified, then these cognitive–behavioural variables must define the area in which we should look. Since the effects of personality traits on behaviour are cumulative, it would be desirable to employ a composite measure of these cognitive–behavioural variables were a theoretically grounded instrument available. However, before Adaption–Innovation theory and the Kirton Adaption–Innovation Inventory are introduced as relevant devices, the problem of terminological confusion must be addressed.

TERMINOLOGICAL CONFUSION AND ITS RESOLUTION

The scope for confusion in the use of terms such as 'innovator' and 'innovativeness' will already be apparent to the reader. At its simplest, it takes the form of quite distinct conceptual levels being described in similar terms, from the hypothetical and abstract 'innate innovativeness' and 'inherent innovativeness', to the concrete and observable 'actualized innovativeness'. To use the same term in each case, whilst claiming that the former provides an explanatory basis for the latter, is to prejudge the issue of whether innovative behaviour is attributable to an underlying personality trait or system. At the intermediate level, there is a plethora of terms to refer to measurable intervening variables: sensory innovativeness, cognitive innovativeness, hedonic innovativeness, adaption–innovation, etc. (Hirschman, 1984; Kirton, 1976). Finally, at the level of consumption rather than purchasing, the term 'use innovativeness' has been suggested to refer to the deployment of a product that has already been adopted to solve a new problem of consumption (Hirschman, 1980).

Foxall (1989) proposed the substitution of 'market initiators' for 'purchase innovators'. The term emphasizes that such adopters are initial purchasers but also that they have an initiating role in the communication and diffusion of new brands and products. The diffusion literature ascribes to this group the functions of earliest adoption of a new product plus its communication to the later adopters who comprise the bulk of the market. This usage is in line with that found in both marketing studies of adoption and diffusion and the wider analysis of these phenomena in a broad range of other fields (Foxall and Bhate, 1993a; Rogers, 1983). A synonym is 'initial adopters'. Both designate an observable level of analysis, the relationship of which to a trait of personality or a group of associated traits that predispose a consumer towards new product buying is an empirical question rather than a matter of preordination.

Market initiation also covers consumers' reactions to the range of newness available in new brands and products more successfully than the blanket term 'innovators'. The word 'innovation' describes an entire spectrum of new products from the discontinuous, which has highly disruptive consequences for consumer behaviour, to the continuous, which requires almost no accommodation on the part of the consumer (Robertson, 1967). Compare the adoption of television in the 1950s with the more recent adoption of fluoride toothpaste. To refer to the earliest purchasers of both types of new product as 'innovators' is misleading and requires constant clarification of the degree of innovativeness exhibited in each case (and the many cases that lie between these extremes). However, to define the behaviour of these first adopters functionally, as initiation, removes this confusion, separating the specification of the degree of continuity/discontinuity possessed by the new product itself from the consumer's subjective reaction to it.

Similarly, the term 'use initiation' might cover the phenomenon of so-called 'use innovativeness'. Again, it describes the behavioural level on which the consumer initiates novel functions for an accepted product, without confusing this observable action with any underlying personality trait or system that might account for it. But it again has the advantage of covering uses of an already adopted product that range from radically inventive, qualitative changes to the more quantitative deployment of a product in a number of more mundane alternative functions (Foxall and Bhate, 1991). An example of the former is consumers' using household bleach as a germicide (which involves a high degree of discontinuity and dissimilarity); the latter is exemplified by the use of a home computer for spreadsheet analysis in addition to word processing (a more continuous re-application which involves much greater similarity of behaviour). Once again, the continuity/discontinuity of the product function is conceptually separate from the consumption behaviour of the consumer.

These terms are used in the following description of a research programme concerned with both market initiation and use initiation, which incorporated as explanatory cognitive/personality variables the adaptive–innovative cognitive styles defined by Kirton. In the following account, the first purchasers of a new brand/product are called *market initiators* or *initial adopters*; consumers who turn a product they already own to novel uses are called *use initiators*. The generic term to cover both types is consumer initiators. Only those who score appropriately on the KAI are called *innovators* and this term is used to refer to consumers whose cognitive style is innovative as defined by Kirton.

ADAPTION–INNOVATION THEORY

Adaption–Innovation theory (Kirton, 1976; see also Chapter 1) suggests a means of understanding both the disappointing outcomes of previous research into the personality-based precursors of consumer innovativeness and the persistence of personality constructs as explicators of early adoption. The Kirton Adaption–Innovation Inventory (KAI), which provides an operational measure of the adaptive–innovative cognitive style continuum posited by Kirton (1976), appears also to be a suitable instrument for further empirical research given its externally validated links with the personality traits known to determine, consistently albeit weakly, initial adoption.

Cognitive style refers to an individual's way of processing information, his or her preferred approach to decision making and problem solving as distinct from his cognitive level, ability or complexity (Chapter 1). The Adaption–Innovation theory, which originated in the context of organizational behaviour, proposes a continuum of such styles and relates them to the individual's characteristic manner of approaching change. The more adaptive person refers order and precision, and is concerned with the accuracy of details, prudence, soundness, efficiency and a degree of conformity. The adaptor is happiest working within a well-established pattern of rule and operating procedures.

By contrast, the more innovative person refers to think tangentially, challenges rules and procedures, and is less uninhibited about breaking with established methods and advocating radically novel perspectives and solutions. The innovator is easily bored by routine and seeks novelty and stimulation in discontinuous change; he or she tends towards risk taking, exploration and trial (Kirton, 1976; see also Chapter 1 of present volume). The KAI's suitability for research in consumer innovativeness is confirmed by its positive correlation with validated measures of category width, tolerance of ambiguity, flexibility, self-esteem and sensation seeking.

As relatively narrow categorizers, adaptors are more likely than innovators to seek to avoid mistakes, even if this means missing some positive opportunities (Foxall, 1988). Their need for structure (Gryskiewicz, 1982) and reluctance to radical change (Chapter 2 of this volume) leads them to take a more cautious view. Adaptors tend, therefore, in making decisions, to be conservative, usually confining their search for information within the frame of reference dictated by their direct personal experience. Since adaptors are more intolerant than innovators of the more disruptive change, unwilling to accept as much ambiguity, more dogmatic and inflexible (Kirton, 1976; see also Kirton, Chapter 1; Goldsmith, Chapter 2 of this volume; Gryskiewicz, 1982), they are predictably less amenable to disruptively new product trial. Their consequent lack of experience of new-different, as distinct from new-improved products further reinforces their unwillingness to explore the former as opposed to the latter. Innovators, who by contrast are broad categorizers, risking errors and costs to take advantage of potential positive chances, are more likely to try radically new products, accepting the risk of buying an unsatisfactory item. They use more environmental stimuli, taking in more of the data that impinge on them and using them more actively to find a solution. Their more abstract thinking leads them to ask more questions, search widely for information, and investigate more relationships. Seeing new-variant as distinct from new-different products as more alike than adaptors, they are less brand loyal.

The KAI requires respondents to estimate on 32 five-point ratings how easy or difficult they would find it to sustain particular adaptive and innovative behaviours over long periods of time. The measure is scored from a theoretical adaptive extremes 32 to an innovative extreme 160, and with a theoretical mean suggested by the scale midpoint 96. Six general population samples, for the UK, USA, Italy, Slovakia and the Netherlands and Flanders, and the three Francophone countries of France, Belgium and Canada, have observed means of within the range 94–96, about which scores are approximately normally distributed over a restricted range from 43 to 149. The KAI shows high levels of internal reliability and validity (e.g., Bagozzi and Foxall, 1993; Foxall and Hackett, 1992a; also Kirton in Chapter 1 of this volume) and test–retest stability (Clapp, 1993; Kirton in Chapter 1) both over periods of years.

IMPLICATIONS FOR NEW PRODUCT ACCEPTANCE

Both academic consumer research into the psychographic segmentation of initial markets for products and services and practical attempts to influence demand for these items have often assumed a homogeneous consumer profile. It is evident from the findings presented in this chapter that both research and marketing management must henceforth take into account the existence of both adaptors and innovators among consumer initiators.

In particular, it is essential to consider the probable differences in decision-making styles from high adaptors to high innovators as they influence product perceptions and responses to persuasive marketing communications. The following propositional inventory for further pure and applied consumer research rests on substantial bodies of knowledge concerning the personality basis of adaptive–innovative cognitive style (Goldsmith in Chapter 2 of this volume; Gryskiewicz *et al.*, 1987; Kirton in Chapter 1) and the relationship of cognitive style to consumer behaviour (Foxall, 1988; Foxall and Bhate, 1993b; Foxall and Goldsmith, 1988; Pinson, 1978; Pinson *et al.*, 1988).

Category width is the extent to which the consumer perceives a new product to differ from the norm established by existing products or practices. The range of difference from the norm or core of the paradigm, according to Kirton (see Preface to 2nd Edition: Five Years On, at the start of book, and Chapter 1), parallels the differing interest exhibited by the range of adaptors and innovators towards something new. He posits that all people like novelty but no one likes everything that is new. Adaption–Innovation is one variable, as is self-interest generally, that accounts for the variance in discrimination. This aspect of the consumer's cognitive framework also partly determines the degree of risk he or she perceives in buying and using something new. Broad categorizers are more willing than narrow categorizers to embrace new products that diverge from the norm (Donnelly and Etzel, 1973; Venkatesen, 1973). Broad categorizers are also likely to adopt 'genuine' new products (radical or discontinuous), even at the risk of being dissatisfied, while narrow categorizers prefer 'artificially' (adaptively) new items, minimizing the possibility of a mistake. Adaptors are likely to be narrow categorizers, seeking to avoid mistakes even if this means their missing some positive opportunities (Foxall, 1988). Their need for structure (Gryskiewicz, 1982) and reluctance to change radically (Goldsmith in Chapter 2 of this volume) leads them to take a more cautious view.

Hence we would expect adaptors to tend, in making decisions, to be conservative, confining their search for information within the frame of reference dictated by their direct personal experience. Moreover, adaptors' relatively narrow category width means that they are more likely to be attracted to relatively continuous new products than discontinuous ones. Adaptors are also more intolerant of change and disruption, unwilling to accept ambiguity, more dogmatic and inflexible than innovators (Kirton, 1976; Kirton in Chapter 1; Goldsmith, 1984; Goldsmith in Chapter 2; Gryskiewicz, 1982). Hence, it is to be expected that adaptors will be less amenable to radical-new product trial. Their resulting lack of experience of new products further reinforces their unwillingness to explore.

Innovators, by contrast, are likely to be broad categorizers, risking errors and costs to take advantage of potential positive chances. They are likely to try discontinuously new products, accepting the risk of buying an unsatisfactory item. They may also use more environmental stimuli, taking in more of the data that impinge on them and using them more actively to find a solution. Their more abstract thinking leads them to ask more questions, search widely for information, and investigate more relationships. Seeing continuous (improved) products as more alike than do adaptors, they are likely to be less brand loyal (Foxall and Goldsmith, 1988).

METHOD

Five studies have employed the KAI in consumer research with the intention of relating a pattern of personality traits to market and use initiation. The first three concern the initial adoption of food brands/ products; the fourth concerns use initiation in the context of home computer use; and the last concerns computer use initiation in organizations. Data for the food studies were collected by an independent market research firm which recruited convenience samples of respondents, administered the measures, advised on the selection of new products/ brands and their availability at sampling points. Sampling points were selected supermarkets in the south of England. For the fourth study, the same organization obtained a systematic sample and responses but the products were selected by the respondents. The last study involved students on graduate courses in a university business school, specializing in marketing, business information technology or legal studies. Methodological details can be found in the original reports: Foxall, 1988; Foxall and Bhate, 1991; 1993a; 1993c.

RESULTS

Study 1: new food brands

Results This exploratory study tested the broad proposition that innovators would evince a greater volume of market initiation than adaptors, i.e., buy more new brands of food products. This hypothesis was not confirmed but the results pointed to a more complicated pattern of initial adoption than either the researchers or the literature of adoption and diffusion had assumed (Foxall and Haskins, 1986). The KAI mean of the 101 female respondents was 95.06. The observed range of new-brand purchases was 1–8; those not buying any of these new brands were not included in the sample. The sample mean was significantly more innovative than that of the UK female general population: $z = 2.27$, p <0.025, non-buyers being excluded. A positive but extremely weak and non-significant correlation was found between the number of new brands purchased and KAI: $r = 0.09$, $p = 0.22$.

Purchasers of four or five brands ($m = 99.31$, s.d. $= 15.96$, $n = 29$) scored more innovatively than purchasers of 1–3 ($m = 93.83$, s.d. $= 14.25$, $n = 60$). However, purchasers of the highest number of new brands (6–8) scored unexpectedly adaptively ($m = 90.75$, s.d. $= 19.48$, $n = 12$). One-way ANOVA gives $F_{2,98} = 1.76$, $p = 0.18$. The mean of purchasers of four or five new brands was notably higher than those of the other two groups; it alone differed significantly from that of the female general population ($z = 2.67$, p <0.01). Moreover, the sample contained 40 adaptors (whose KAI mean was equal to or less than the female general population mean) and 61 innovators.

A panel of consumers divided the thirteen brands into three groups, based on a classification of new products put forward by Robertson

(1967): those judged qualitatively to be discontinuous (i.e., radically new), continuous (incrementally new) and dynamically continuous (in intermediate classification inferring brands that differed by a step function from existing brands). Mean interjudge reliabilities were 0.81. The discontinuous brands were found to have been purchased by innovators rather than adaptors (the difference in KAI means was statistically significant); continuous brands, by adaptors rather than innovators (again the difference was significant). Dynamically discontinuous brands were each bought by innovators rather than adaptors but the differences in means was not significant (see Foxall, 1988; Foxall, 1989; Foxall and Haskins, 1986 for the complete methodology).

Conclusions The results suggest three main conclusions which, because they fly in the face of accepted adoption theory and findings, invite further research:

1 Contrary to expectations, there is no correlation between KAI and the overall number of new brands purchased.
2 Both adaptors and innovators are substantially represented among the initial purchasers of recently launched brands.
3 Buyers of the largest number of recently launched brands are adaptors.
4 The KAI may provide an operational measure of Robertson's qualitative classification of new products as discontinuous, dynamically continuous and continuous.

Study 2: new 'healthy' food products

Results The first study produced weak evidence of a tendency for the heaviest purchasers of new brands to be adaptive rather than innovative. The second study pursued this possibility by investigating initial purchase within a coherent product field, namely 'healthy' food products. The KAI mean of the 345 female respondents, 95.01, was significantly higher than that of the female general population: $z = 3.20$, $p = <0.001$. New product purchasing was again not linearly related to KAI: $r = 0.04$, $p = 0.26$. The sample consisted of 142 adaptors and 203 innovators. The range of products purchased was 0–19, though only four respondents reported not having purchased any of the items (Foxall and Haskins, 1987).

Neither the KAI mean of purchasers of up to two new products, nor that of purchasers of 16 to 19 differs significantly from the female general population mean. Means of both of these groups are distinctly adaptive. However, means of the purchasers of intermediate quantities of new products are significantly higher than that of the female general population. Moreover, in this study stronger evidence of the adaptive cognitive styles of members of the group of purchasers of the highest number of new products is apparent. One way ANOVA, $F_{5,339} = 3.35$, $p = 0.006$. A post hoc Sheffé procedure indicates that the means of the extreme groups (purchasers of 0–2 and purchasers of 16–19) differ significantly from that of purchasers of intermediate levels ($p < 0.05$).

Conclusions The conclusions are similar to those for Study 1 and are based on much firmer evidence which relates this time to the product level. Once again, contrary to expectations based on adoption theory and the literature on personality and initial purchase:

1 KAI is not correlated with the overall volume of initial purchasing.
2 Adaptors as well as innovators are found among the primary segment that displays initial purchasing.
3 The purchasers of the highest number of products recently introduced into supermarkets are adaptors.

Study 3: new 'healthy' food brands

Results The third study provided an opportunity to refine the research in two ways (Foxall and Bhate, 1993a). First it was expected (Foxall, 1988) that adaptors who had become committed to the cause of healthy eating and therefore to this product field would indeed be more likely than innovators or other, less involved adaptors to seek out assiduously not a few but as many as possible relevant food items. This was operationalized in terms of personal involvement with healthy eating, which was measured by the Zaichkowsky Personal Involvement Inventory (PII). This instrument consists of ten 7-point scales on which the individual indicates the degree of interest as opposed to boredom and other aspects of ego involvement with the product field (Zaichkowsky 1987). These instruments and a questionnaire with respect to recent food brand purchasing, representing the second focusing of the research, were administered to 151 female grocery shoppers; the KAI sample mean at 93.1 (s.d. = 16.06) was not significantly different from that of the UK female general population, $z = 1.4$.

Purchase initiation was not linearly related to adaption–innovation: $r = 0.04$. Two-way ANOVA with number of 'healthy' food brands purchased as the dependent variable and KAI and PII as the independent variables showed no significant main effects for either adaption/innovation ($F_{1,47}$ <1) or for personal involvement ($F_{1,147}$ = 1.88, p >0.17). A significant interaction effect was observed, however: $F_{1,147}$ = 4.27, p <0.05). A post hoc Sheffé procedure indicated a significant difference between the mean volume of purchase of the more involved adaptors (3.10, s.d. = 1.53, n = 40) and that of the less involved adaptors (2.20, s.d. = 1.30, n = 44) (p <0.05). The means of the less involved innovators (2.83, s.d. = 1.83, n = 24) and that of the more involved innovators (2.65, s.d. = 1.54, n = 43) fell between those of the adaptor groups but were not significantly different.

Conclusions Two additional conclusions can be drawn from these results, which strengthen the emerging theoretical basis for understanding the relationship between adaptive–innovative cognitive style and consumer initiation:

1 The recurrent pattern of findings has now been shown to obtain at the brand level of a coherent product group.
2 The importance of consumers' involvement with the product has been shown to relate to adaption in determining initial adoption.

Study 4: software applications in home computing

Results This study extended the research in several ways (Foxall and Bhate, 1993b). It investigated use initiation. The research design was developed at this stage to include products that were intrinsically more involving than foods, namely computing software applications. The sample KAI and PII means for 151 male home computer users were 99.05 (s.d. = 17.90) and 49.69 (s.d. = 10.02) respectively. This KAI mean did not differ significantly from that of the male general population sample for the United Kingdom (98.12, s.d. 16.75, n = 290): z = 0.52. Respondents used between one and seven software applications. KAI is not linearly related to use initiation: r = −0.01. Following the example of Mudd (1990), the KAI and PII means of users of up to four applications were compared with those of users of five to seven. The KAI mean of the latter group (111.00, s.d. = 18.69, n = 7) was significantly more innovative than that of the users of one to four (98.47, s.d. = 17.72, n = 143): z = 1.82, p <0.05.

While the KAI mean of the group of users of five to seven applications was significantly more innovative than that of the male general population (z = 1.81, p <0.05), that of the users of only one to four applications was not (z = 0.20). The PII mean of users of five to seven software applications (56.00, s.d. = 9.1) was significantly higher than that of the users of one to four (49.40, s.d. = 10.00): z = 1.72, p <0.05. Seventy-one members of the sample (47.3 per cent) were adaptors; 78 (52.7 per cent) were innovators: the gap narrows! Two-way ANOVA revealed no significant main effects or significant interactions among the independent variables (KAI × PII) on the number of computer applications used (F < 1). Two sources of situational influence affected significantly the number of applications to which the computer had been put. The length of time the current computer had been owned correlated significantly with use initiation (r = 0.23, p <0.01). In addition, the degree of use initiation varied with the make of computer owned.

Conclusions The conclusions draw attention to two important determinants of computer use:

1 Both innovative cognitive style and a high level of personal involvement with computing are significantly related to the number of software packages used – but only for a small segment of users who score very highly on both KAI and PII.
2 Situational variables, as well as cognitive factors, are closely related to computer use.

Study 5: software applications in organizational contexts

Results The final study developed the theme of situational influence on use initiation (Foxall and Bhate, 1991). The Business Information Technology Systems programme (BITS) simulated situations of required use of computers; the Marketing programme, situations of discretionary use; and the Legal Practice programme, situations of minimal use. The sample KAI mean at 98.56 (s.d. = 13.39) did not differ significantly from that of students (*c.* 100) or managers (*c.* 97). The PII mean was 44.65 (s.d. = 15.26).

KAI scores were skewed towards the innovative pole (range 70–138), while the range of PII scores covered the entire theoretical range. The convenience sample contained more adaptors (N = 57, i.e., 53 per cent) than innovators. Multiple regression analysis was used since the standardized βs allow the influence of different independent variables to be directly assessed. The dependent variables studied were programming experience, frequency of computer use, number of packages used, length of computing experience, and a weighted index of all of these, namely overall computer use. When situational factors are ignored – i.e., KAI and PII are the independent variables – overall computer use correlates with both KAI (β = 0.17, p <0.05) and PII (B = 0.24, p <0.01), though these relationships are rather weak. Number of packages used correlates with KAI (β = 0.17, p <0.05) and PII (β = 0.34, p <0.001). PII correlates with programming experience (β = 0.33, p <0.001), and with frequency of computer use (β = 0.56, p <0.001).

Neither independent variable is related significantly to duration of computing experience. When organizational influence is included (as three dummy variables representing course affiliation), this factor assumes greater explanatory significance than either cognitive variable. (The full results are available in Foxall and Bhate, 1991.) However, PII remains significantly correlated with overall computer use (β = 0.29, p <0.001) and KAI is marginally correlated with this variable (β = 0.14, p <0.1). Neither cognitive variable is related to programming experience, though each shows a unique relationship to one other dependent variable: KAI with number of packages used (β = 0.27, p <0.01), PII with frequency of computer use (β = 0.33, p <0.001). Both cognitive variables correlate with duration of computing experience (in both cases, β = 0.19, p < 0.05).

The sample was divided into four 'style/involvement' groups based on whether their KAI and PII scores exceeded or fell short of the sample means. One-way ANOVA was used to examine the relationship of each group's KAI and PII scores to each of the dependent variables. Significant F ratios were found for overall computer usage ($F_{3,103}$ = 8.38, p = 0.000), programming experience ($F_{3,103}$ = 3.16, p = 3.027), frequency of computer use (F = 11.13, p = 0.000), and number of packages used (F = 5.03, p = 0.002). In the case of duration of computing experience, $F_{3,103}$ = 0.53, p = 0.66. For each dependent variable where F was significant, post hoc Sheffé tests indicate that highly involved groups, whether innovative or adaptive, have a group mean that differs from each of the low involved group means (p <0.05).

Conclusions The findings of the previous study with respect to both cognitive and situational influences on use initiation are confirmed and extended:

1 Regardless of cognitive style, a high level of involvement with computing is positively related to overall extent of computer use.

2 But both adaptors and innovators are represented in both low and high involvement conditions.

3 While situational influences are determinative of overall computer use levels, adaptive–innovative cognitive style and personal involvement are differentially related to specific uses of the computer such as number of packages used and frequency of computer use.

IMPLICATIONS

Theoretical implications

The findings resolve the problem of low correlations between measures of personality and consumer behaviour which were repeatedly a feature of early research. Low correlations were presumably the outcome of researchers' measuring the traits of personality embodied by innovators and overlooking those of the adaptors, who are also substantially represented among consumer initiators. Low correlation of KAI and consumer initiation would be a problem for this measure only if it operationalized innovativeness alone; however, as a bipolar measure of adaptiveness as well as innovativeness, it has consistently produced results that are intelligible once the coexistence of adaptors and innovators among market initiators is recognized. This finding has several important implications: for the conceptualization of 'consumer innovativeness'; for the depiction of the adoption decision process; for the psychographic segmentation of new product markets; and for further research.

The view that the behaviour of consumer initiators is explained by a set of personality traits that define 'innate' or 'inherent' innovativeness is naive (incomplete!).

The Midgley–Dowling thesis that actualized innovativeness is explicable by reference to innate innovativeness, mediated by product field interest and situational factors, is upheld in the case of computing (Foxall and Bhate, 1991; 1994), a result which has led Steenkamp and Baumgartner (1992) to refer to 'the Midgley–Dowling–Foxall model'. Even here, only some aspects of use initiation in computing (such as number of packages used) were related to innovative cognitive style. Moreover, the results may be interpreted as implying that now that operational measures related to innate innovativeness have been found (the Kirton and Zaichkowsky inventories), reliance on an abstract construct, innate innovativeness, should surely be relaxed in favour of these more concrete operationalizations (Foxall and Bhates, 1991).

However, the import of the results of the food studies is that consumer initiators may manifest either adaptive or innovative personality characteristics (i.e., the full range of cognitive styles) rather than the profile suggested by research in marketing and cognitive/personality psychology. Although psychometric techniques will continue to improve, it seems infeasible that traits other than those investigated in the five studies will emerge as related to 'innate innovativeness'. In the case of new foods, any notion that consumer initiators' behaviour can be explained by reference to an underlying trait of innate or inherent *innovativeness* is, therefore, disconfirmed. Far from indicating that actualized innovativeness is a function of an underlying personality configuration, the results show that *Adaption–Innovation*, a dimension of cognitive style that correlates reliably with traits generally associated with initial adoption, is only weakly and usually non-linearly related to market initiation (operationally measured as the number of new brands purchased or as use initiation).

Moreover, in the case of new foods, the cognitive style profiles of market initiators were approximately evenly divided between the adaptive and the innovative, while a subset of the adaptors were responsible for the highest level of purchase. In the case of use initiators for software products, both adaptors and innovators were again well represented; although, in the organizational context, personal involvement in computing played a dominant role in determining the extent of use initiation, both adaptors and innovators were present in substantial proportions. The results also suggest that Midgley and Dowling were right in calling attention to the mediation of innovative behaviour by situational events, but do not confirm those authors' preoccupation with an ultimately trait-based explanation of observed early adoption.

Why is the Midgley–Dowling thesis confirmed for one product type (computer software) and consumer behaviour (use initiation) but not for another product (food) and behaviour (initial adoption of either brands or foods)? A possible explanation is that the thesis applies principally to products and situations that are inherently highly involving (computer software under task orientations requiring externally enforced adoption versus food choice under discretionary control and, even then, enabling several competing brands/products to be used as substitutes). This possibility is borne out by the finding reported by Foxall and Bhate (1994; see also Foxall and Hackett, 1992b) that Adaption–Innovation was most closely associated with computer usage in the case of the Business Information Technology Programme.

Further research should concentrate on the paradoxical finding that both systematic buyers and systematic non-buyers may be the same kind of people: *adaptors* who differ according to their personal involvement with the product field. This result, since replicated (Mudd, 1990) for the adoption of new educational practices by college professors in the United States, flies in the face of conventional adoption theory. It emphasizes the need, which further research should recognize, to treat Adaption–Innovation as a continuum rather than as the dichotomy that work to date has assumed in order to simplify analysis. Since a unique configuration of personality traits can no longer be expected to characterize initial adopters; researchers should additionally turn their attentions to the interactions with situational influences on consumer initiation. These have been especially powerful explicators of use initiation where further research might, for instance, profitably refine the sources of contextual pressure inherent in different task orientations. There is clearly a need for replication of the finding (Study 1) that brands adjudged discontinuous are purchased by innovators and that those adjudged continuous are purchased by adaptors.

Implications for adoption modelling

Accounts of consumers' information processing must recognize the differences in cognitive style and personal involvement that distinguish adaptors and innovators at each stage of the decision-making sequence.

By confirming that market initiators may have one of two diametrically opposed personality profiles, only one of which is predicted by adoption theory, the results have profound implications for the understanding of consumers' cognitive processing. They disconfirm the widely held view that initial buyers are inevitably highly involved and engaged in extended problem solving, while low involvement, manifesting in routine decision making and purchasing, is characteristic of later adopters. Both high- and low-involved consumers have been identified at the earliest stage of the diffusion process. Moreover, in the case of new foods, while involvement makes no difference to the purchase level of innovators, for adaptors it marks a crucial distinction.

The problem-solving behaviours of consumer initiators can be expected to differ at each stage of the adoption decision process depending on the adaptive–innovative style and, in the case of adaptors, their level of involvement with the product field (Foxall and Bhate, 1991; 1993a; 1993b; 1993c). Table 19 illustrates the differences by reference to the decision styles of the three segments found in innovative food markets.

Table 19 Psychographic segments of new foods markets

Stage in adoption process	Less-involved adaptors	Innovators	More-involved adaptors
Problem recognition	Reactive	Active	Proactive
Search	Restricted to known brand set	Superficial for any given item but wide ranging within product class and across classes	Assiduous exploration within accepted product category
Evaluation	Cautious and slow, based on tried and tested criteria	Short, personal and subjective, impulsive	Meticulous but confident
Decision	Conservative choice within acceptable range of brands/products: continuous innovations preferred	Radical, discontinuously – new products attractive. Frequent trial, assessment and discontinuance	Prudent but goal-oriented even if this entails dynamically continuous innovations
Post-purchase behaviour	Detailed evaluation, tendency towards brand loyalty	Little brand loyalty, constant search for novel experience	Loyal if satisfied but tendency for exploration _within_ product class

Further research should seek to elucidate the behavioural implications of the coexistence of adaptive and innovative segments within markets for new brands and products. Adaptors' narrow category width, relative inflexibility, intolerance of ambiguity, lower self-esteem and sensation seeking suggest they are more likely to be attracted to relatively continuous (improved) new products than to discontinuous ones. Foxall (1989) reported evidence that consumers' perceptions of the degree of continuity/discontinuity of new food brands were reflected in the predominance of adaptors and innovators respectively among their purchasers.

This result, if replicated by further work, would explain why more-involved adaptors bought the highest numbers of food brands/products – items which, at their most radically new, tend still to be fairly continuous. By comparison, the more discretely new software applications could be expected to be used in the largest volumes by more-involved innovators. The use of new products in alternative functions is, however, more likely to be determined by involvement and situational imperatives. Research aimed at testing these propositions is not only relatively straightforward to carry out but capable of clarifying the place of adaptive–innovative cognitive style in models of adoption.

Implications for new product marketing

The post-launch market for new products includes both adaptors and innovators whose reactions to marketing communications and other elements of the marketing mix are likely to be diametrically opposed.

The research has identified not only market segments whose coexistence at the beginning of the product life-cycle may be inimical to the successful introduction of a unified launch marketing mix, but also the psychographic basis on which they differ. The practical import of the five studies lies not in the weak correlational relationships between KAI and consumer behaviour but in the reason for their prevalence, which the Adaption–Innovation theory makes clear. The consistent finding that both adaptive and innovative market segments must be addressed at the launch stage of the product life cycle raises obvious questions for marketing strategy. According to the received wisdom of the product development and marketing texts, the initial market for new products consists of innovators.

Yet Table 19 suggests that the market for new 'healthy' foods can be psychographically segmented three ways, while that for computing applications software contains both adaptive and innovative subsegments for both more- and less-involved consumer segments. It is essential, therefore, to consider the probable differences in decision-making styles for adaptors and innovators as they influence product perceptions and responses to persuasive marketing communications. Advertising, for instance, plays a crucial role in the persuasion of initial adopters, since it is virtually the sole means by which new brands and products can be communicated to this primary market. Yet adaptors and innovators will likely respond quite differently to the same new product advertising.

Further research at the managerial level should seek solutions to the problem of accommodating marketing strategy for new products to the psychographic segments revealed in the research. One possibility is that the product development process may produce novel items that are tailor-made for one segment – on the conventional wisdom, this would be the 'innovative' but, better, the 'initial' segment – but which are simply ignored as inappropriate by the other. At worst, persuasive appeals aimed towards one segment may simply alienate the other. Authoritarian appeals, likely to appeal to extreme adaptors, might stimulate anti-pathetic feelings in innovators which precluded their trying the new item; and more freewheeling appeals, aimed at innovators, which stressed the novelty and radical difference of a new product or brand could similarly alienate adaptors. However, the extent to which these considerations actually influence market take-up of specific new offerings remains to be empirically established product market by product market. If confirmed, they may suggest why most new products fail. But, more hopefully, research may indicate how new product marketing appeals might be made simultaneously to the segments of new markets.

Several guidelines for such research emerge from the findings reported above. Considerations of category width, boredom with the familiar, and a capacity to work with several paradigms rather than within one frame-work implies that innovators would respond more positively than adaptors to two-sided appeals. It is possible that innovators actually appreciate messages that embody pro and con arguments and that they become easily bored with repeated messages that are consistent with their current beliefs.

Adaptors are more likely than innovators to respond favourably to one-sided messages, consistent with their current attitudes and habits. They are more likely than innovators to need credible sources of information to handle discrepant advertising messages and to change their attitudes and behaviour. Innovators, being more flexible, can accommodate more discrepant information. They therefore can cope with cognitive dissonance and indeed may be motivated by it. They are more likely than adaptors, who have strong needs for clarity, to remember incomplete messages. Their tolerance of ambiguity might render them more susceptible to postmodern advertising.

Since adaptors are more cautious and analytical in their judgements, more reflective and tentative in their decision making, they are open to rational, apparently objective appeals based on reasoned arguments. It appears likely that adaptors will be more amenable to reasoned argumentative advertising, even if it leads to allegedly incontrovertible conclusions (that would appear dogmatic and authoritarian to innovators). The more impulsive innovator is likely to be more open to personalized, affective advertising.

SUMMARY AND CONCLUSION

Theoretical and practical studies of 'consumer innovativeness' are currently beset by two problems. First is the proliferation of terms referring to 'innovators', 'use-innovators', 'innovative personality traits' and so on, which are both confusing and conceptually inexact. Second is the failure to account for the mass of weak evidence on which the notion of an innovation-prone personality is based.

This chapter has proposed a more coherent set of terms to designate the behavioural and psychological dimensions of 'innovative' consumer behaviour. Five empirical studies have been presented of the cognitive style/personality profiles related to new brand/product purchasing and the use of computers for novel purposes. Contrary to the literature on adoption and diffusion, while many of the consumers with a propensity for these behaviours showed the cognitive/personality styles widely attributed to 'consumer innovators', a substantial proportion, sometimes a majority, had the obverse profile. In terms of Kirton's Adaption– Innovation theory, so-called consumer innovators might exhibit either adaptive or innovative cognitive styles. Personal involvement with the product field also emerged as a powerful explicator of 'innovative' consumer behaviour.

Hence purchasers of the highest level of new food products were adaptors who were also highly involved in the product field; and while the heaviest users of software applications were those who were highly involved, both adaptors and innovators figured strongly among them. The findings suggest a more complicated psychographic composition of initial consumers than is generally appreciated in managerial prescriptions for new product development and marketing, and in theoretical explanations of consumer behaviour which rely on conceptual abstractions such as 'innate' or 'inherent' innovativeness. The argument has been advanced for the use of a more precise terminology, for empirically based theories and for sound measures. The overall conclusion is the need to reject emphatically the idea that the behaviour of consumer initiators can be explained by a set of personality traits that uniquely defines 'innate' or 'inherent' innovativeness.

The study of consumer initiation has been dogged for too long by loose terminology and simplistic reasoning. As a field that has prided itself on its scientific approach to the acquisition of knowledge, consumer research ought now to reject those hypothetical constructs and tenuous relationships among variables that are no longer relevant to a field in which knowledge rather than speculation is demonstrably possible. This chapter has not only suggested a resolution of the problem of inexact and misleading terminology; it has also shown a way forward through the incorporation of operational variables rather than abstract conjecture into our models of consumer initiation.

7

ADAPTION–INNOVATION AND CHANGES IN SOCIAL STRUCTURE: ON THE ANATOMY OF CATASTROPHE

P.P. van der Molen

SOME CONSEQUENCES OF LIVING SOCIALLY

This chapter deals with the questions: 'Why do social structures tend to harden and ossify in time?' or 'Why do social structures appear to have a limited life span?' and 'What can Adaption–Innovation theory teach us about these phenomena?'

Kirton has suggested that Adaption–Innovation differences are set very early in life and are relatively stable. As will be pointed out below, this is not surprising, since similar individual differences, and their genetic basis, can even be traced in non-human mammals that have social group life. Therefore the underlying biological organization must, from an evolutionary point of view, be very old and elementary. Insight into these underlying biological mechanisms and their effects in social groups may increase our understanding of a wide range of intriguing, and sometimes disquieting, phenomena. These phenomena range from educational and organizational strategies to the emergence and the, sometimes catastrophic, collapse of companies and other social group structures, including the way social roles and positions tend to be distributed, and the evolutionary consequences.

First, this chapter suggests why, from a biological point of view, Adaption–Innovation differences between individuals are theoretically to be expected among social mammals. Second, the chapter investigates the consequences of these behavioural differences on the level of social interaction. A lifespan theory of social structures and organizations will be introduced, which includes the likelihood of catastrophic collapses as a major implication. Third, these assumptions are related to some experimental results and data from the literature. Experimental and empirical findings from biological and psychological research will be presented which support the notion of a biological basis of Adaption–Innovation, and related inter-individual differences. Finally, the chapter explores how this type of understanding may enable us to map the processes underlying periodic catastrophe and may teach us how to exercise a degree of control on the process.

Starting with the biological and theoretical viewpoint, let us focus on the basic requirements of social behaviour. Each individual among social mammals is by necessity saddled with a conspicuous bipolarity in behavioural urges. First, being a social animal, drives for social contact and interaction are by definition an important part of its behaviour-genetical endowment. Second, it also has a set of perhaps even more basic drives to ensure the fulfilment of a range of non-social personal needs, e.g., water, food, cover, warmth, sex, territory, etc. As far as these latter needs are concerned, the amount of resources is often limited, thus causing competition and social conflict. This basic functional conflict exists in every social individual, who inescapably has to reconcile these two sets of urges much of the time. Whenever some of the needed resources are scarce, the ensuing competition will put a strain on social relations. Under such conditions an individual frequently has to choose between either striving for continuation of peaceful social relations or getting an appropriate share of the resources, eventually at the cost of social peace and harmony. Most of the time this dilemma boils down to the question of whether or not to submit to the initiative of other individuals at the cost of fulfilling personal urges and desires.

In any social species this conflict of needs is inescapably present in each individual day after day, the outcome determining how the individual will deal, by and large, with the social situation at hand. It is most desirable to have one's own way most of the time and still maintain close social contact and interaction. But that is more or less identical to what is generally understood by a 'dominant' social role, and such roles are comparatively scarce. It is therefore more interesting to know what happens to the majority of individuals, the various types of subordinates who are under regular pressure to comply and postpone or even abandon part of their individual desires and initiatives. For such non-dominant individuals, the balance between the strength of the desire for social contact and interaction, and the strength of the desires to fulfil other biological needs, determines the outcome of this continuous process of weighing one need against the other. Given a certain pressure to comply, it largely depends on this equilibrium of basic sensitivities within the subordinate individual, as to what the behavioural outcome will be, either drifting gradually into an outcast position or assuming a compliant and socially accepted subordinate position. Such differences between subordinates have indeed frequently been observed in mammals.

What is important for us to note here is that for any social mammal, the competing sets of needs under discussion are very general and basic. We must therefore assume that the variance in the balance between these sets of basic needs has strong genetic roots. The equilibrium discussed above is therefore also an equilibrium between functionally competing parts of the genetic programme. As such, we may consider this equilibrium, varying over individuals, as a trait in the classical sense. We could therefore express this set of behavioural polarities as a set of (*inter alia* genetically based) trait differences, which do have a clearly defined impact on the distribution of social roles, or – mathematically speaking – as $p(\omega/\text{not } \alpha)$ or as $1-p$ ($\beta/\text{not } \alpha$) see Figure 6). (In the cross-specific behavioural literature the symbols α, β and ω are used for: dominant role (α), compliant and tolerated subordinate role (β), and non-compliant, non-tolerated type of subordinate, frequently leading to an outcast role (ω); the p stands for probability and refers to the indeterminancy of the social roles to be acquired, because of environmental influences).

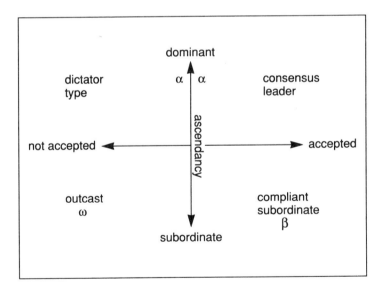

Figure 6 Two dimensions of social role behaviour
© P.P. van der Molen

Up to this point, three basic assumptions have been made about the behaviour of social mammals in general:

1 There is a strong functional link between, on the level of behavioural orientation, the frequency of social behaviour versus thing-orientated individualistic behaviour, and, on the level of the distribution of social roles, conformity and compliance with authority versus a self-willed attitude. These two polarities cannot be separated; they do have the same behavioural basis. Therefore a range of personality characteristics have to be strongly intercorrelated, e.g., self-will, thing-orientatedness, individualism, and innovative creativity on the one pole, and compliance, person-orientatedness, sociability, conformity, and creative adaptiveness within rules and traditions, on the other.

2 Individuals differ from one another as far as the balance between these polarities is concerned.

3 This variation between individuals must have genetic components.

Later in this chapter we will check these assumptions against experimental data, but before doing that, we will first investigate their logical consequences.

At this point one might justly retort: 'Why so much ado about nothing?' It seems self-evident that these polarities in behaviour are interconnected, and since for most broad behavioural characteristics it is likely that differences in behaviour are partly caused by genetic differences, in particular if they are of very old phylogenetic origin, which these behaviours apparently are, it is rather tautological to state that they have genetic roots.

The point is, first, that this notion of a biological basis of certain behaviours may be self-evident to behaviour biologists, it is certainly not for large groups of sociologists and psychologists. Second, these three assumptions do have peculiar and important consequences if applied to the sociology of group structures, the incrowd–outcast dynamism, and the concomitant behavioural reflexes in particular.

In order to discuss these consequences we have to add one more assumption, which is rather a definition, namely:

4 In what follows, 'social groups' will mean groups over which individuals are distributed discretely. In other words, individuals can recognize one another as either belonging to the 'social group' in question or not – and treat each other accordingly.

HYPOTHESIS: LIFE CYCLES OF SOCIAL GROUPS AND STRUCTURES

If defined this way, the previous four assumptions imply that within such 'social groups' – and other discrete social structures for that matter – there is exercised a more or less continuous selection pressure in favour of compliance and sociability. This is so because the most compliant – and thus most socially orientated and rule-adaptive – individuals are most likely to establish long-lasting accommodation within the group. Self-willed individualists, on the other hand (also being innovative and thing-orientated according to assumption 1), are most likely to run into trouble and disagreement with the dominant individuals and/or habits and rules in the group. They are least prepared to pay time and again the price of postponing or giving up personal urges and initiatives in order to keep the peace and social harmony. As a consequence, such individuals are most likely either to fight hard for attaining a dominant position, or if failing, to drift into marginal omega-like social positions and eventually become outcasts and leave the social structure.

For any eventual influx of individuals into the social group or structure, the opposite holds. Individuals will be most readily accepted if they do not pose a threat to the individuals and/or habits ruling group life, which of course favours rule-adaptive compliants. The effect of such a continuous selection pressure is that the behavioural make-up of a group will shift gradually towards compliance and sociable rule-adaptiveness. Because of assumption 1, this also implies a shift towards less and less independent creativity and thing-orientated innovativeness. And because of assumption 3, this shifting of group characteristics is (genetically) consolidated.

What then automatically happens with every social group and structure is a gradual loss of innovativeness and behavioural flexibility. In the end such a gradual ossification reduces the effectiveness of the group (structure), whether its function be the preservation of a territorial area with sufficient resources to keep a deme of mice alive, or, in man, the enhancement of some sport, the maintenance of political ideals, the aim to get a better share of the market, or the preservation of a political state. At any level of organization, a price has to be paid in the end. Such ossification especially matters whenever novel challenges turn up in the form of environmental changes or the emergence of competing groups. The disadvantages of a lowered flexibility and innovative creativity weigh most when, because of changing circumstances, innovations and a change of habits are urgently required.

141

In such circumstances the advantages of the old social system in terms of experience, solidly established routines, compliance, malleability of all members, and sheer size, may easily be outdone by the innovativeness, flexibility and efficiency of a younger, and often much smaller, social group (structure), on which these selection pressures have not yet been working for such a long period of time. At such a moment the old structure will yield to the younger structure in a relatively sudden way.

Therefore, provided the above-mentioned assumptions are valid, social groups and structures only have a limited lifespan. The life cycle of a social institution then, e.g., in human society, can roughly be indicated as: Foundation $\rightarrow$ Consolidation $\rightarrow$ Internal selection pressure $\rightarrow$ Increasing ossification and a reduction of flexibility of the social structure $\rightarrow$ Eventual attempts to compensate these effects by means of more striving for growth and power $\rightarrow$ Further increase of rigidity and ossification $\rightarrow$ Catastrophic collapse by sudden environmental changes or competition (see Figure 7).

This model implies a departure from notions of mere gradual changes in societal structures. The probability of sudden catastrophic turnover events, increasing in time with cumulating selection effects, can graphically be represented and mathematically be described with help of the bistable models from the mathematical branch of catastrophe theory (Thom and Zeeman, 1974; Zeeman, 1976; Woodcock and Davis, 1978). Figure 8 shows a cusp catastrophe, visualizing the relation between the continuous and the discontinuous part of the cycle. After foundation of a social structure, the level of overt challenges tends to decrease and the stability of the structure tends to increase until the inefficiency begins to take its toll, after which the stability of the structure decreases again. During the process the average level of self-will (percentage of innovators) necessarily decreases. An increase in the level of radical challenge may then sooner or later lead to a catastrophic turnover event. In the new structure the percentage of innovators (average level of self-will) starts at a high level again, and so on.

The selection rate determines the speed of ossification, and the life expectancy of a social structure is therefore roughly inversely proportional to the internal selection pressure. Such sudden turnovers of social structures are therefore bound to happen at any level at which discrete social group structures are operating, as long as individuals can be recognized by one another as either belonging or not belonging to that group, and as long as there is some outflow or neutralization (and eventually a selected influx) of individuals. Depending on the level of organization, such a turnover goes by the labels 'conquest',

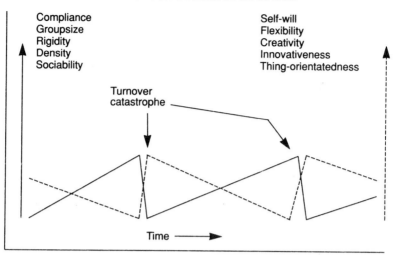

Figure 7 Group membership and catastrophe
© P.P. van der Molen

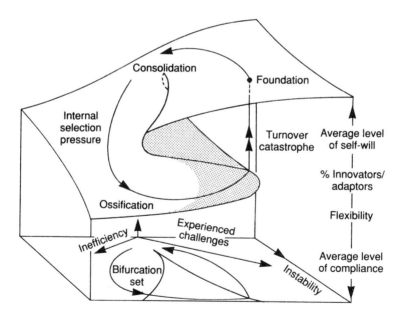

Figure 8 Turnover cycles, personality and institutional functioning
© P.P. van der Molen

'close-down', 'discontinuance', 'bankruptcy', 'revolution', 'subjugation', 'extermination', or 'genocide'.

Once the old, ossified social structure has been replaced by one or more younger competitor-structures, the individuals from the population as a whole have been reshuffled in favour of resourceful self-willed innovators, who now occupy the 'in-crowd' positions. The rule-adaptive compliants, who formed the bulk of the establishment of the former social structure in power, have drifted by then into marginal positions and run the worst risks from then on. Thus the previous internal shift in genetic make-up has been undone, and a new selection cycle is started in these new structures.

The selective advantages for individuals are therefore different within and outside of social groups and structures, and also different depending on the stage of the life cycle an institution is in. A compliant, adaptive and sociable temperament gives a selective advantage within large, and especially within older social systems, whereas a thing-orientated, innovative and self-willed temperament is selectively advantageous outside of the protective maze of established structures, or within small and young systems.[1]

EVOLUTIONARY ADVANTAGES

Notwithstanding the above-mentioned unpleasant aspects of turnover catastrophes, such a scheme of automatic and unavoidable cyclic changes in social-behavioural structures does have conspicuous evolutionary advantages. It is, for instance, clear that this mechanism keeps everything moving: structures, individuals and, finally, genes. After every turnover event (or catastrophe) there occurs a thorough reshuffling of individuals. And when in the ensuing chaos new combinations of individuals reassemble in the newly emerging social group (structures), novel combinations of gene sets are also eventually formed.

Apart from this advantage at the level of interpersonal social reorganization and consequently of ensuing recombination of gene sets, there is also an advantage at the level of migration, exploration and colonization of the environment (e.g., Lancaster, 1986). Most mammals are reluctant to go beyond the limits of familiar territory – their home range – and generally must be forced one way or other to do so (Christian, 1970).

Every time an old structure breaks down, a large number of individuals is forced to move and is therefore added to the extra-group surplus population. This will produce a sudden increase in inter-individual competition outside of the group (structures), and therefore also a sudden increase in the pressure on other established group (structures), catalizing the eventually impending catastrophic collapse of more systems, thus locally adding to the already existing chaos. This spatial synchronization causes migratory and related pressures to occur spasmodically and strongly instead of continuously and rather weakly. This may be an advantage where geographical barriers, for example, need to be overcome in order to enable further migratory moves of the population or species as a whole. Many authors have commented on the importance of surplus out-group individuals for the production of strong dispersal pressures (Darlington, 1957), and from the model discussed above it may be clear that social hierarchies constitute by themselves a major force for dispersion.

This is also stressed by Christian (1970) in a review of population dynamics research in mammals. He adds the conclusion that it is primarily on outcasts that the process of evolution can really work. The implication is that the Darwinian 'struggle for life' is in fact a process with much irony and relativity, since those individuals with, apparently, maximum reproductive success, the dominants, create by the very violence of their success the outcasts that carry on the process that we call evolution (Hoffschulte, 1986). The ethologist and social psychologist Calhoun (1974) comments on our own origins:

> The strong remain where conditions are most salubrious to preserving the old life-style. The weak must emigrate – bodily, behaviourally or intellectually. Our most distant ancestors swung from trees. Slightly less distant ones lost that race and won another. Population pressure forced them out of forest islands to wander across the African plains in search of another patch of forest where they could renew the old ways. Successive losses and successive demands for adjusting culminated in upright walking creatures like ourselves. So it has been through all of evolution; the weak (eventually) survive, changed, to open new routes into the future. The meek do inherit the earth.
>
> (Calhoun, 1974: 302–3)

The importance of deviants and scapegoats for these processes, on the level of culture and social organization in man, is emphasized in the comprehensive works of Coser (e.g., 1956; 1968) and Girard (e.g., 1982). Girard describes how throughout human history the distribution of social role positions has been brought about by means of violent acts of social repression. Not only is the dramatic shifting of non-average, deviant subordinate persons into outcast positions just as common as in lower mammals, but, according to Girard, the very development of our culture even depended on it. Only through acts of violence and the collective commemoration of the victim-outcast or scapegoat do human groups find the social-cognitive norms and unanimity from which culture can develop. Culture in our species is therefore not to be considered as an immaculate attainment with which we have overcome primitive forms of violence. On the contrary, it is precisely through the violent social collisions themselves that human culture emerged from the animal background. The threatening circle around victims who are found guilty of social disorders is, so to say, the daily bread of social cultural order (Hoffschulte, 1986, on Girard).

In summary, if a similar mechanism of population and group-cycles exists, it would facilitate speciation through genetic adaption to marginal habitats, would help to overcome migratory bottlenecks, and even would, in the case of man, serve to motor the evolution of culture. It would also have significant effects on other levels of social organization. On the level of industrial companies, for instance, such periodic outbursts of organizational turnover may cause an enormous series of 'domino bankruptcies', but they also trigger synchronized waves of entrepreneurial creativity and innovative initiatives, thus inducing large-scale industrial reshuffling and renewal. Similar considerations apply to the other levels of social organization.

The actual turnover catastrophes themselves may not be pleasant for the participants at all, but that is irrelevant from an evolutionary perspective. On this grand scale it is not the feeling and suffering of the individual involved that counts, but the long-term behavioural and behavioural-genetic output that does.

These evolutionary considerations suggest that if in the case of man his superior capacity for learning plays a modifying role in these matters, that the organization of his intellectual capacities will probably have evolved in such a way as to enhance the occurrence of the cyclic changes under discussion, rather than thwart it. (We shall return later to this particular consequence, i.e., the peculiar phenomenon of blind spots in our cognitive system as far as social role interactions are concerned.)

Having outlined these intriguing, and also somewhat disquieting consequences of the four assumptions made, I will now present some data that may help us assess the validity of those four assumptions. First, some ethological research on behavioural differences between individual mice will be presented, especially in so far as these data shed light on the probabilities of non-dominant animals drifting into an omega-role (outcast-like) or adapting to a subordinate (beta) role. Then a short

146

literature review will be presented on inter-individual differences in (innovative) self-will versus (adaptive) compliance and its correlates in other socially living mammals and especially in man.

EXPERIMENTS WITH HOUSE MICE

As is reported in more detail elsewhere (van der Molen, 1973; 1988), data supporting these assumptions were obtained from mouse research. This research investigated:

1 how social role differences could be manipulated;
2 which part of the behavioural differences had to be ascribed to those role differences; and
3 which part of the behavioural differences was due to innate 'trait'-factors.

Dominance appeared to determine the behaviour of an individual to a great extent, thus being an indispensable tool for ethological descriptions of inter-individual differences. It could also be shown experimentally that becoming dominant or subordinate was mainly dependent on coincidence and contingencies, and only to a limited extent on individual characteristics such as body-weight, social-and-fighting experience, self-will, etc. Within the categories of dominants and subordinates there appeared large differences in tolerance for other individuals. Some dominant mice behaved far more aggressively towards their subordinates than did others and these differences determined to a large extent the number of subordinates eventually holding out with such a dominant. Another role difference which can easily be manipulated experimentally is the 'in-crowd/outcast' difference in subordinates, or rather, the difference between betas and omegas (the usual terms in mouse research). These differences in tolerance versus aggressiveness among dominants and subordinates largely determined the population density in the observation areas.

'Self-willed conflict-proneness' was found to be strongly correlated with a high frequency of 'exploratory' and 'thing-orientated' behaviour, whereas 'compliance' was found to be strongly correlated with a high frequency of 'social' and 'partner-orientated' behaviour. Every time a group of four males and two females was placed in a large observation cage for the first time, there were at first no clear alpha, beta, or omega roles. In the course of the following days (or weeks) an alpha male would emerge and the differences in behaviour between the subordinate males would still be rather vague. Subsequently, differences would gradually evolve between the behaviour patterns of the subordinates. The subordinate mice who adapted to the initiatives of the alpha behaved submissively more regularly and underwent the manipulations of the alpha more often. They were, however, less often disturbed by aggressive attacks from the alpha, and did not much care whether the alpha was awake or asleep. The subordinates who put up more resistance towards the alpha showed, on the other hand, a conversely adjusted type of activity pattern; they kept silent as long as they sensed that the alpha was active, and walked around when he was asleep.

These gradually developing behavioural differences between subordinates can be described as differences in 'staying' (beta types) and 'fleeing' (omega types), since the latter type showed a tendency to flee the territory if possible. In experimental situations in which opportunities for fleeing are provided, a large proportion of the (young) subordinate males flee from the territory (van Zegeren, personal communication). This is similar in many other rodent species (e.g., Healey, 1967; Ewer, 1971; Wilson, 1977: 278; Barash, 1977).

In the process of a subordinate gradually becoming an omega, the behaviour of the alpha gradually changes towards treating the omega ever more as a stranger. What is important to note here however, is that the behavioural differences between betas and omegas seemed to develop before the alpha in question would begin to treat the subordinates in a different way. This suggests that these beta/omega differences are caused by differences between the individual subordinates themselves. It could, in principle, also be explained by assuming that an alpha male initiates these differences by having a dislike for one of the subordinates, and that this subordinate thereupon avoids the alpha more than the other subordinates do. These differences in treatment by the alpha might initially be of such a subtle nature that even though the subordinate in question reacts promptly with increased avoidance behaviour, these differences have escaped our attention.

In cross-breeding experiments it could, however, be demonstrated that strong hereditary factors determine the likelihood of drifting into a compliant subordinate ($\beta-$) position versus the likelihood of drifting into an outcast ($\omega-$) position. Consequently, differences between omegas and betas of the same population appeared to originate, at least for a greater part, from genetic differences between the subordinate individuals. We label these differences accordingly as 'self-will', 'intolerance', 'tendency to have one's own way', or for that matter, 'tendency to dominate'. And these temperamental differences appeared to determine in a similar way the style of an individual's dominant behaviour.

148

In the mouse experiments some of the populations were manipulated in such a way that some males shifted through subordinate as well as through dominant social positions. It was found that 'tolerant', 'compliant' males, apt to take up a beta role instead of an omega role when in a subordinate position, were tolerant of (their) subordinates when performing an alpha role, contrary to males with a high level of 'self-will' or 'tendency to dominate'. The latter would sooner end up in an outcast or omega position when subordinate, and when they achieved dominance, they would tend to perform their dominant roles with much intolerant aggressiveness. Besides, self-willed individuals, when either in a dominant or in a subordinate position, tended to display more thing-orientated and explorative (innovative) behaviour, whereas compliant, adaptive individuals tended to display more social-interactive behaviour. And when in a dominant position, compliant, adaptive individuals tended to maintain a more peaceful reign than did self-willed individuals, though the peacefulness of the social group involved was of course also strongly influenced by the level of self-willedness of the other (non-dominant) group members.

ETHOLOGICAL AND ENDOCRINOLOGICAL DATA

The plausibility of this 'self-will versus compliance' or 'individualistic, thing-orientated versus social' dimension in the domain of temperament traits is furthermore corroborated by a substantial amount of other ethological and personality-psychological literature.

In practice, it is often difficult to distinguish successfully between temperamental traits and social-role dimensions, since it is clear that amount and kind of 'social' behaviour never merely depend on con-genital trait differences, but by definition also depend strongly on the actually assumed roles. Our aim here is to look for the trait 'explorative versus social' as a label for basic individual predilections, and as far as it indicates within-role variance in personal style between individuals (see e.g., Strelau (1974) on the differences between these two classes of inter-individual (differences)). Only then can we be sure to be dealing with differences in temperament in the sense of behavioural traits with a stable and inherited component (Buss and Plomin, 1975).

In many species, differences between individuals have been found which resemble the above-mentioned differences between male mice. From ethological field research it appears to be a general characteristic of social mammals that some individuals exert a lot of aggressive dominance, bullying their subordinates much of the time, whereas other dominants act as sort of 'social controllers', governing the social relations in the group by social skill, sustained by appreciation from companions rather than by aggressive intimidation. These differences are for instance reported from ethological research on mountain gorillas by Fossey (1972); on chimpanzees by Reynolds and Luscombe (1969); on a number of species including man by Chance and Jolly (1970) and Wilson (1977: 311–13); and on man by Lippit and White (1958), Krech *et al.* (1962; Ch. 12), Gibb (1969), Strayer and Strayer (1976), Hold (1976), and Sluckin and Smith (1977). Wilson comments on these differences:

> It is not wholly imprecise to speak of much of the residual variance in dominance behaviour as being due to 'personality'. The dominance system of (e.g.) the Nilgiri langur (Presbytis johnii) is weakly developed and highly variable from troop to troop. Alliances are present or absent, there is a single adult male or else several animals coexist uneasily, and the patterns of interaction differ from one troop to another. Much of this variation depends on idiosyncratic behavioural traits of individuals, especially of the dominant males.
>
> (Poirier, 1970: 294)

To continue with non-human primates, Itani *et al.* (1963) and Yamada (1966) describe the behaviour of extreme beta-type males in Japanese Monkeys (Macaca fuscata) and indicate that a compliant temperament seems to be conditional for assuming such a role. Yamada further points out that, when eventually achieving a dominant position, a tendency for independence sometimes seems to exclude a tolerant attitude towards subordinates.

Differences between dominant males of this sort have also been described in stumptail macaques (Macaca speciosa) by Bertrand (1969), who describes both 'bullies' and 'fair alpha males' (ibid.: 127) and stresses that aggressiveness is not always a necessary factor for dominance (ibid.: 261). She states that stumptail macaques differ considerably in the amount of intolerance and aggression displayed, and that in certain cases the sustained aggressiveness of some individuals who were followed up for several years seemed a personality trait appearing originally early in childhood (ibid.: 126, 127, 261). She concluded too that the amount of investigative behaviour shown by an individual depended, apart from social rank, age and conditions of captivity, also on the predisposition of each monkey. Some individuals were far more adventurous than others (Bertrand, 1969: 153, 154, 262). This personality dependence of investigative behaviour overruled age- and rank-dependent behaviour in particular when the stimuli were frightening or ambivalent.

Earlier it was pointed out that in socially living mammals at least two sets of basic urges have to be postulated, which, independently from one another, vary over individuals, thus producing *inter alia* the adaptor/innovator differences. The first set contains drives for social contact and interaction, leading to gregarious types of behaviour. The second set contains the drives for thing-orientated behaviour. From recent neuro-anatomical and endocrinological research it appears that there is probably a strong link between these two distinct sets of drives on the one hand and specific neuro-endocrine systems on the other. Cloninger (1986; 1987) presented a biosocial theory of personality, based on a synthesis of information from family studies, studies of personality structure, as well as neuropharmacologic and neuroanatomical studies of behavioural conditioning and learning in man and other animals. He describes three dimensions of personality that are genetically independent, two of which, the 'novelty seeking' dimension and the more socially orientated 'reward dependence' dimension, relate to the two distinct sets of basic drives mentioned above.

One of his dimensions of personality trait differences is principally ruled by the monoamine neuromodulator 'dopamine'. This system determines the heritable tendency toward intense exhilaration and excitement, leading to frequent exploratory activity (novelty seeking) and avoidance of monotony. Individuals high on this dimension are generally also characterized as impulsive, quick-tempered and disorderly. They tend to neglect details and are quickly distracted or bored. They are also easily provoked to prepare for fight or flight. The other dimension is principally ruled by the monoamine neuromodulator norepinephrine. This system determines the heritable tendency to respond intensely to signals of social reward and approval, sentiment and succour. Individuals high on this dimension are generally characterized as eager to help and please others, persistent, industrious, warmly sympathetic, sentimental, and sensitive to social cues, praise and personal succour, but also able to delay gratification with the expectation of eventually being socially rewarded.

According to Cloninger, a person high on 'novelty seeking' (the dopamine system) and low on 'reward dependence' (the norepinephrine system), is characterized as:

seeking thrilling adventures and exploration; disorderly and unpredictable; intolerant of structure and monotony, regardless of

151

consequences; frequently trying to break rules and to introduce change; quick tempered and strongly engaged with new ideas and activities; socially detached; independent nonconformist; content to be alone; minimal ambition and motivation to please others, and insensitive to social cues and pressures anyway.

Conversely, a person low on 'novelty seeking' (dopamine) and high on 'reward dependence' (norepinephrine) is characterized as:

dependent on emotional support and intimacy with others; sensitive to social cues and responsive to social pressure; sentimental; crying easily; rigid; orderly and well organized; trying to impose stable structure and consistent routine; rarely becoming angry or excited; an analytical decision maker who always requires detailed analysis of complete information; slow to form and change interests and social attachments.

This is strikingly similar to descriptions of Kirton's innovator v. adaptor dimension, which illustrates once more the biological roots of A–I differences.

FURTHER RESEARCH DATA ON HUMAN BEHAVIOUR

Gibb (1969), Strayer and Strayer (1976), Hold (1976) and Sluckin and Smith (1977) report similar differences in dominance styles of children, and of adolescents (Savin-Williams, 1979; 1980). Hold labels these differences thus:

there are two opposite leadership styles, called by Gibb (1969) 'leadership' and 'domination'. With leadership, authority is spontaneously accorded by fellow group members whereas with domination there is little or no shared feeling or joint action and authority derives from some extra-group power.

(Hold, 1976: 194)

Turning from dominance styles to more general differences in behavioural style, Abrams and Neubauer (1976) report that human infants differ considerably in the way they divide their attention between persons and objects. This trait dimension, which they called 'Thing – versus Human Orientatedness', was manifest as early as in the second month of life. They found that the more thing-orientated child shows a greater freedom in exploration. Therefore we might label this dimension of 'Thing – versus Human Orientatedness' (or sociability) also as 'explorative versus social', parallel to the vocabulary in Bertrand's (1969) longitudinal research on macaques. Abrams and Neubauer suggest furthermore that learning processes are shaped in a way that is different for each type of child:

> Training issues are characterized essentially as 'tasks' for the more thing-oriented child; for the human-disposed infant, they are characterized as acts in the spectrum of approval or disapproval. . . . If earlier impressions were that the more thing-oriented children are more outer-directed, by the third year of life they appeared more inclined to be motivated by inner determinants and resources, a distinction which seems to persist thereafter. . . . The dispositions of infants are re-inforced in the milieu, as implements in evolving strategies are cycled back into the psychological system and thus inevitably emerge as traits of character.
>
> (Abrams and Neuberger, 1976)

Hold (1976) reports that children who rank high in the attention structure tend to set initiatives instead of complying to the initiatives of other children and that they 'prefer to play alone when the leading role was already taken by another high-ranking child. It seems that these children do not like to be commanded by other children.' This runs essentially parallel to what has been said in the introduction, in that self-willed individuals are more prone to become either dominants or 'loners' than beta-type, compliant subordinates. Hold's findings also suggest that such self-willed individuals are prone to become more thing-orientated and less social, since 'loners' are by definition less sociable.

A similar trait contrast is employed by McClain (1978) in his study on the behaviour of adult women. He distinguishes between women (e.g., feminists) who are dominated by a need for independence and women who are dominated by a need for affiliation. McClain, like Ausubel (1952), points out that two basically opposing patterns of maturation occur in the parent–child relationship during a youngster's early years. He terms the resulting personality types as 'satellizers', who tend to adapt to existing rules, versus 'nonsatellizers', who tend to behave more individualistically (hence feminists' irritation at failing to imbue all women with their views).

> The satellizing child establishes her life orbit about her parents, whom she perceives as the benign source of all that is good in her life. In contrast, the nonsatellizing child rejects this kind of

dependency because she 'believes' that her welfare lies in her freedom to choose her own course.

(McClain, 1978: 436)

The material of McClain's study was derived from behaviour of women. Kirton (1976; 1987a) investigates the phenomenon of adaptiveness and innovativeness in adults in general. For Kirton, a person confronted with a problem has a choice: he can do things 'better' or 'more' to solve the problem (adapt) or he can do things 'differently' (innovate). Doing things 'better' (Drucker, 1969) implies the acceptance of the old framework, while doing things 'differently' means breaking accepted patterns. As Kirton says:

The Adaptor is right at home in bureaucracies, which tend to become more adaptor-oriented as time goes on . . . whereas . . . the natural position of high Innovators seems to be out on a limb.

Kirton's work is of special significance if for the performance of leaders it can be argued that innovators tend to become initiating and directing 'task'-leaders whereas adaptors tend to become consideration-orientated 'maintenance-specialists' of social relations. This is in line with differences between leader types as described by Bales (1953), Halpin and Winer (1957), Thibaut and Kelley (1959), Krech et al. (1962) and Reddin (1987). From a conceptual point of view, innovativeness may furthermore be considered as a positively appreciated creative variant of nonconformism and disobedience.

'Conformity' as defined by Krech et al. (1962) in their research on the dimensions of social interactive behaviour, is related to the trait dimension 'thing-orientated and self-willed versus social and compliant'. They state: 'For another thing, some people are more resistant to group pressures and demands (the hard-core independents and the deviants) than are others (the easy conformists)' (Krech et al., 1962: 486). They also conclude, 'The above findings offer strong support for the proposition that conformity tendencies are significantly related to enduring personality factors in the individual, (ibid.: 527). The relevance for our model becomes especially clear where they define Conformity as a 'trait of the person' as opposed to conformity as a 'trait of the situation' (or 'social role' dimension in our words).

conformity might be thought of as a 'trait of the situation'. . . . There are also marked individual differences in general readiness to conform, over a wide variety of situations. These differences . . . reflect conformity as a 'trait of the person'. This distinction

154

between conformity as reflecting the conformity-inducing properties of a situation and as reflecting the conforming propensity of a
person should be kept well in mind. Much of the controversy and
misunderstanding about the facts and theories of conformity stems
from a confusion of these two aspects of conformity.

(Krech *et al.*, 1962: 527)

FACTORANALYTIC RESEARCH

Of particular interest is the existence of a similar dimension in factoranalytic personality trait research. Feij (1978) compares the trait models
of Heymans (1932), Eysenck (1953), Zuckerman (1974), Strelau (1974),
Buss *et al.* (1973) and Buss and Plomin (1975), amongst others. Although
these authors often use different classes of subjects and prefer different
final rotations of their resulting factorial personality models, some of
their dimensions appear closely related to our trait dimension 'self-
willed and individualistic and thing-orientated and explorative' versus
'compliant and social'.

For instance, a high score on Zuckerman's (1974) and Feij's (1978; Feij
et al. 1981) trait dimension of 'sensation seeking' indicates a strong need
for change, exploration and new experiences; a tendency towards
independence of other people and an anti-authoritarian attitude, while
'low sensation seeking' implies a tendency to comply with conventional
values and rules. Feij (1978: 293) stresses that extreme sensation
seekers may on the one hand be anti-social, drop-out delinquents but
may on the other hand be unconventional but fully accepted creative
innovators (For Goldsmith's empirical support, see Chapter 2). This is in
agreement with what was postulated above, namely that highly self-willed
individuals have a tendency to become either drop-outs (omega role)
or accepted innovators in the focus of attention (alpha role), and that
individuals with a low self-will have a higher tendency to assume beta roles
compliantly, i.e., fit into groups and systems.

Buss and Plomin's (1975) trait dimension 'sociability' indicates a strong
need to be together with others, a high responsiveness towards others,
and a predilection for social interaction above non-social reinforcers
(Feij, 1978).

In most other factoranalytical classification systems one or more
dimensions may also be discerned which are related to our concept of
'self-will and thing-orientatedness versus compliant and social'. In
Cattell's sixteen-personality-factor set, for instance, the dimension
labelled as 'liberalism' (Q1), indicating among other things behavioural

155

differences like 'conservative' and 'experimenting', is supposed to measure an underlying tendency towards nonconformity and indepen- dence versus a need for affiliation (Cattell *et al.*, 1970; Karson and O'Dell, 1976; McClain, 1978). At least three other dimensions from his 16PF battery also relate to concepts discussed here, namely Cattell's higher-order factor IV, indicating 'subduedness versus independence', the factor 'assertiveness' ('E') indicating 'cautious humbleness versus abrasive assertiveness', and the factor 'Superego' ('G'), indicating 'conscientiousness versus expedience' (Kirton and de Ciantis, 1986; Kirton, 1987a).

From all these data it would appear that the personality trait dimen- sion for which we are looking does indeed emerge systematically in one form or other in most factoranalytic personality research. Moreover, it appears from the empirical work of, *inter alia*, Goldsmith (see Chapter 2) that the concepts emerging in all these dimensions from the various authors on personality are indeed related, forming a coherent web of conceptually intertwined behavioural characteristics. Kirton (in Chapter 1) reports numerous different studies, which investigated the interrelations of the KAI with various established dimensions fitting into this mesh of conceptually intertwined personality characteristics. This resulted in over 60 significant correlations with 25 of these different personality trait dimensions. This is the more interesting because Kirton's A–I theory provides a conceptual framework linking all these aspects of personality in a meaningful way, a framework that ties in seamlessly with the theory as outlined in the previous sections. We shall return to Kirton's research in the following sections.

GENETICS

These data from personality research are the more relevant because various writers point out that a genetic basis of these dimensions has repeatedly been established firmly (Eysenck, 1967; Buss *et al.*, 1973; Feij, 1978; Claridge *et al.*, 1973; Eaves and Eysenck, 1975; Wilson, 1977; Plomin and Rowe, 1977; 1979).

Feij uses, for instance, two more or less orthogonal dimensions with a hereditary component which seem to be related to our dimension 'self- willed, individualistic, thing-orientated, explorative, versus compliant, social' (See Figure 9). These are labelled by Feij as 'extraversion' and 'sensation seeking'. His topological system does not include a genetically based dimension 'activity' like Buss and Plomin's (1975), for example, but both these dimensions of Feij may be conceived as correlated with 'activity' because a high activity enhances a higher score on either scale (Feij, 1978; Feij *et al.*, 1981). Therefore Feij's two dimensions 'extraversion' and 'sensation seeking', both with hereditary components, appear to be similar (spanning the same two-dimensional personality space) to the dimension we are looking for, together with the dimension 'activity-level' (see Figure 9).

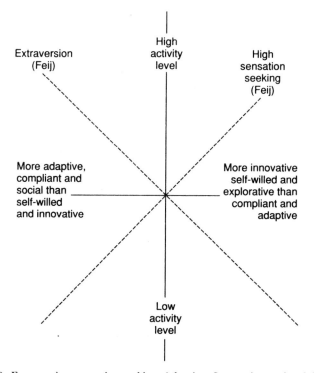

Figure 9   Extraversion, sensation seeking, Adaption–Innovation and activity
© P.P. van der Molen

The empirical findings of Kirton (1976; 1978a; 1987b: 90–9, 114–19) and Ettlie and O'Keefe (1982) are also in line with the notion of a biological basis. They report that differences in innovativeness versus adaptiveness are not significantly related to IQ, level of education, exam results or previous experiences, but are definitely of a more basic personality nature (see Chapter 2). What is clear is that Kirton's concept indicates the 'type' of creativity, and so differs from instruments which measure 'level' of creativity (Kirton, 1978c; Torrance and Horng, 1980)

Kirton (1987a) further marshals the evidence that, at the least, the adaption–innovation characteristics must be set early in life. The biological links of the adaptor/innovator differences also show in a correlation with hemispheric preference (Torrance, 1982; Kirton, 1987a; Prato Previde and Carli, 1987). The more methodical, planned approach of the left-brain dominated individual relates to adaption, and the more intuitive style of the right-brain dominated individual relates to innovation.

In summary, the available data support the view that a genetically based trait dimension 'thing-orientated, explorative versus social' or, in different terms, 'self-willed versus compliant' is indeed conspicuously present.

SELECTION

As the first three assumptions made at the beginning of this chapter find ample support in ethological and psychological literature, one would conclude that in any class of social (group) systems in which there are clear differences between members and non-members (prerequisite 4), cyclic changes should occur in the sense that each separate social group or structure only has a limited lifespan, which lifespan is inversely proportional to the effectiveness of the selection pressure in favour of compliance within the (group) structure. The separate lifecycles are then separated by turnover catastrophes which go by various names, depending on the level of organization: territorial conquest, close-down, discontinuance, bankruptcy, revolution, subjugation, extermination, genocide. etc.

In the literature on animal ecology and population dynamics the research data on population explosions and emigration waves at more or less regular time intervals are renowned (see e.g., Christian, 1970, on various species of lemmings, mice and voles). Whereas Christian points to the importance of these periodic changes in density and migration activity for evolution, the proximal causation of these conspicuous phenomena has, up to this moment, not yet been explained satisfactorily. It will be clear that the present model constitutes, among other things, an attempt to fill this gap.

Turning to man, we can, in the psychological literature, find many comments referring to the relevance of the discussed personality dimensions (and the selection thereupon) for the way our human society is run, including data on the selective processes involved (see also, apart from the authors quoted here, Snow, 1961; Etzioni, 1964; Weick, 1969; Tiger, 1987). Milgram, on the first page of his book on the compliance of people in situations where obedience and conformity conflict with ethics and sympathy, states:

> Obedience is the psychological mechanism that links individual action to political purpose. It is the dispositional cement that binds men to systems of authority. Facts of recent history and observation in daily life suggest that for many people obedience may be a deeply ingrained behaviour tendency, indeed, a prepotent impulse overriding training in ethics, sympathy, and moral conduct.
>
> (Milgram, 1974: 1)

This dependence of strongly repressive systems on a strong and dependable compliance of its employees and 'agents', explains what is often considered a paradox in the literature on holocausts like e.g., in 'das Dritte Reich', namely that, surprisingly, the people who were in charge of the extermination machinery quite generally appeared to be extremely docile, middle-class, adapted, morally rigid and reliable house-fathers and exemplary husbands, with an aversion to adventure and violence. As shall be clear from the present theory, this is the only type of person – the highly compliant, non-innovative, non-self-willed adaptor – that can be relied upon to carry through orders ('Befehl ist Befehl!') in situations where obedience strongly conflicts with morals and ethics. Under such extreme circumstances the selection pressure on personality characteristics is therefore also extreme, the not-extremely-compliant individuals trying to avoid such ghastly 'responsibilities' (see e.g., van der Dennen, 1987). As Koestler eloquently stated:

> It is not the murderers, the criminals, the delinquents and the wildly nonconformists who have embarked on the really significant rampages of killing, torture and mayhem. Rather it is the conformist, virtuous citizens, acting in the name of righteous causes and intensely held beliefs who throughout history have perpetrated the fiery holocausts of war, the religious persecutions, the sacks of cities, the wholesale rape of women, the dismemberment of the old and the young and the other unspeakable horrors. ... The crimes of violence committed for selfish, personal motives are historically insignificant compared to those committed '*ad majorem gloriam Dei*', out of a self-sacrificing devotion to flag, a leader, a religious faith, or a political conviction.
>
> (Koestler, 1967)

It should be stressed here that this tendency towards obedience and conformity is not the exclusive domain of adaptors. It is a general

159

human characteristic. In fact, it is an undispensable basic characteristic of any social mammal. It is the glue that keeps individuals together in social structures. The difference between adaptors and innovators is a relative one. Adaptors are more often willing to pay the price of giving up personal urges and convictions in favour of social coherence and compliance with authority, whereas innovators are more often prepared to pay the price of social isolation for not giving up personal convictions and desires (note that Adaption–Innovation is a continuum).

Milgram labels the compliant, subordinate style of functioning the 'agentic mode', which expresses that somebody in that mode functions as the 'agent' of some (personal or impersonal) authority. He points out that individuals tend to function in any one situation in either this mode or in its opposite, the 'autonomous mode'. Milgram explains that the readiness to shift from the 'agentic mode' into the 'autonomous mode' in certain conflict situations differs considerably between adults, and that people differ in the amount of time they spend in either 'mode'.

This discontinuity in the way antagonistic social modes of functioning reverse into each other, is also highlighted by the phenomenological work of Apter and co-workers on 'reversal theory' (Apter, 1982 Ch. 9; 1983; Apter and Smith, 1976; 1985; Lachenicht, 1985). They label these antagonist meta-motivational modes of functioning as the 'negativistic' and the 'conformist' state. Apter defines:

> When high arousal is associated with the negativistic state in the telic (goal-directed, need-motivated, reactive) mode, then the emotion experienced is likely to be that of anger. Indeed, it would appear that it is the operation of the negativistic state which transforms anxiety into anger. Anything which increases the arousal at such a time, e.g., frustration, will also increase the intensity of the anger experience. . . . Negativism in an individual always involves three related components in his or her phenomenal field. The first consists of some other individual, or some social group or situation, which is perceived as exerting some pressure on him or her. This can be called the 'source'. The second component consists of some perceived expectation, norm, convention, suggestion, request, requirement, rule, law, command, order, injunction, prohibition, threat or dictate, deriving from the source. . . . The third component is a feeling on the part of the individual who perceives the requirement (etc.) and the source, as a desire or need to reject it and act against it. . . . Put at its simplest, then, the feeling

160

of being in a negativistic state can be defined as 'wanting, or feeling compelled, to do something contrary to that required by some external agency'. The conformist state can be defined most simply as the absence of this feeling.

(Apter 1982: 198)

Since individuals tend to reverse from one meta-motivational state into the other in a discrete, all-or-none way, as was also shown by Milgram, negativist/conformist differences between individuals should not so much be regarded as differences in the 'degree' of conformism with which individuals generally operate in their social environment, but rather as differences in the relative frequencies of the antagonist meta-motivational states, *viz.* the relative frequency of the 'conformist' versus the 'negativist', or, in Milgram's terms, the 'agentic' versus the 'autonomous' state. It is in these frequent or less frequent instances of negativistic states, with all the possibilities of social friction and evoked conflicts involved, that the selective forces exert their systematic pressure.

The differences between individuals in their tendencies either to comply with social standards most of the time, or to act autonomously and independently most of the time, are also important for the way in which bureaucratic structures and other social institutions are run. Kirton elaborates

the 'adaptor' personality . . . who can be relied upon to carry out a thorough, disciplined search for ways to eliminate problems by 'doing things better' with a minimum of risk and a maximum of continuity and stability. . . . whereas . . . innovative change . . . leads to increased risk and less conformity to rules and accepted work patterns (Bright, 1964), and for this reason it rarely occurs in institutions on a large scale (Kirton 1978c: 611).

It is said that organisations in general (Whyte, 1957; Bakke, 1965; Weber, 1970; Mulkay, 1972) and especially organisations which are large in size and budget (Veblen, 1928; Swatez, 1970) have a tendency to encourage bureaucracy and adaption in order to minimise risk. Weber (1970), Merton (1957) and Parsons (1951) wrote that the aims of a bureaucratic structure are precision, reliability, and efficiency. The bureaucratic structure in its nature exerts constant pressure on officials to be methodical, prudent, and disciplined, resulting in an unusual degree of individual conformity in that situation.

(Kirton, 1987c: 284)

Therefore institutions tend to become more adaptor-orientated as time goes on (see Chapter 3) because a selection pressure is continuously exerted against innovators. Hayward and Everett (1983) found empirically that in the case of an adaptive cognitive climate, innovators are more likely to resign than adaptors, which consolidates and strengthens the adaptive climate. But the present model goes even further and predicts also that in the case of an innovative cognitive climate the average level of innovativeness of individuals coming into and staying in the organization will tend to be a little lower than the current general average, which causes the cognitive climate gradually to shift towards adaptiveness. This is not to deny that in general there is a selection pressure in the direction of the existing cognitive climate, it just means that there must also be another overall selection pressure in the direction of more adaptiveness. In other words, a slight deviance from the average cognitive climate in the adaptive direction should be more acceptable to the established in-crowd than a slight deviance in the innovative direction. One of the reasons for the latter effect is the innovator's lower level of social skills. Even when an innovator finds badly needed novel solutions for pressing problems, it will often fail to render him social approval, because of inherent (sometimes insurmountable) communication problems with his more adaption-orientated colleagues (Kirton, 1987a).[1]

Instead of winning social approval when coming up with the badly needed novel solutions for pressing problems, the innovator rather experiences that tolerance for his innovative style of approach is at its lowest ebb when his adaptor-type colleagues feel under pressure from the need for quick and consensually accepted change (Kirton, 1987c). Even when the novel solutions in question are accepted, it does not generally lead to a suspension of the above-discussed selective forces. In an empirical study to investigate the ways by which ideas, which had led to radical changes in some companies, were developed and implemented, Kirton found that:

> There was a marked tendency for the majority of ideas which encountered opposition and delays to have been put forward by managers who were themselves on the fringe, or were even unacceptable to the 'establishment' group. This negativism occurred not only before, but after the ideas had not only become accepted, but had even been rated as highly successful. At the same time other managers putting forward the more palatable (i.e., conventional) ideas were themselves not only initially acceptable, but remained so even if their ideas were later rejected or failed.
>
> (Kirton 1984)

It can thus be seen how the failure of ideas is less damaging to the adaptor than to the innovator, since any erroneous assumptions upon which the ideas were based were also shared with colleagues and other influential people (Kirton, 1984).

PARADIGM CONSISTENCY, COGNITIVE BIASES AND OSSIFICATION

This relative advantage for adaptors in terms of social selection pressures can even more easily be understood if we take into account the fact that adaptors and innovators are also different in their cognitive functioning. As Kirton showed (1985), innovators are more inclined towards consistency between (as distinct from within) paradigms than are adaptors. Adaptors are more likely to use different paradigms at different times, bothering less with their mutual inconsistency, in particular if the use of such different and incompatible paradigms is in line with local habits and expectations.

For instance, it is no problem for many people to go to church on Sundays in snug conviction of their own good Christian faith, while behaving in a rather unchristian fashion during the rest of the week. This results in a conflict of conscience, because nobody is totally indifferent to the contradiction between his Sunday's creeds and his daily deeds. The adaptors have to pay a price for their adherence to consensus and their wish to stick to established but mutually incompatible paradigms for different situations. In order to avoid too much cognitive dissonance, they have to keep the paradigms functionally well separated and thus the situations in which each one is applied. As a consequence they also have to accept a lower overall level of rationality. In terms of cognitive logic, adaptors tend towards applying 'sufficiency-orientated' paradigms with an empirical *ad hoc* character in contrast to the bent of the typical innovator for 'necessity-orientated' paradigms with a more general and broad causal validity.

The consequence of the innovator's need for consistency between paradigms is that he appears of necessity less rigidly committed to any one separate paradigm. He will sooner start to explore its limits and reconsider its validity (see Goldsmith and Matherley (1986b) for example). Since his concern is primarily with mutual consistency, he is less concerned with minor details. He will rather squeeze at least one paradigm a bit to make more paradigms fit together into one new encompassing model than have to accept a multitude of different paradigms for different occasions. But his preference for few novel encompassing models above many established models of limited scope, no matter the unavoidable initial lack of sufficient detail of the new paradigms, brings with it the social risk of being regarded a heretic by colleagues. By this cognitive bias the typical innovator is likely to run into trouble with at least three different categories of people.

First, he will clash with supporters of each separate established classical paradigm which he tries to incorporate in his novel grand design, and these supporters are likely to be a majority. Second, he will clash with anybody who is slow at accepting new ideas – typical adaptors fit into the category, but also anybody feeling too insecure to let go of the anchorage of fixed old ideas and beliefs. In itself, this category is also likely to be a majority. Third, standing out by his deviant points of view, he is, as pointed out in the section on ethological and endocrinological data, likely to be sought out by people who are on the look-out for scapegoats.

All in all, the innovator is apt to run into social trouble just because he is trying to solve his personal paradigm inconsistencies, let alone the rest of his less-appreciated behavioural predilections. Little wonder then that the innovator, on average, is unlikely to beat the adaptor within the system, be it science (Kuhn, 1970) or organization (Whyte, 1957).

As a consequence of this continuous selection pressure, discussed in the previous two sections, ageing institutions suffer in the end from the disadvantages of not having innovator-type creative input available in times of change when policy and methods are required to change as well. Such necessary changes are therefore often brought about only when a 'precipitating event', or a crisis, occurs when at last the adaptor needs, and so collaborates with, the innovator (Kirton, 1961). Therefore,

> although the adaptor clearly has qualities essential to any institution, he should not be the only type to be rewarded by promotion. Despite the fact that the innovator has weaknesses – he is erratic, insensitive to the needs of others, impatient, and a risk-taker – which are potentially dangerous to an organization, he also has qualities essential to that organization.
>
> (Kirton, 1978c: 661)

Scientific research is one of the areas where the effects of the selective forces as discussed earlier can clearly be recognized. The very goal of scientific research is to find ever better conceptual and instrumental frameworks. But, as Kuhn (1970) points out, changing the paradigms that are hitherto accepted without question by an entire scientific community requires a breakdown of previously accepted rules. Such breakdowns are the very process of scientific revolution and this revolutionary process is also fundamental to scientific advance.

In scientific institutions, the innovator-type input is therefore not only needed in rarely occurring times of change, but very regularly, since 'precipitating events' or conceptual crises are the very thing that scientific efforts are supposed to be aimed at. Some ageing institutions, like production or administrative units, that have an unconscious adaptive bias in selection and in promotion policies may initially not be very disadvantaged. For as long as no drastic external challenges turn up, they can go on producing their output ever more efficiently with excellent results. But in ageing research units it is eventually disastrous if the 'cognitive climate' becomes more and more adaptor-orientated. The innovator-type creative output, consisting of (often disquieting) conceptual challenges and explorations of the unknown and 'unthought', will in that case gradually be replaced by adaptor-type output consisting of residual puzzle solving and intra-paradigm discoveries with lesser conceptual threat. After an initially fruitful phase of consolidation, the prevailing paradigms will become overpowerful. It is clear that in a government-protected scientific community, even more than in government-protected industrial companies, competition does not operate freely. On the contrary, the scientific community tends to be controlled by people whose career and existence depend on the dominant paradigms and who, as a consequence, are neither able nor willing to view the world and its phenomena in a different way. This may postpone organization-structural turnover considerably, and thus the timely rejuvenation and deossifications science continually needs; eventually catastrophe intervenes. Oddly, until then, efficiency predominates.

SOCIAL ROLE BLINDNESS

Apart from these specific ossification phenomena, many more areas in human society can be found where the effects of the selection mechanisms are manifest. These selection mechanisms are apparently operative in lower social mammals as well as in man. They must therefore be anchored quite solidly in the behavioural system. This is not surprising because this mechanism does indeed have considerable evolutionary advantages not only in animals, but, at least up to recent times, also in the case of man. As mentioned earlier, it facilitates speciation through genetic adaption to marginal habitats, helps in many species to overcome migratory bottlenecks, and even serves to motor the evolution of culture in the case of man. It seems, therefore, plausible that if, in the case of man, our superior capacity for learning plays a modifying role in these matters, that the organization of our intellectual capacities will have evolved in such a way as to enhance the occurrence of selection cycles, rather than to thwart them. The mechanism of selection cycles and periodic turnover catastrophes is basically powered by the involuntary forces of attraction and repulsion within social groups and structures. Therefore it must have been evolutionarily advantageous for behavioural and cognitive 'master-programmes' to develop, serving to prevent the intellectual capacities from interfering with the involuntary biases in social interactions.

As we shall see, this is indeed what can be found. Generally speaking, people are quite well able to assess their own as well as other people's basic behavioural tendencies and personality characteristics. People are found to be quite proficient in the utilization of personality descriptive adjectives and other personality descriptive language (Norman, 1963; Goldberg, 1978; Brokken, 1978; de Raad, 1985). From an evolutionary point of view this ability is not surprising. After all, it is extremely important for us, as a socially living and intelligent mammal species, to predict other people's actions correctly. People are for instance quite well able to estimate their own and other's relative position on the adaptor–innovator dimension accurately (Kirton and McCarthy, 1985).

Knowing this, one would suggest that it should be even easier to assess one's own and other people's characteristics at the level of overt social behaviour, and still easier to evaluate objectively and reliably one's own and other's social actions in hindsight. This, however, is contrary to what is found. Human beings appear to be peculiarly unable to assess objectively the quality of their own social role behaviour and the role behaviour of other people they are dealing with in the social group. There is, it appears, a sort of 'social role blindness', of specific blind spots in our cognitive capacities, safeguarding primitive, elementary tenden-cies of being either attracted or repulsed by other people, depending on their own and on the other's social role and position. As in the experi-ments with mice described earlier, the omega-like subordinates, the peripheral non-conforming types, are also in humans most likely to be disliked by the established leaders as well as by the conforming and compliant other subordinates. This is of course a tautological statement, since drifting into a marginal or an outcast position (omega-type in Figure 6), is just another way of saying that one is less acceptable to, and less accepting of, the in-group as Lindsay's (1985) KAI case study shows.

What is important to note here, however, is that human individuals are hardly aware that the way they assess the other person's qualities is to a large extent coloured by their positive or negative feelings towards that other person, resulting from the involuntary forces of attraction and repulsion in operation. A considerable part of human communication consists not of transferring pure information, but of more or less involuntary emotional expressions of praise, admiration, criticism, ridicule and insults, as is shown for instance in the ethological work of Weisfeld (1980) on social role behaviour in adolescent boys, or in the sociological investigations by Segerstrale (1986) into the Wilson–Lewontin 'scientific' debate as part of the sociobiological controversy. To a large extent the use of language serves to support or to camouflage non-verbal actions, actions for manipulating other people and for staking out and sustaining social roles (Scheflen and Scheflen, 1972; Mehrabian, 1972; Argyle, 1976a; 1976b).

In fact analytic research on the social interactions between people, the first and by far the largest principal component, is in general the so-called 'evaluation–' or 'positive–negative dimension', describing to what extent one appreciates or disappreciates the rated other. In questionnaire research where elucidation of the actual social behavioural attitudes and social-role distributions is the primary goal, the raw data are therefore in general first 'corrected' for the 'positive–negative evaluation' or 'social desirability' dimension by partialling out its influence (Smith-Benjamin, 1974: 419). Raters colour their judgements with 'appreciation' or 'disapproval' to indicate, 'explain' and consolidate the social relations between themselves and the rated person (e.g., Kipnis, 1976: Ch. 9).

The importance of this negative or positive bias in the way we think about our companions is also expressed in the fact that most behavioural attitudes and personality characteristics can be expressed in positive as well as in negative terms, giving us virtually a double set of conceptual labels for other people's actions and behavioural attitudes. This cumbersome and at first sight inefficient cognitive organization, in which the pure assessment of other people's behavioural qualities is blurred to a great extent by the strong involuntary bias of 'appreciation' or 'disappreciation', can only be evolutionarily advantageous if it serves an essential purpose. This purpose may be the protection of the involuntary attraction and repulsion reflexes, which direct our social behaviour, against our intelligent faculties. Indeed, people do not generally realize that their, say, negative labelling of (the behaviour of) an important other, can easily be changed into its positive counterpart by simply regarding the same behaviour from the point of view of a supporter, and vice versa. They tend instead to attach a sense of permanence and absoluteness to their (negative) judgement, and they are in particular not aware of the relativity of the judgement in terms of its dependence on the mutual social positions of the rater and the ratee.

In summary, the postulated blind spots and 'no entry' signs in our intellectual faculties apparently do indeed exist. Despite our vaunted intellect and our protestations of rational and scientific know-how, we humans show a disturbing tendency to reserve our intellectual powers strictly for certain specific tasks. In other specific areas of functioning, like the mechanisms of social attraction and repulsion mentioned above, we tend to rely on intuitive biases while allowing the intellectual faculties to be effectively blocked.

The result of these cognitive biases is that, in many instances, we cannot help to foster involuntarily a lower esteem for other persons if they happen to be less 'in-crowd' than ourselves. And in more extreme cases, we cannot help tending to join others in 'mobbing' or in 'scapegoating'. We tend to justify the actions taken through our (biased) evaluations of the outcast's or scapegoat's qualities, attitudes and behaviour (unless we incidentally happen to be one of the outcast's supporters). Being in the 'agentic' or 'systemic' (Milgram, 1974) or 'compliant' (Apter and Smith, 1976; 1985) motivational mode while dealing with a victim, we involuntarily tend to see the person in question to a larger or lesser extent as inferior, or even repulsive, detestable or evil. This tendency is so powerful it is considered the behavioural basis of torture by Amnesty International (1973).

We cannot help hating our (self-created) enemies and we cannot help loving, primarily, those individuals whom the selection cycle mechanism urges us to appreciate. On the level of the behaviour of managers, for instance, this can be illustrated by the findings of Kirton:

> Problems of fruitful collaboration between innovators and adaptors are not infrequently based on the coloured and often inaccurate perceptions which each group has of the other. Innovators tend to be seen by adaptors as abrasive, insensitive and disruptive, unaware of the havoc they are causing. Adaptors are seen by innovators, on the other hand, as stuffy and unenterprising, wedded to systems, rules and norms of behaviour which (in the opinion of the innovators) are restrictive and ineffectual. Consequently, disagreement and conflict are likely to arise when the more extreme types of innovator and adaptor come into working contact. . . . When the extreme types view each other pejoratively (as they tend to do – see also Myers 1962: 76) the innovator claims that the adaptor originates with a finger on the stop button; the adaptor sees the innovator as an originator who cannot find such a button.
>
> (Kirton 1987c: 284)

168

When it comes to evaluating the contributions of adaptors versus those of innovators, the effect of systematic evaluative distortions becomes even more apparent. Kirton points out that when ideas fail, initiators who are adaptors are less likely to be blamed than those who are innovators, since the former share with the establishment the same set of basic assumptions. To condemn them would be, in the eyes of the establishment, to condemn themselves. As a consequence, such failure is likely to be written off as 'bad luck' or due to 'unforeseeable events', thereby directing the blame away from the individuals concerned. The opposite is found for the authors of innovative ideas, ideas that depart from and may even challenge the beliefs, values and practices of the group. They tend to be viewed with suspicion, and may be subjected to derision, and such rejection or virtual hostility may very well persist even after those ideas have been shown to be successful. Nonconformists are not forgiven for being right. Authors of adaptive ideas, being themselves in most cases adaptors, generally appear to be in a relationship of mutual admiration with the establishment, which leads those managers of the opposite turn of mind – the innovators – to assert that adaptors owe their success to and maintain their position simply by agreeing with their superiors. Kirton (1977) showed, however, that such opinions are not supported by empirical evidence. They are part of the systematic cognitive distortions, in this case cherished by the typical innovators.

NATURE AND NURTURE

It could be argued that, at least in man, social structure cycles with their turnover catastrophes might occur merely because of mechanisms on the cognitive psychological level. In that case one would not need to postulate a genetic background for these gradual shifts in social structures to occur. Indeed, as we saw above, social role blindness and related cognitive biases are a very powerful influence in man. Moreover, we can also find a wealth of empirical and experimental data on the various constraints on learning in man, on habit forming, traditions and the transfer of cultural information, on perceptual biases like the cognitive dissonance theory, etc., all showing that our behaviour is organized in such a way that a great inertia of ideas, concepts and habits is safeguarded in spite of our capacity to keep learning. These data would suggest that enough mechanisms at a purely cognitive and cultural level can be traced as to make social-structural cycles likely to occur. Indeed, the basic requirement for the postulated selection cycles is not so much that there is a genetic basis to it, but rather that individuals, once their phenotypes in these areas of functioning have established themselves, cannot be reshaped into their opposites. As we saw above, this inflexibility aspect, irrespective of its causes, has been firmly established by psychological research. Moreover, the evidence for genetic influence cannot be neglected. These mechanisms are therefore most probably implemented on the genetic as well as the learning level. That in man, the learning animal *par excellence*, the influence of learning will be important goes without saying.

Another, related, critique is the argument that where a multi-gene basis of these differences should be expected, a strong enough selection pressure and a quick selection response are difficult to imagine. However, no high mortality, or low fecundity or whatever on the part of the declining morph needs to be assumed at all. Basic to the model is rather the existence of differences between in-crowd and outcast individuals. No physical elimination whatsoever needs to be assumed to let the cycles run. The only thing that needs to be postulated is that the in-group/out-group and the in-crowd/outcast distribution of social roles and positions is subject to reshuffling. It depends on the level of organization we are talking about whether the postulate of a genetic effect needs to be included in a description of the cycles or not. In man this will, in my view, probably only be indispensable in the case of very long-term cycles on a very large scale. On most levels of human social structures, the individuals selected against just need to be shifted into outgroup or outcast positions, relative to the unit(s) of organization in question. The very presence of the removed individuals in the organizational periphery then represents the growing danger of a turnover catastrophe.

As was pointed out above, the duration of social-structural cycles is predicted to be roughly inversely proportional to speed and intensity of selection for the trait under discussion. In an industrial company the intensity of selection and the take-on/dismissal percentages are much higher than the selection intensity and the immigration/emigration percentages in the much larger units of political states, for instance. Therefore the average cycle periods are likely to vary from a few decades in companies (refer for illustrative material on cycles to Schumpeter, 1939; Kirton, 1961; 1976) or in political parties (Ostrogorski, 1982) to a few centuries in political states (Olson, 1982), or even to one or two millennia in the case of whole civilizations (for illustration refer to Spengler, 1918; Toynbee, 1972),[2] Darlington, 1969; Davis, 1974). The small-scale turnover cycles, with a relatively stronger and quicker selection effect, are thus superimposed on the larger-scale turnover cycles with a longer lifespan. Individuals may therefore be outcasts in terms of some small-scale social structure while at the same time being totally accepted 'in-crowd' members in terms of some larger-scale social structure. The small-scale cycles may thus be seen as the ripples on the surface of the long-range waves of the large-scale cycles. What happens with a person at the social role level of a sports club is not necessarily paralleled at the level of the village community or the nation.

This chapter has, however, argued that the sociological theory of a mechanism of cyclic changes and periodic turnover catastrophes is anchored firmly and intricately in our behavioural system, rooted in genetically based social patterns and protected against rational enquiry by specific awareness blocks. This leads to a rather gloomy perspective. A limited lifespan for industrial companies and other social organizations does seem natural, ending in their bankruptcy or takeover. In the case of animals, this natural course of events in social structures would seem inevitable. They can do nothing about their behavioural programme. The human case, however, is an altogether different matter. Man's saving grace is his unparalleled capacity to learn. Once a sufficient number of people succeed in gaining a clear understanding of these mechanisms and come to grips with them, the opportunity exists to mitigate these biological tendencies.

The aim to keep harvesting the benefits of the periodic widespread change to new and novel circumstances (which is progress), without suffering so much damage from catastrophe. (e.g., Weisbord, 1987) such as global economic slump or devastating war. Mankind as a whole has up to now been able to survive these self-induced disasters. But it must be worthwhile to search for ways to replace or short-circuit nature's hitherto applied selection tricks with which it powered our evolution, and to substitute alternative and less dangerous mechanisms for it. As Kirton (1987c) points out, individuals may acquire coping strategies, compensating for the set-backs, concomitant with their particular cognitive style. Similarly, society as a whole may learn to overcome the catastrophic events, concomitant with the unchecked progression of the cyclic social changes, if the mechanisms are better understood. This elaboration of Adaption–Innovation theory is admittedly still tentative, but its relevance for our very existence might urge us to search for further experimental evidence for or against it.

This elaboration contains several related parts. Initially Kirton's suggestion that Adaption–Innovation differences are set up early in an individual's life is taken up, and it is demonstrated that most probably they are innate and, certainly, basically not confined to man. Then the argument develops by reference to the already well-established research

171

on changes in animal groups. It highlights the gradual 'ageing' effect in social structures, leading to disastrous destabilization from intruding, less compliant individuals and groups, a situation paralleled in human institutions and described in earlier chapters. In short, the concept of individual preferred style to solve basic social problems has explanatory power in understanding group phenomena. Kirton and his associates have been concerned with the influence of these individual differences on industrial-type organizations but there is no apparent reason why the same influences should not bear on the state itself. Organizations, however large, can be affected by selection drift into adaption domination, first establishing 'evolutionary' -type change which is orderly, safe and largely acceptable, then gradually slowing the pace of that change. As the pace of change slows, the range of flexibility narrows closer to well-chosen, but 'ageing' paradigms, so the pressure for innovative change banks up until drastic 'revolutionary' -type catastrophe threatens discontinuous rupture of whole societies. What can be tolerated in small groups of social animals – however uncomfortable to the individual – cannot be readily accepted for whole swathes of mankind.

This chapter suggests that the same mitigating processes that aid individuals and small groups again applies on larger scales: insight through knowledge and a wide range of learnt, acceptable forms of coping behaviour may enable society to avoid catastrophic events.

NOTES

1 Since this chapter was written, further evidence has become available, e.g., Vicere, 1992; Buttner and Gryskiewicz, 1993.

2 Toynbee disagrees with what he calls Spengler's 'determinism'. Though Toynbee gives abundant material to illustrate the point made here, he emphasizes that one cannot convincingly speak of some or other pre-determined and fixed 'lifespan' of societies. The present theory would support Spengler's view. But it would also give room for something that Toynbee stresses, namely that, as far as their lifespan and their spin-off in terms of disseminative effect towards other societies is concerned, societies differ greatly from one another. According to the present theory, it very much depends on incidental environmental factors how effective selective emigration can be, and how strong the differential propagation within the structures themselves. And it depends on the actual presence of competing structures how quickly the effects of the internal selection processes will precipitate an eventual turnover catastrophe.

BIBLIOGRAPHY

Abrams, S. and Neubauer, P.B. (1976) 'Object orientedness: the person or the thing', *The Psychoanalytic Quarterly*, 45: 73–99.

Amabile, T.M. (1983) 'The social psychology of creativity: a componential conceptualization', *Journal of Personality and Social Psychology*, 45: 357–76.

Amnesty International (1973) Report on Torture, London.

Apter, M.J. (1982) *The Experience of Motivation*, London, New York, etc.: Academic Press.

Apter, M.J. (1983) 'Negativism and the sense of identity', in G. Breakwell (ed.), *Threatened Identities*, London: Wiley.

Apter, M.J. and Smith, K.C.P. (1976) 'Negativism in adolescence', *The Counsellor*, 23/24: 25–30.

Apter, M.J. and Smith, K.C.P. (1985) 'Experiencing personal relationships', in M.J. Apter, D. Fontana and S. Murgatroyd (eds) *Reversal Theory: Applications and Developments*, Cardiff, UK: University College Cardiff Press.

Argyle, M. (1976a; second edition 1987), *Bodily Communication*, London: Methuen.

Argyle, M. (1976b) 'Personality and social behaviour', in R. Harre (ed.), *Personality*, Oxford: Blackwell.

Ausubel, D.P. (1952) *Ego Maturation and the Personality Disorders*, New York: Grune & Stratton.

Bagozzi, R.P. and Foxall, R.G. (1993) 'Construct validity and generalizability of the Kirton Adaption–Innovation Inventory', working paper, Research Centre for Consumer Behaviour, University of Birmingham.

Baker, M.J. (1983) *Market Development*, Harmondsworth: Penguin Books.

Bakke, E.W. (1965) 'Concept of the social organization', in M. Haire (ed.), *Modern Organization Theory*, New York, Wiley.

Bales, R.F. (1953) *Interaction Process Analysis*, Reading, Mass.: Addison-Wesley.

Barash, D.P. (1977) *Sociobiology and Behaviour*, New York: Elsevier.

Barron, F. (1953) 'Complexity–simplicity as a personality dimension', *Journal of Abnormal and Social Psychology*, 48:163–72.

Beene, J.M. (1985) *Compatibility of Self-Actualization and Anxiety and the Relationship to Adaptors and Innovators*,. M.Sc thesis, The Graduate School of East Texas State University.

Beene, J.M. and Zelhart, P.F. (1986) *Factor Analysis of the Kirton Adaption–Innovation*

173

Inventory, Working paper, Department of Psychology, East Texas State University.

Bertrand, M. (1969) *Behavioural Repertoire of the Stumptail Macaque, Macaca Speciosa*, Basel: S. Karger AG.

Bieri, J., Atkins, A.L., Briar, S., Seaman, R.L., Miller, H. and Tripodi T. (1966) *Clinical and Social Judgements: the Discrimination of Behavioural Information*, New York: Wiley.

Billings, R.S., Klimoski, R.J. and Breaugh, J.A. (1977) 'The impact of a change of technology on job characteristics: a quasi-experiment', *Administrative Science Quarterly*, 22: 318–39.

Bowers, K.S. (1973) 'Situationism in psychology: an analysis and a critique', *Psychological Review*, 80: 307–36.

Boyatzis, R. (1982) *The Competent Manager*, New York: John Wiley & Sons.

Bray, B.W., Campbell, R.J. and Grant, D.L. (1974) *Formative Years in Business: A Long Term AT&T Study of Managerial Lives*, New York: John Wiley & Sons.

Brief, A.P. and Aldag, R.J. (1975) 'Employee reactions to job characteristics: a constructive replication', *Journal of Applied Psychology*, 60:182–6.

Bright, J.R. (1964) *Research, Development and Technological Innovation*, Homewood, Ill.: Irwen.

Brokken, F.B. (1978) *The Language of Personality*, thesis, State University Groningen.

Brunswick, E. (1956) *Perception and the Representative Design of Psychological Experiments*, Berkeley: University of California Press.

Budner, S. (1962) 'Intolerance of ambiguity as a personality variable', *Journal of Personality*, 30: 29–50.

Burns, T. and Stalker, G.M. (1961) *The Management of Innovation*, Tavistock, London.

Buss, A.H. and Plomin, R.A. (1975) *A Temperament Theory of Personality Development*, New York: Wiley.

Buss, A.H., Plomin, R. and Willerman, L. (1973) 'The inheritance of tempera-ments', *Journal of Personality*, 41:.513–52.

Buttner, E. Holly and Gryskiewicz, S.S. (1993) 'Entrepreneurs' problem solving styles: an empirical study using the Kirton Adaptation–Innovation Theory', *Journal of Small Business Management*, 31(1): 22–31.

Byrne, D. (1974) *An Introduction to Personality*, Englewood Cliffs, NJ: Prentice-Hall.

Calhoun, J.B. (1974) 'The universal city of ideas', presentation at a Conference on The Exploding Cities, held at Worcester College and the Taylor Institution, Oxford, 1–6 April 1974, Conference Transcripts 301–6.

Campbell, D.P. (1974) *Introversion Extraversion Scale*, Strong Campbell Interest Inventory, Stanford University California.

Campbell, D.T. and Fiske, D.W. (1959) 'Convergent and discriminant validation by the multitrait-multimethod matrix', *Psychological Bulletin*, 56: 81–105.

Carne, J.C. and Kirton, M.J. (1982) 'Styles of creativity: test score correlations between the Kirton Adaption–Innovation Inventory and the Myers–Briggs Type Indicator', *Psychological Reports*, 50: 31–6.

Casbolt, D. (1984) *The Effects of Idea Generation Technique, Problem Type and Creative Thinking Style on Individual Problem Solving Performance*, PhD thesis, University of Ohio.

Cattell, R.B. (1981) *Misurare l'Intelligenza con i Test Culture Fair*, Sirenze, Florence: Organizazzione Speciali.

Cattell, R.B., Eber, H.W. and Tatsouka, M.M. (1970) Handbook for the *Sixteen Personality Factor Questionnaire* 16PF, IPAT, Champaign, Ill.

Chance, M.R.A. and Jolly, C. (1970) *Social Groups of Monkeys, Apes and Men*, London: Cape.

Chapman, L.J. and Campbell, D.T. (1957) 'An attempt to predict the performance of three-man teams from attitude measures', *Journal of Social Psychology*, 46: 277–86.

Christian, J.J. (1970) 'Social subordination, population density and mammalian evolution', *Science*, 168: 84–90.

Clapp, R.G. (1991) 'The fate of ideas that stimulate change in a large organisation', PhD thesis, University of Hertfordshire.

Clapp, R.G. (1993) 'The stability of cognitive style in adults: a longitudinal study of the KAI', *Psychological Reports*, 73: 1235–45.

Clapp, R.G. and de Ciantis, S. (1987) 'The influence of organisational climate on the relationship between cognitive style and observed behaviour', working paper, Occupational Research Centre, Hatfield Polytechnic.

Clapp, R.G. and Kirton, M.J. (1994) 'The relationship between cognitive style and psychological climate: some comments on the article by Isaksen and Kaufmann', *Studia Psychologica*, in press.

Claridge, G.A., Canter, S. and Hume, W.J. (1973) *Personality Differences and Biological Variations: A Study of Twins*, New York: Pergamon Press.

Cloninger, C.R. (1986) 'A unified biosocial theory of personality and its role in the development of anxiety states', *Psychiatric Development*, 3: 167–226.

Cloninger, C.R. (1987) 'A systematic method for clinical description and classification of personality variants', *Archives of General Psychiatry*, 44: 573–88.

COMA, (Committee on Medical Aspects of Food Policy) (1984) *Diet and Cardiovascular Disease*, Department of Health and Social Security Report No. 28, London: HMSO.

Cooper, R. and Foster, M. (1971) 'Sociotechnical systems', *American Psychologist*, 26: 467–74.

Coser, L.A. (1956) *The Functions of Social Conflict*, New York: Free Press.

Coser, L.A. (1968) *Gulzige Institutes: Patronen van Absolute Toewijding*, Deventer: van Loghum Slaterus, translation of Greedy Institutions, 1974.

Crockett, W.H. (1965) 'Cognitive complexity and impression formation', in D.A. Maher (ed.) *Progress in Experimental Personality Research* (Vol. 2) New York: Academic Press.

Cronbach, L.J. and Meehl, P.E. (1955) 'Construct validity in psychological tests', *Psychological Bulletin*, 52: 281–302.

Crowne, D. and Marlowe, D. (1964) *The Approval Motive*, New York: Wiley.

Csikszentmihály, M. (1990) 'The domain of creativity' in M.A. Runco and R.S. Albert (eds) *Theories of Creativity*, New York: Sage.

Darlington, C.D. (1969) *The Evolution of Man and Society*, London: Allen & Unwin.

Darlington, Jr., P.J. (1957) *Zoogeography: The Geographical Distribution of Animals*, New York: Wiley.

Davidson, M.J. (1982) *Occupational Stress in Female Managers*, PhD thesis, UMIST.

Davis, K. (1974) 'The migrations of human populations', *Scientific American*, 231(3): 93–105.

de Ciantis, S.M. (1987) *The Relationships Between Leadership Style, Cognitive Style and*

Learning Style: An Exposition of Management Style Dimensions. PhD thesis, University of Hertfordshire.

de Ciantis, S.M. and Kirton, M.J. (1994) 'A psychometric re-examination of Kolb's experiential learning cycle construct: a separation of level, style and process', *Journal of Educational and Psychological Measurement* (in press).

Dennis, D.M. (1973) 'Predicting full-scale WAIS IQ's with the Shipley', *Journal of Clinical Psychology*, 29: 366–8.

de Raad, B. (1985) 'Person-talk in everyday life: pragmatics of utterances about personality', thesis, State University Groningen, Netherlands.

Dershimer, E.L. (1980) *Study to Identify the Characteristics of Teachers Willing to Implement Computer Based Instruction using Microcomputers in the Classroom.* EdD thesis, Memphis State University.

Dewan, S. (1982) *Personality Characteristics of Entrepreneurs*, PhD thesis, Institute of Technology, Delhi.

Donnelly, J.H. and Etzel, M.J. (1973) 'Degrees of product newness and early trial', *Journal of Marketing Research*, 10: 295–300.

Donnelly, J.H. and Ivancevich, J.M. (1974) 'A methodology for identifying innovator characteristics of new brand purchasers', *Journal of Marketing Research*, XI (August): 331–4.

Drucker, P.F. (1969) 'Management's new role', *Harvard Business Review*, 47: 49–54.

Eaves, L. and Eysenck, H.J. (1975) 'The nature of extraversion: a genetical analysis', *Journal of Personality and Social Psychology*, 32: 102–12.

Ekvall, G.A. and Waldenström-Lindbald, I. (1983) *Creative Organizational Climate: Construction and Validation of a Measuring Instrument*, Stockholm: The Swedish Council for Management and Organizational Behaviour.

Eisner, E.W. (1965) 'Children's creativity in art: a study of types', *American Educational Research Journal*, 2: 125–36.

Epstein, S. (1986) 'Does aggregation produce spuriously high estimates of behaviour stability?' *Journal of Personality and Social Psychology*, 50: 1199–210.

Epstein, S. and O'Brien, E.J. (1985) 'The person–situation debate in historical perspective', *Psychological Bulletin*, 98: 513–37.

Ettlie, J.E. and O'Keefe, R.D. (1982) 'Innovative attitudes, values and intentions in organizations', *Journal of Management Studies*, 19: 163–82.

Etzioni, A. (1964) *Modern Organizations*, in Foundation of Modern Sociology Series, A. Inkeles (ed.), New York: Prentice-Hall.

Ewer, R.F. (1971) 'The biology and behaviour of a free-living population of black rats (*rattus rattus*)', *Animal Behaviour Monographs*, 4(3): 127–74.

Eysenck, H.J. (1953) *The Structure of Human Personality*, London: Methuen.

Eysenck, H.J. (1967) *The Biological Basis of Personality*, Springfield: Thomas.

Eysenck, H.J. and Eysenck, S.B.G. (1964) *Manual of the Eysenck Personality Inventory*, London: University of London Press.

Feij, J.A. (1978) *Temperament: Onderzoek Naar de Betekenis van Extraversie, Emotionaliteit, Impulsiviteit en Sapnningsbehoefte*, Amsterdam: Academic Press.

Feij, J.A., Orlebeke, J.F., Gazendam, A. and van Zuilen, R. (1981) 'Sensation seeking: measurement and psychophysiological correlates', in J. Strelau, F.H. Farley, and A. Gale (eds) *Biological Foundation of Personality and Behaviour*, New York: Hemisphere Press.

Feshbach, S. (1978) 'The environment of personality', *American Psychologist*, 33: 447–55.

Forbes, J.B. (1975), 'The relationship between management styles and functional specialization', *Group and Organizational Studies*, 10: 95–111.

Fossey, D. (1972) 'Living with mountain gorrillas', in R.P. Marler (ed.), *The Marvels of Animal Behaviour*, Washington DC: National Geographic Society.

Foxall, G.R. (1984) *Corporate Innovation*, London: Routledge.

Foxall, G.R. (1986a) 'Managers in transition: an empirical test of Kirton's Adaption–Innovation theory and its implication of mid-career MBA', *Technovation*, 4: 219–32.

Foxall, G.R. (1986b), 'Managerial orientations of adaptors and innovators', *Journal of Managerial Psychology*, 1: 24–7.

Foxall, G.R. (1988) 'Consumer innovativeness: creativity, novelty-seeking and cognitive style', in E.C. Hirschman and J.N. Sheth (eds) *Research in Consumer Behaviour*, 3: 79–113.

Foxall, G.R. (1989) 'Adaptive and innovative cognitive styles of market initiators', in M.J. Kirton (ed.) *Innovators and Adaptors* (1st edn), London and New York: Routledge, 125–57.

Foxall, G.R. (1994) 'Consumer initiators: both adaptors and innovators', *British Journal of Management*, 5(2).

Foxall, G.R. and Bhate, S. (1991) 'Cognitive style, personal involvement and situation as determinants of computer use', *Technovation*, 11: 183–200.

Foxall, G.R. and Bhate, S. (1993a) 'Cognitive styles and personal involvement of market initiators', *Journal of Economic Psychology*, 14: 33–56.

Foxall, G.R. and Bhate, S. (1993b) 'Cognitive styles of use-innovators for home computing software applications: implications for new product strategy', *Technovation*, 13: 311–23.

Foxall, G.R. and Bhate, S. (1993c) 'Cognitive style and personal involvement as explicators of innovative purchasing of "healthy" food brands', *European Journal of Marketing*, 27(2): 5–16.

Foxall, G.R. and Bhate, S. (1994) *How Task Orientation and Individual Differences Influence Computer Utilization: the Effects of Cognitive Style and Personal Involvement in Three Situational Contexts*, report by the Research Centre for Consumer Behaviour, University of Birmingham.

Foxall, G.R. and Goldsmith, R.E. (1988) 'Personality and consumer choice: another look', *Journal of the Market Research Society*, 30: 111–29.

Foxall, G.R. and Goldsmith, R.E. (1994) *Consumer Psychology for Marketing*, London and New York: Routledge.

Foxall, G.R. and Hackett, P. (1992a) 'The factor structure and construct validity of the Kirton Adaption–Innovation Inventory', *Personality and Individual Differences*, 13: 967–75.

Foxall, G.R. and Hackett, P. (1992b) 'Cognitive style and extent of computer use in organizations', *Perceptual and Motor Skills*, 74: 491–97.

Foxall, G.R. and Haskins, C.G. (1986) 'Cognitive style and consumer innovativeness on empirical test of Kirton's Adaption–Innovation theory in the context of food purchasing', *European Journal of Marketing*, 20: 63–80.

Foxall, G.R. and Haskins, C.G. (1987) 'Cognitive style and discontinuous consumption: the case of "Healthy Eating"', *Food Marketing*, 3(2): 19–32.

French, J.R.P., Rodgers, W. and Cobb, S. (1974), 'Adjustment as person-environment fit', in G.V. Coehlo and D.A. Hamburg (eds), *Coping and Adaption*, New York: Basic Books.

Gardner, H. (1983) *Frames of Mind: The Theory of Multiple Intelligences*, Basic Books: New York.

Gatignon, H. and Robertson, T.S. (1991) 'Innovative decision processes', in T.S. Robertson and H.H. Kassarjian (eds) *Handbook of Consumer Behavior*, Englewood Cliffs, NJ: Prentice-Hall, 316–46.

Geen, R.G. (1976) *Personality: The Skein of Behavior*, Saint Louis: C.V. Mosby.

Gershon, A. and Guilford, J.P. (1963) *Possible Jobs: Scoring Guide*. Orange, CA: Sheridan Psychological Services.

Getzels, J.W. and Jackson, P.W. (1962) *Creativity and Intelligence: Explorations with Gifted Students*, New York: Wiley.

Gibb, C.A. (1969) 'Leadership', in G. Lindzey and E. Aranson (eds), *Handbook of Social Psychology*, Reading, Mass.: Addison-Wesley.

Girard, R. (1982) *Le Bouc Emissaire*, Paris: Bernard Grasset.

Goldberg, L.R. (1978) 'Attribution of trait-descriptive terms to oneself as compared to well liked, neutral and disliked others', *Journal of Personality and Social Psychology*, 36: 1012–28.

Goldsmith, R.E. (1983) *Dimensions of Consumer Innovativeness: An Empirical Study of Open Processing*, PhD dissertation, University of Alabama.

Goldsmith, R.E. (1984) 'Personality characteristics associated with adaption–innovation', *Journal of Psychology*, 117: 159–65.

Goldsmith, R.E. (1985) 'A factorial composition of the KAI Inventory', *Educational and Psychological Measurement*, 45: 245–50

Goldsmith, R.E. (1986a) 'Convergent validity of four innovativeness scales', *Educational and Psychological Measurement*, 46: 81–7.

Goldsmith, R.E. (1986b) 'Adaption–innovation and cognitive complexity', *Journal of Psychology*, 119: 461–7.

Goldsmith, R.E. (1986c) 'Personality and adaptive–innovative problem solving', *Journal of Personality and Social Behaviour*, 1: 95–106.

Goldsmith, R. E. and Matherley, T. A. (1986a) 'The Kirton Adaption–Innovation Inventory, faking and social desirability. A replication and extension', *Psychological Reports*, 58: 269–70.

Goldsmith, R.E. and Matherley, T.A. (1986b) 'Seeking simple solutions: assimilators and explorers, adaptors and innovators', *Journal of Psychology*, 120: 149–55.

Goldsmith, R.E. and Matherley, T.A. (1987a) 'Adaption–innovation and creativity. A replication and extension', *British Journal of Social Psychololgy*, 120: 149–55.

Goldsmith, R. E. and Matherley, T. A. (1987b) 'Adaption–innovation and self-esteem', *Journal of Psychology*, 127: 351–2.

Goldsmith, R.E., Matherley, T.A., and Wheatley, W.J. (1986) 'Yeasaying and the Kirton Adaption–Innovation Inventory', *Educational and Psychological Measurement*, 36: 433–6.

Goldstein, K.M. and Blackman, S. (1978) *Cognitive Style: Five Approaches and Relevant Research*, New York: Wiley.

Goldstein, K.M. and Blackman, S. (1981) 'Cognitive styles in personality', in F. Fransella (ed.), *Theory Measurement and Research*, London: Methuen.

Goodenough, D.R. (1985) 'Styles of cognitive-personality functioning', in H.J. Bernardin and D.A. Bownas (eds), *Personality Assessment in Organizations*, New York: Praeger.

Gough, H.G. (1956 and 1975) *California Psychological Inventory*, Palo Alto, Calif.: Consulting Psychologists' Press.

Gryskiewicz, S.S. (1982) 'The Kirton Adaption–Innovation Inventory in Creative Leadership Development', invited paper for the occupational psychology conference of the British Psychological Society, Sussex University.

Gryskiewicz, S.S., Hills, D.W., Holt, K. and Hills, K. (1987) *Understanding Managerial Creativity: The Kirton Adaption–Innovation Inventory and Other Assessment Measures*, Greensboro, NC: Center for Creative Leadership.

Guilford, J.P. (1950) 'Creativity', *American Psychologist*, 5: 444–54.

Guilford, J.P. (1967) *The Nature of Human Intelligence*, New York: McGraw-Hill.

Guilford, J.P. (1969) *Seeing problems: Manual for Administration and Interpretation*, Orange, CA: Sheridan Psychological Services.

Guilford, J.P. (1980) 'Cognitive styles: What are they?' *Educational and Psychological Measurement*, 40: 715–35.

Gul, F.A. (1986) 'Differences between adaptors and innovators attending accountancy courses on their preferences in work and curricula', *Journal of Accounting Education*, 4: 203–9.

Hackman, J.R. and Lawler, E.E. III (1971), 'Employee reactions to job characteristics', *Journal of Applied Psychology Monograph*, 55: 259–86.

Hackman, J.R. and Oldham, G.R. (1975) 'Developments of the job diagnostic survey', *Journal of Applied Psychology*, 60: 159–70.

Hackman, J.R. and Oldham, G.R. (1976) 'Motivation through the design of work: test of a theory', *Organizational and Human Performance*, 16: 250–79.

Hage, J. and Dewar, R. (1973) 'Elite values versus organizational structure predicting innovation', *Administrative Science Quarterly*, 18: 279–90.

Halpin, A.W. and Winer, B.J. (1957) 'A factorial study of the leader behavior descriptions', in R.M. Stagdill and A.E. Coons (eds), *Leader Behavior: Its Description and Measurement*, Bur. Bus. Res. Monogr. 88 Columbus: Ohio State University.

Hammerschmidt, P. and Jennings, A.C. (1993) 'The impact of personality characteristics on leadership effectiveness ratings', *Personality and Leadership Effectiveness*, 38: 469–75.

Hammond, S.M. (1986) 'Some pitfalls in the use of factor scores: the case of the Kirton Adaption–Innovation Inventory', *Personality and Individual Differences*, 7: 401–7.

Hannaway, J. (1985), 'Managerial behaviour, uncertainty and hierarchy: a prelude to a synthesis', *Human Relations*, 38:1085–100.

Hardin, E. (1967) 'Job satisfaction and desire for change', *Journal of Applied Psychology*, 51: 20–7.

Hayes, J. and Allinson, C.W. (1994) 'Cognitive style and its relevance for management practice', *British Journal of Management*, 5: 53–71.

Hayward, G. and Everett, C. (1983) 'Adaptors and innovators: data from the Kirton Adaption–Innovation Inventory in a local authority setting', *Journal of Occupational Psychology*, 56: 339–42.

Healey, M.C. (1967) 'Aggression and self-regulation of population size in deer-mice', *Ecology*, 48: 377–92.

Heller, F.A. (1976) 'Decision processes: an analysis of power sharing at senior organizational levels', in R. Dubin, (ed.), *Handbook of Work, Organization and Society*, Chicago: Rand McNally.

Hertz, M.R. (1946) *Frequency Tables to be Used in Scoring Responses to the Rorschach Ink Blot Test* (3rd ed.) Cleveland, OH: Western Reserve University.

Heymans, G. (1932) *Inleiding tot de Speciale Psychologie*, Haarlem: Bohn.

Hickson, D.J., Pugh, D.S. and Pheysey, D.C. (1969) 'Operations technology and organization structure: an empirical reappraisal', *Administrative Science Quarterly*, 14: 378–97.

Hinrichs, J.R. (1978) 'An eight year follow up of a management assessment center', *Journal of Applied Psychology*, 63: 596–601.

Hirschman, E.C. (1980) 'Innovativeness, novelty seeking and consumer creativity', *Journal of Consumer Research*, 7: 283–95.

Hirschman, E.C. (1984) 'Experience seeking: a subjectivist perspective of consumption', *Journal of Business Research*, 12: 115–36.

Hoffschulte, B. (1986) 'The Scapegoat Theory and Sociobiology', paper presented at the 8th meeting of the European Sociobiological Society (ESS), Bussum, Netherlands.

Hofstede, G. (1984) *Cultures Consequences: International Differences in Work-Related Values*, London: Sage Publications.

Hold, B.C.L. (1976) 'Attention structure and rank specific behaviour in preschool children', in M.C.R. Chance and R.R. Larsen (eds), *The Social Structure of Attention*, London: Wiley.

Holland, P.A. (1987) 'Adaptors and innovators: application of the Kirton Adaption–Innovation Inventory to bank employees', *Psychological Reports*, 60: 263–70.

Holland, P.A., Bowskill, I. and Bailey, A. (1991) 'Adaptors and innovators: selection vs. induction', *Psychological Reports*, 68: 1283–90.

Honey, P. and Mumford, A. (1982) *The Manual for Learning Styles*, Berkshire, UK: Honey.

Horton, R.L. (1979) 'Some relationships between personality and consumer decision making', *Journal of Marketing Research*, 16: 233–46.

Howard, J.A. (1989) *Consumer Behavior in Marketing Stratetgy*, Englewood Cliffs, NJ: Prentice-Hall.

Howell, D.C. (1982) *Statistical Methods for Psychology*, 2nd edn., Boston, MA: Duxbury Press.

Huff, S., Lake, D.G. and Schaalman, M.L., (1982) *Principal Differences: Excellence in School Leadership and Management*, Florida Council on Educational Management Report, Department of Education, State of Florida, Tallahassee, FL.

Hunt, R.G. (1970) 'Technology and organization', *Academy of Management Journal*, 13: 235–52.

Hurt, H.T., Joseph, K., and Cook, C.D. (1977) 'Scales for the measure of innovativeness', *Human Communication*, Research, 4: 58-65.

Hyland, M.E. (1985) 'Traits, processes and the purpose of templates', *Journal of Research in Personality*, 19: 72–7.

Isaksen, S.G. (ed.) (1987) *Frontiers of Creativity Research: Beyond the Basics*, Buffalo, NY: Brearly, 11.

Isaksen, S.G. and Dorval, B.K. (1993) 'Toward an improved understanding of creativity within people: the level-style distinction', in S.G. Isaksen *et al.* (eds) *Understanding and Recognizing Creativity: the Emergence of a Discipline*, Norwood, NJ: Ablex.

Isaksen, S.G. and Kaufmann, G.(1990) 'Adaptors and innovators: different perceptions of the psychological climate for creativity', *Studia Pschologica*, 32: 129–41.

Itani, J., Tokuda, K., Furuya, Y., Kano, K. and Shin, Y. (1963) 'The social construction of natural troops of Japanese monkeys in Takasakiyama', *Primates*, 4: 1–42.

Ivancevich, J.M. and Donnelly, J.H. (1974), 'A study of role clarity and need for clarity for three occupational groups', *Academy of Management Journal*, 17: 28–36.

Jackson, D.N. (1976) *Jackson Personality Inventory Manual*, Goshen, New York: Research Psychologists' Press.

James, L.R. and Jones, A.P. (1974) 'Organizational climate: a review of theory and research', *Psychological Bulletin*, 81: 1096–112.

Jorde, P. (1984) 'Change and Innovation in Early Childhood Education: The Relationship Between Selected Personal Characteristics of Administrators and Willingness to Adopt Computer Technology', PhD thesis. Stanford University, California.

Kagan, J. and Kogan, N. (1970) 'Individual variation in cognitive processes', in P.H. Mussen (ed.), *Carmichael's Manual of Child Psychology*, vol. 1. New York: Wiley.

Kahneman, D. and Tversky, A. (1982) 'The psychology of preferences', *Scientific American*, 246: 160–73.

Karson, S. and O'Dell, J.W. (1976) *A Guide to the Clinical use of the 16 PF*, Champaign: Institute for Personality and Ability Testing.

Katz, D. and Kahn, R.L. (1978) *The Social Psychology of Organizations*, (2nd edn), New York: Wiley.

Keller, R.T. (1984) 'A cross-national validation study for research and development professional employees', *IEEE Transactions on Engineering Management*, EM–31, 162–5.

Keller, R.T. (1986) 'Predictors of project group performance in Research and Development organisations', *Academy of Management Journal*, 29: 715–26.

Keller, R.T. and Holland, W.E. (1978a) 'Individual characteristics of innovativeness and communication in Research and Development organizations', *Journal of Applied Psychology*, 63: 759–62.

Keller, R.T. and Holland, W.E. (1978b) 'A cross-validation study of the Kirton Adaption–Innovation Inventory in three Research and Development organizations', *Applied Psychological Measurement*, 2: 563–70.

Keller, R.T. and Holland, W.E. (1979) 'Towards a selection battery for Research and Development professional employees', *IEEE Transactions on Engineering Management*, vol. EM–26: 4.

Khatena, J. and Torrance, E.P. (1976) *Manual for Khatena-Torrance Creative Perception Inventory*, Chicago: Steolting Co.

Kiggundu, M.N. (1983) 'Task interdependence and job design: test of a theory', *Organizational Behaviour and Human Performance*, 31: 145–72.

Kipnis, D. (1976) *The Powerholders*, Chicago/London: University of Chicago Press.

Kirton, M.J. (1961) *Management Initiative*, London: Acton Society Trust.

Kirton, M.J. (1976) 'Adaptors and innovators: a description and measure', *Journal of Applied Psychology*, 61: 622–9.

Kirton, M.J. (1977) 'Adaptors and innovators and superior–subordinate identification', *Psychological Reports*, 41: 289–90.

Kirton, M.J. (1978a) 'Have adaptors and innovators equal levels of creativity?', *Psychological Reports*, 42: 695–8.

Kirton, M.J. (1978b), 'Field dependence and adaption–innovation theories', *Perceptual and Motor Skills*, 47: 1239–45.

Kirton, M.J. (1978c) 'Adaptors and innovators in culture clash', *Current Anthropology*, 19: 611–12.

Kirton, M.J. (1980) 'Adaptors and innovators in organizations', *Human Relations*, 3: 213–24.

Kirton, M.J. (1984) 'Adaptors and innovators – why new initiatives get blocked', *Long Range Planning*, 17: 137–43.

Kirton, M.J. (1985) 'Adaptors, innovators and paradigm consistency', *Psychological Reports*, 57: 487–90.

Kirton, M.J (1987a) *Kirton Adaption–Innovation Inventory (KAI)*, Manual 2nd Edition Hatfield UK: Occupational Research Centre.

Kirton, M.J. (1987b) 'Reply to R.L. Payne's article: "Individual differences and performance amongst R&D Personnel"', *R&D Management*, 17:163–6.

Kirton, M.J. (1987c) 'Adaptors and innovators: cognitive style and personality', in S.G. Isaksen (ed.), *Frontiers of Creativity*, Buffalo, NY: Brearly Ltd.

Kirton, M.J. and de Ciantis, S.M. (1986) 'Cognitive style and personality: the Kirton Adaption–Innovation and Cattell's Sixteen Personality Factor Inventories', *Personality and Individual Differences*, 7: 141–6.

Kirton, M.J. and McCarthy, R. (1985) 'Personal and group estimates of the Kirton Inventory scores', *Psychological Reports*, 57: 1067–70.

Kirton, M.J. and McCarthy, R. (1988) 'Cognitive climate and organizations', *Journal of Occupational Psychology*, 61: 175–84.

Kirton, M.J. and Mulligan, G. (1973) 'Correlates of managers' attitudes towards change', *Journal of Applied Psychology*, 58: 101–7.

Kirton, M.J. and Pender, S.R. (1982) 'The adaption–innovation continuum: occupational type and course selection', *Psychological Reports*, 51: 883–6.

Kirton, M.J., Bailey, A.J. and Glendinning, J.W. (1991) 'Adaptors and Innovators: preference for educational procedures', *Journal of Psychology*, 125(4): 445–55.

Koeske, G.F., Kirk, S.A. and Koeske, R.D. (1993) 'Coping with job stress', *Journal of Organizational Psychology*, 66: 319–35.

Koestler, A. (1967) *The Ghost in the Machine*, London: Pan.

Kogan, N. (1971) 'Educational implications of cognitive styles', in G.S. Lesser (ed.), *Psychology and Educational Practice*, Glenview, Il: Scott Foresman.

Kogan, N. (1973) 'Creativity and cognitive style: a life-span perspective', in P.B. Baltes and K.W. Schaie (eds), *Life-Span Developmental Psychology: Personality and Socialization*, New York: Academic Press.

Kogan, N. (1976) 'Sex differences in creativity and cognitive styles', in S. Messick (ed.) *Individuality in Learning*, San Francisco: Jossey-Bass.

Kolb, D.A., Rubin, I.M. and McIntyre, J.M. (1979) *Organizational Psychology: An Experiential Approach*, Englewood Cliffs, NJ: Prentice-Hall.

Krech, D., Crutchfield, R.S., and Ballachey, E.L. (1962) *Individual in Society: A Textbook of Social Psychology*, New York: McGraw Hill.

Kubeš, M. and Benkovič P. (1994) 'Realities, paradoxes and perspectives of human resource management in Eastern Europe: the case of

Czechoslovakia', in P.S. Kirkbride (ed.) *Human Resource Management in Europe*, London and New York: Routledge.

Kubeš, M. and Spillerová, D. (1992) 'The effects of personality characteristics on communication patterns in R&D teams', *Creativity and Innovation Management*, 1(1): 33–40.

Kuhn, T.S. (1970) *The Structure of Scientific Revolutions* (2nd ed.) Chicago, IL: University of Chicago Press.

Lachenicht, L. (1985) 'A reversal theory of social relations applied to polite language', in M.J. Apter, D. Fontana and S. Murgatroyed (eds) *Reversal Theory: Applications and Developments*, Cardiff, UK: University College Cardiff Press.

Lancaster, J.B. (1986) 'Primate social behavior and ostracism', *Ethology and Sociobiology*, 7: 215–25.

Lawler, E.E., Hall, D.T. and Oldham, G.R. (1973) 'Organisational climate: relationship to organisation structure, process and performance', *Organisational Behaviour and Human Performance*, 10: 118–27.

Leavitt, H. (1972) *Managerial Psychology*, (3rd edn), Chicago: University of Chicago Press.

Lewin, K. (1935) *A Dynamic Theory of Personality*, New York: McGraw-Hill.

Lindsay, P.R. (1985) 'Counselling to resolve a clash of cognitive styles', *Technovation*, 3: 57–67.

Lippitt, R. and White, R.K. (1958) 'An experimental study of leadership and group life', in E.E. Maccoby, T.M. Newcomb and E.L. Hartley (eds), *Readings in Social Psychology* (3rd edn.), New York: Holt.

Lowe, E.A. and Taylor, W.G.K. (1986) 'The management of research in the life sciences: the characteristics of researchers', *R&D Management*, 16: 45–61.

Loy, J.W. Jnr. (1969) 'Social psychological characteristics of innovators', *American Sociological Review*, 34: 73–82.

McCarthy, R. (1993) 'The relationship of individual characteristics of women managers to the pressures experienced at work and choice of coping strategy', PhD thesis, The University of Hertfordshire.

McClain, E. (1978) 'Feminists and nonfeminists contrasting profiles in independence and affiliation', *Psychological Reports*, 43: 435–41.

Maccoby, M. (1976) *The Gamesman, the New Corporate Leaders*, New York: Simon & Schuster.

MacDonald, A.P. Jnr. (1970) 'Revised scale for ambiguity tolerance', *Psychological Reports*, 26: 791–8.

McHale, J. and Flegg, D. (1985) 'How Calamity Jane was put in her place', *Transition*, November, 14–16.

McHale, J. and Flegg, D. (1986) 'Innovators rule OK – or do they?' *Training and Development Journal*, Oct. 10–13.

McKenna, F.P. (1983) 'Field dependence and personality: a re-examination', *Social Behaviour and Personality*, 11: 51–5.

McKenna, F.P. (1984) 'Measures of field dependence: cognitive style or cognitive ability?' *Journal of Personality and Social Psychology*, 47: 593–603.

MacKinnon, D.W. (1962) 'The personality correlates of creativity: a study of American architects', in G.S. Neilson (ed.), *Proceedings of the XIV International Congress of Applied Psychology, Copenhagen, 1961*, 2: 11–39.

MacKinnon, D.W. (1978) *In Search of Human Effectiveness: Identifying and Developing Creativity*, Buffalo, NY: Brearly.

MacKinnon, D.W. (1987) 'Some critical issues for future research in creativity', in S.G. Isaksen (ed.) *Frontiers of Creativity Research: Beyond the Basics*, Buffalo, NY: Brearly.

McNemar, Q. (1964) 'Lost: our intelligence? Why?' *American Psychologist*, 19: 871–82.

Malloy, T.E. and Kenny, D.A. (1986) 'The social relations model: an integrative method for personality research', *Journal of Personality*, 54: 199–225.

Matherley, T.A. and Goldsmith, R.E. (1985) 'The two faces of creativity', *Business Horizons*, 28: 8–11.

Meehl, P.E. (1945) 'The dynamics of "structured" personality tests', *Journal of Clinical Psychology*, 1: 296–303.

Mehrabian, A. (1972) *Nonverbal Communication*, Chicago/New York: Aldine, Altherton.

Mehrabian, A. and Russell, J.A. (1974) *An Approach to Environmental Psychology*, Cambridge, Mass.: The MIT Press.

Merton, R.K. (ed.) (1957) *Bureaucratic Structure and Personality in Social Theory and Social Structure*, New York: Free Press of Glencoe.

Messick, S. (1976) *Individuality in Learning: Implications of Cognitive Styles and Creativity for Human Development*, San Francisco: Jossey-Bass.

Messick, S. (1984) 'The nature of cognitive styles: problems and promise in educational practice', *Educational Psychologist*, 19: 59–74.

Midgley, D.F. (1977) *Innovation and New Product Marketing*, London: Croom Helm.

Midgley, D.F. and Dowling, G.R. (1978) 'Innovativeness: the concept and its measurement', *Journal of Consumer Research*, 4: 229–42.

Milgram, S. (1974) *Obedience to Authority*, London: Tavistock.

Mischel, W. (1973) 'Toward a cognitive social learning reconceptualization of personality', *Psychological Review*, 80: 252–83.

Mischel, W. (1976) *Introduction to Personality*, (2nd edn) New York: Holt, Rinehart & Winston.

Mohr, L B. (1971) 'Organizational technology and organizational structure', *Administrative Science Quarterly*, 16: 444–57.

Mudd, S.A. (1990) 'The place of innovativeness in models of the adoption process: an integrative review', *Technovation*, 10: 119–36.

Mudd, S.A. and McGrath, K. (1988) 'Correlates of the adoption of curriculum-integrated computing in higher education', *Computers & Education*, 12(4): 457–63.

Mulkay, M.S. (1972) *The Social Process of Innovation*, London: Macmillan.

Mulligan, G. and Martin, W. (1980) 'Adaptors, innovators and the KAI', *Psychological Reports*, 46: 883–92.

Murdock, M., Isaksen, S.G. and Lauer, K.J. (1993) 'Creativity training and the stability and internal consistency of the Kirton Adaption–Innovation Inventory', *Psychological Report*, 72: 1123–30.

Murgatroyd, S. and Evans, P. (1979) *A Negativism-Conformity Scale for Adolescents*, Paper for the Conference of the Psychology of Reversals Study Group, Cardiff.

Myers, I.B. (1962) *The Myers Briggs Type Indicator*, Palo Alto: Calif. Consulting Psychologists' Press.

NACNE (National Advisory Committee on Health Education) (1983) *A Discussion Paper on Proposals for National Guidelines for Health Education in Britain*, London: Health Educational Council.

National Food Survey (1986), London: HMSO.

National Institute of Industrial Psychology Test Battery (1964–1979) Windsor, UK: Nelson – NFER.

Norman, W.T. (1963) 'Toward an adequate taxonomy of personality attributes: replicated factor structure in peer nomination personality ratings', *Journal of Abnormal and Social Psychology*, 66: 574–83.

Nyström, H. (1979) *Creativity and Innovation*, Chichester: John Wiley & Sons.

Olson, M. (1982) *The Rise and Decline of Nations (Economic Growth, Stagflation and Social Rigidities)*, New Haven: Yale University Press.

Osborn, A.F. (1963) *Applied Imagination*, (3rd edn) New York: Charles Scribner's.

Ostrogorski, M. (1982) *Democracy and the Organization of Political Parties*, Brooklyn: Haskell House.

O'Toole, J.J. (1979) 'Corporate and managerial cultures', in C.L. Cooper (ed.) *Behavioural Problems in Organizations*, Englewood Cliffs, New Jersey: Prentice Hall.

Parsons, T. (1951) *The Social System*, Glencoe: Free Press.

Payne, R.L. (1987) 'Individual differences and performance amongst R&D personnel: some implications for management development', *R&D Management*, 17: 153–61.

Payne, R.L. and Pugh, D.S. (1973) 'Organisational climate and organisational structure', in M.D. Dunnette (ed.) *Handbook of Industrial and Organisational Psychology*, (2nd edn), New York: Wiley.

Perrow, C. (1967) 'A framework for the comparative analysis of organizations', *American Sociological Review*, 32: 194–208.

Peters, T.J. and Waterman, R.H. (1983) *In Search of Excellence*, New York: Warner Books.

Petrinovich, L. (1979) 'Probabilistic functionalism: a conception of research method', *American Psychologist*, 34: 373–90.

Pierce, J.L.(1984) 'Job design and technology: a sociotechnical perspective', *Journal of Occupational Behaviour*, 5: 147–54.

Pinson, C. (1978) 'Consumer cognitive styles: review and implications for marketers', in E. Topritzhofer (ed.) *Marketing: Neue Ergebnisse aus Forschung und Praxis*, Wiesbaden: Gabler, 163–84.

Pinson, C., Malhotra, N.K. and Jain, A.K. (1988) 'Les styles cognitifs des consommateurs', *Recherche et Applications en Marketing*, III: 53–73.

Plomin, R. and Rowe, D.C. (1977) 'A twin study of temperament in young children', *The Journal of Psychology*, 97: 107–13.

Plomin, R. and Rowe, D.C. (1979) 'Genetic and environmental etiology of social behaviour in infancy', *Development Psychology*, 15: 62–72.

Poirier, F.E. (1970) 'Dominance structure of the Nilgiri langur (Presbytis johnii) of South India', *Folia Primatologica*, 12: 161–86.

Prato Previde, G. (1984) 'Adattatori ed Innovatori: i risultati della standardizzazione italiana del KAI', *Ricerche di Psicologia*, 4: 81–134, Validated Italian translation of the KAI.

Prato Previde, G. and Carli, M. (1987) 'Adaption–Innovation typology and right–left hemispheric preferences', *Journal of Personality and Individual Differences*, 8: 681–6.

Pulvino, C.A.F. (1979) 'Relationship of principal leadership behaviour to teacher motivation and innovation',. PhD thesis, University of Wisconsin, Madison.

Raju, P.S. (1980) 'Optimum stimulation level: its relationship to personality, demographics and exploratory behavior', *Journal of Consumer Research*, 7: 272–82.

Reddin, W.J. (1970) *Managerial Effectiveness*, London: McGraw-Hill.

Reddin, W.J. (1987) *Effective Management*, New Delhi: McGraw-Hill.

Reynolds, V. and Luscombe, G. (1969) 'Chimpanzee rank order and the function of displays', in C.R. Carpenter (ed.), *Proceedings of the Second International Congress of Primatology*, Basel: Karger.

Rickards, T. (1990) 'The KAI and a survey-feedback instrument', *Journal of European Industrial Training*, 14(6): 3–7.

Rickards, T. and Moger, S. (1994) 'The resolution of diversity: a case study report of a diadic work relationship', *Journal of Applied Behavioural Science*, 30(1): 108–31.

Roberts, K.H. and Glick, W. (1981) 'The job characteristics approach to task design: a critical review', *Journal of Applied Psychology*, 66: 193–217.

Robertson, I.T. (1985) 'Human information-processing strategies and style', *Behaviour and Information Technology*, 4: 19–29.

Robertson, T.S. (1967) 'The process of innovation and the diffusion of innovation', *Journal of Marketing*, 31: 14–19.

Robertson, T.S. (1971) *Innovative Behavior and Communication*, New York: Holt, Rinehart & Winston.

Robey, D. and Taggart, W. (1981) 'Measuring managers' minds: the assessment of style in human information processing', *Academy of Management Journal*, 6: 375–83.

Rodger, A. and Cavanagh, P. (1962) 'Training of occupational psychologists', *Occupational Psychology*, 36: 80–8.

Rogers, C.R. (1959) 'Towards a theory of creativity', in H.H. Anderson (ed.) *Creativity and its Cultivation*, New York: Harper.

Rogers, E.M. (1983) *Diffusion of Innovations*, (3rd edn), New York: The Free Press.

Rogers, E.M. and Shoemaker, F.F. (1971) *Communication of Innovations A Cross-Cultural Approach*, (2nd edn), New York: The Free Press.

Rokeach M. (1960) *The Open and Closed Mind*, New York: Basic Books.

Rosenberg, M. (1965) *Society and the Adolescent Self-Image*, Princeton, NJ: Princeton University Press.

Russell, B. (1946) *History of Western Philosophy*, London: Allen & Unwin.

Rydell, S.T. and Rosen, E. (1966) 'Measurement and some correlates of need cognition', *Psychological Reports*, 90: 139–65.

Sackett, P.R. and Dreher, G.F. (1982) 'Constructs and assessment center dimensions: some troubling empirical findings', *Journal of Applied Psychology*, 67: 401–10.

Savin-Williams, R.C. (1979) 'Dominance hierarchies in groups of early adolescents', *Child Development*, 67: 923–35.

Savin-Williams, R.C. (1980) 'Dominance hierarchies in groups of middle to late adolescent males', *Journal of Youth and Adolescence*, 9: 75–85.

Schaefer, C.E. (1971) *Similies Test Manual*, Research Psychologist Press, New York: Goshen.

Scheflen, A. and Scheflen, A. (1972) *Body Language and Social Order*, New Jersey: Prentice Hall.

Schiffman, L.G. and Kanuk, L.L. (1987) *Consumer Behavior*, Englewood Cliffs, NJ: Prentice–Hall.

Schneider, B. (1983) 'Work climates: an interactionist perspective', in N.R. Feimer and E.S. Geller (eds), *Environmental Psychology: Directions and Perspectives*, New York: Praeger.

Schneider, B. (1985) 'Organizational behaviour', *Annual Review of Psychology*, 36: 573–611.

Schneider, B. and Snyder, R.A. (1975) 'Some relationships between job satisfaction and organisational climate', *Journal of Applied Psychology*, 60: 318–27.

Schoen, D.R. (1960) 'Managing technological innovation', *Harvard Business Review*, May–June, 156–68.

Schroder, H.M. (1985) *Manual for Assessing Managerial Competencies*, Tampa, FL: Center for Organizational Effectiveness, University of South Florida.

Schroder, H.M. (1986) *The Development of Managerial Competencies*, Tampa, FL: Center for Organizational Effectiveness, University of South Florida.

Schroder, H.M. and Croghan, J.H. (1984) *The Reliability and Validity of Assessment Center Measures*, Florida Council on Educational Management Report, Department of Education, State of Florida, Tallahassee, FL.

Schroder, H.M., Driver, M.J. and Streufert, S. (1969) *Human Information Processing*, New York: Holt, Rinehart & Winston.

Schroder, H.M., Croghan, J.H. and Michaels, C.E. (1986) *Situational Manuals for Measuring Managerial Competencies*, Tampa, FL.: Center for Organizational Effectiveness, University of South Florida.

Schumacher, E. F. (1975) *Small is Beautiful: Economics as if People Mattered*, New York: Harper & Row.

Schumpeter, J.A. (1939) *Business Cycles, a Theoretical, Historical and Statistical Analysis of the Capitalist Process*, London: McGraw Hill.

Segerstrale, U. (1986) 'Colleagues in conflict: an "In Vivo" analysis of the socio-biological controversy', *Biology and Philosophy*, 1: 53–87.

Shipley, W.C. (1940) 'A self-administering scale for measuring intellectual deterioration', *Journal of Psychology*, 9: 371–7.

Slocum, J.W. and Sims, H.P. (1980) 'A typology for integrating technology, organization, and job design', *Human Relations*, 33: 193–212.

Sluckin, A.M. and Smith, P.K. (1977) 'Two approaches to the concept of dominance in preschool children', *Child Development*, 48: 917–23.

Smith-Benjamin, L. (1974) 'Structural analysis of social behavior', *Psychological Review*, 81: 392–425.

Snow, C.P. (1961) 'Either – or', *Progressive*, 24.

Snyder, M. (1979) 'Self-monitoring processes', in L. Berkowitz (ed.), *Advances in Experimental Social Psychology*, vol. 12, New York: Academic Press, 85–128.

Snyder, M. and Gangestad, S. (1986) 'On the nature of self-monitoring: matters of assessment, matters of validity', *Journal of Personality and Social Psychology*, 51: 125–39.

Spengler, O. (1918) *Der Untergand des Abendlandes*, Vienna and Leipzig: Wilhelm Braunmuller.

Steenkamp, J.-B. and Baumgartner, H. (1992) 'The role of optimum stimulation level in exploratory consumer behaviour', *Journal of Consumer Research*, 19: 434–48.

Stein, M.I. (1975) *Manual: Physiognomic Cue Test*, New York: Behavioral Publications.

Strayer, F.F. and Strayer, J. (1976) 'An ethological analysis of social agonism and dominance relations among preschool children', *Child Development*, 47: 980–9.

Strelau, J. (1974) 'Temperament as an expression of energy level and temporal features of behaviour', *Polish Psychological Bulletin*, 5: 119–27.

Streufert, S. and Swezey, R.W. (1986) *Complexity, Managers and Organisations*, New York: Academic Press.

Swatez, G.M. (1970) 'The social organization of a university laboratory', *Minerva: A Review of Science Learning and Policy*, VIII: 36–58.

Taylor, J. (1994) 'The stability of schoolchildren's cognitive style – a longitudinal study of the KAI Inventory', *Psychological Reports*, 74: 1008–10.

Tefft, M.E. (1990) 'A factor analysis of TTCT, MBTI and KAI: the creative level/style issue re-examined', Master's thesis, State University of New York College at Buffalo.

Tellegan, A. (1987) 'TCI, control-impulse in Tellegan's research scale' in S. Gryskiewicz *et al. Understanding Managerial Creativity: the Kirton Adaption–Innovation Inventory and Other Assessment Measures*, Greensboro, NC: Center for Creative Leadership.

Thibaut, J.W. and Kelley, H.H. (1959) *The Social Psychology of Groups*, New York: Wiley.

Thom, R. and Zeeman, E.C. (1974) 'Catastrophe theory: its present state and future perspectives', in A. Manning (ed.), *Dynamical Systems: Proceedings of a Symposium Held at the University of Warwick 1973/1974*, Springer-Verlag.

Thomson, D. (1980) 'Adaptors and innovators: a replication study on managers in Singapore and Malaysia', *Psychological Reports*, 47: 383–7.

Thomson, D. (1985) 'A study of Singaporean executives: their attitudes, dispositions and work values', PhD thesis, Henley Management College/Brunel University.

Thornton, G.C. and Byham, W.C. (1982) *Assessment Center and Managerial Performance*, New York: Academic Press.

Tiger, L. (1987) *The Cerebral Bridge from Family to Foe*, Presentation at the 9th meeting of the European Sociobiological Society (ESS) Jerusalem.

Torrance, E.P. (1971) *Technical Norms Manual for the Creative Motivation Scale*, Athens GA: Georgia Studies of Creative Behavior, University of Georgia.

Torrance, E.P. (1974) *Norms Technical Manual: Torrance Tests of Creative Thinking*, Bensenville, ILL.: Scholastic Testing Service.

Torrance, E.P. (1982) 'Hemisphericity and creative functioning', *Journal of Research and Development in Education*, 15: 29–37.

Torrance, E.P. and Horng, R.Y. (1980) 'Creativity, style of learning and thinking characteristics of adaptors and innovators', *The Creative Child Adult Quarterly*, V: 80–5.

Torrance, E P., Reynolds, C.R., Ball, O.E. and Riegel, T.R. (1978) *Revised Norms-Technical Manual for Your Style of Learning and Thinking*, Athens, GA: Georgia Studies of Creative Behavior, University of Georgia.

Toynbee, A. (1972) *A Study of History*, Oxford: Oxford University Press.

Trist, E.L. and Bamforth, K.W. (1951) 'Some social and psychological consequences of the Longwall method of coal-getting', *Human Relations*, 4: 1–38.

Troldahl, V. and Powell, F. (1965) 'A short-form dogmatism scale for use in field studies', *Social Forces*, 44: 211–14.

Trumbo, D.A. (1961) 'Individual and group correlates of attitudes to work-related change', *Journal of Applied Psychology*, 45: 338–44.

van der Molen, P.P. (1973) *Verslag van een Ontdekkingsreis door het Gebied van het Sociale Gedrag*, Internal Research Report, Dept. of Behavioural Genetics, Rijks Universiteit Groningen (RUG) Netherlands.

van der Molen, P.P. (1988) 'Biological mechanisms precluding the establishment of social equilibria and their effects on the emergence of conflict and disaster' in J.M.G. van der Dennen, V.S.E. Falger, M. Hopp and C.J. Irwin (eds), *The Sociobiology of Conflict*, London: Croom Helm.

Vannoy, J.S. (1965) 'Generality of cognitive complexity–simplicity as a personality construct,' *Journal of Personality and Social Psychology*, 2: 385–96.

Veblen, T. (1928) *The Theory of the Leisure Class*, New York: Vanguard Press.

Venkatesen, M. (1973) 'Cognitive consistency and novelty-seeking' in S. Ward and T.S. Roberston (eds) *Consumer Behavior: Theorectical Sources*, Englewood Cliffs, NJ: Prentice-Hall, 354–84.

Vicere, A.A. (1992) 'The strategic leadership imperative for executive development', *Human Resource Planning* 15(1): 15–31.

Wallach, M.A. and Kogan, N. (1965) 'A new look at the creativity–intelligence distinction', *Journal of Personality*, 33: 348–69.

Walling, M., Robertson, E.D., Higgins, P. and Fournet, G.P. (1987) 'Relationship between time perception and Kirton's Adaption–Innovation Inventory', paper presented at the 1987 Annual Convention of the Southwestern Psychological Association.

Watts, W. (1985) 'Relationship between specific skills and managerial performance', M Phil thesis, North East London Polytechnic.

Weber, M. (1970) in H.H. Gerth and C.W. Mills (eds and trans.) *From Max Weber: Essays in Sociology*, London: Routledge & Kegan Paul.

Weick, E.I. (1969) *The Social Psychology of Organizing*, Reading, MASS.: Addison-Wesley.

Weisbord, M.R. (1987) 'Managing and consulting beyond the design limits: a third wave action product' in M.R. Weisbord (ed.), *Productive Workplaces: Organizing and Managing for Dignity, Meaning and Community*, San Francisco/London: Jossey-Bass.

Weisfeld, G.E. (1980) 'Determinants and behavioral correlates of dominance in adolescent boys', in D.R. Omark, F.F. Strayer and D.G. Freedman (eds), *Dominance Relations: An Ethological Perspective on Human Conflict*, New York: Garland.

Wells, W.D. (1961) 'The influence of yeasaying response style', *Journal of Advertising Research*, 1: 1–12.

Wesley, E.L. (1953) 'Preservative behaviour in a concept-formation task', *Journal of Abnormal and Social Psychology*, 8: 129–34.

Whyte, W.H. (1957) *The Organization Man*, London: Cape.

Wilson, E.O. (1977) *Sociobiology, The New Synthesis*, Cambridge, MASS: Harvard University Press.

Wilson, G.D. and Patterson, J.R. (1968) 'A new measure of conservatism', *British Journal of Social and Clinical Psychology*, 7: 274–9.

Wind, Y. (1981) *Product Policy: Concepts, Methods and Strategy*, Read, MA: Addison-Wesley.

Winer, B.J. (1971) *Statistical Principles in Experimental Design*, (2nd edn), New York: McGraw-Hill.

Witkin, H.A. and Goodenough, D.R. (1977) *Field Dependence Re-visited*, (ETS RB–77–16) Princeton, NJ: Educational Testing Service.

Witkin, H.A., Dyk, R.B., Faterson, H.F., Goodenough, D.R. and Karp, S.A. (1962) *Psychological Differentation*, New York: Wiley.

Witkin, H.A., Moore, C.A., Goodenough, D.R. and Cox, P.W. (1977) 'Field-dependence and field-independent cognitive styles and their educational implications', *Review of Educational Research*, 47: 1–64.

Woodcock, A. and Davis, M. (1978) *Catastrophe Theory*, New York: Avon.

Woodward, J. (1965) *Industrial Organization: Theory and Practice*, London: Oxford University Press.

Yamada, M. (1966) 'Five natural troops of Japanese monkeys in Shodishama Island', *Primates*, 7: 313–62.

Zaichkowsky, J.L. (1987) *The Personal Involvement Inventory: Reduction, Revision and Application to Advertising*, discussion paper no. 87–08–08, Simon Fraser University, Faculty of Business Administration.

Zaleznik, A. (1977) 'Managers and leaders: are they different?' *Harvard Business Review*, 55(3): 67–78.

Zaltman, G. (1965) *Marketing: Contribution from the Behavioural New Sciences*, New York: Harcourt, Brace & World Inc.

Zaremba, J. (1978) 'Relationship of teacher motivation to innovativeness and job satisfaction', PhD dissertation, University of Wisconsin-Madison.

Zeeman, E.C. (1976) 'Catastrophe theory', *Scientific American*, 234: 1976.

Zuckerman, M. (1974) 'The sensation seeking motive', in B.A. Maher (ed.), *Progress in Experimental Personality Research*, vol. 7, New York: Academic Press, 74–148.

UNPUBLISHED REFERENCES

Thanks are due for the use of their unpublished data to:

Davies, G., The Cambridge Management Centre.

Flegg, D., Industrial Training Research Unit, Cambridge, UK.

Mathews, D., Engineering Industry Training Board, UK.

Pottas, C.D.. University of Pretoria, South Africa.

Rickards, T., Manchester Business School, UK.

Rivera, G. and Prato Previde, G., Bocconi Institute, Milan, Italy.

INDEX